Job Stress
and the Librarian

Job Stress and the Librarian

Coping Strategies from the Professionals

Edited by Carol Smallwood *and* Linda Burkey Wade

Foreword by Julia L. Eisenstein

McFarland & Company, Inc., Publishers

Jefferson, North Carolina, and London

SELECTED RECENT MCFARLAND WORKS FROM CAROL SMALLWOOD AND OTHERS

Continuing Education for Librarians: Essays on Career Improvement Through Classes, Workshops, Conferences and More, edited by Carol Smallwood, Kerol Harrod and Vera Gubnitskaia (2013). *Marketing Your Library: Tips and Tools That Work*, edited by Carol Smallwood, Vera Gubnitskaia and Kerol Harrod (2012). *Mentoring in Librarianship: Essays on Working with Adults and Students to Further the Profession*, edited by Carol Smallwood and Rebecca Tolley-Stokes (2012). *Women on Poetry: Writing, Revising, Publishing and Teaching*, edited by Carol Smallwood, Colleen S. Harris and Cynthia Brackett-Vincent (2012). *Thinking Outside the Book: Essays for Innovative Librarians*, edited by Carol Smallwood (2008). *Internet Sources on Each U.S. State: Selected Sites for Classroom and Library*, compiled by Carol Smallwood, Brian P. Hudson, Ann Marlow Riedling and Jennifer K. Rotole (2005).

LIBRARY OF CONGRESS CATALOGUING-IN-PUBLICATION DATA

Job stress and the librarian : coping strategies from the professionals / edited by Carol Smallwood and Linda Burkey Wade ; foreword by Julia L. Eisenstein.
p.   cm.
Includes bibliographical references and index.

ISBN 978-0-7864-7180-5
softcover : acid free paper ∞

1. Librarians—Job stress.   2. Library personnel management.
3. Stress management.   4. Conflict management.
I. Smallwood, Carol, 1939– II. Wade, Linda Burkey, 1967–
Z682.J59 2013   020.92—dc23   2013026952

BRITISH LIBRARY CATALOGUING DATA ARE AVAILABLE

On the cover: *books and table* Stockbyte/Thinkstock

Manufactured in the United States of America

McFarland & Company, Inc., Publishers
Box 611, Jefferson, North Carolina 28640
www.mcfarlandpub.com

To the contributors for sharing with colleagues, and Dr. Robert P. Holley for suggesting one of his former students as a foreword writer. — *Carol Smallwood*

To Deanne Donley and Megan Welch for their help. Also, a special thanks to Jamie Roth for coming to the rescue when the word processor would not cooperate. This work would not have been completed without them, my family and the wonderful contributors. — *Linda Wade*

Table of Contents

Part IV: Balancing the Professional and the Personal

Part V: Juggling Responsibilities

Part VI: Easing Stress on a Budget

Part VII: Overcoming Challenges

Part VIII: Navigating Career Transitions

Foreword

JULIA L. EISENSTEIN

If you ask the average person to list jobs that are perceived as stressful, you would likely get responses such as fireman or policeman, but I doubt anyone would say librarian. Those of us who work as librarians know better. Our lives are not in unusual danger each day, but stress isn't just the result of physical threat. Stress can arise from any circumstances that cause hardship and emotional upset. If not eliminated or mitigated, over time physical symptoms such as ulcers, high blood pressure, etc., can result. The chapters collected here in this tome reflect multiple sources of stress that come with being a librarian and creative recommendations for coping with them. Dealing with difficult patrons and/or co-workers, ever-shrinking budgets, ever-advancing technologies, and the unceasing pressure to do more with less, are just a few of the challenges librarians face daily in every kind of library.

Most of us spend at least a third of our lives at work with the same people every day. Spending that much time together is bound to lead to occasional conflicts. In Part I, Defusing and Reducing Conflict at Work, Kathleen Clauson, and Lisa A. Forrest give us keen insights as to why some co-workers are harder to deal with than others and they offer practical, helpful suggestions. Sometimes just by understanding, we are empowered to be more patient with, more kind towards and more forgiving of the shortcomings of our co-workers and ourselves.

Physicians know that chronic stress can cause any number of physical symptoms. It's the "fight-or-flight" response that causes adrenaline to surge and over time weakens our immune systems. The essays in Part II, Stress Management, discuss strategies for keeping stress in check. Leigh A. Woznick looks at gender specific approaches and Su Epstein reminds us humor can help to keep everything in perspective. The mind/body connection is so important in stress management. Amy Bodine and Kim Rush Lynch explain how both self-care and proper nutrition are essential. Then John Boyd and Elizabeth Cramer discuss the indispensability of exercise. Finally, Jonathan Frater offers his perspective on how solitude provides rejuvenation.

Offering library programs can often be an additional source of stress for an already over-taxed librarian. In Part III, Library Programs for Patrons and Staff, Beth Nieman considers how to successfully plan and implement library programs for patrons and Kymberly Anne Goodson details how her university library created an employee yoga program.

A strong social support network is often cited as important in relieving stress. Aislinn Catherine Sotelo and Shirley A. Higgins demonstrate how employees can help each other through activities that not only reduce stress but have the added benefit of improving relationships among co-workers.

Part IV, Balancing the Professional and the Personal, provides excellent ideas for handling the challenges we face both at home and at work. Maryann Mori has three words that will change your professional (and perhaps your personal) life. Cristina Hernandez Trotter endorses journaling as a means to appreciate the journey of your professional life, and Samantha Schmehl Hines talks about avoiding and recovering from burnout.

In Part V, Juggling Responsibilities, Pamela O'Sullivan considers the real cost of doing more with less, Marcia E. Rapchak offers advice on meeting the demands of teaching, and James B. Casey shows how employee empowerment is a smart strategy for supervisors.

There are few libraries in these economic times that won't be able to use the ideas for stretching a dollar presented in Part VI, Easing Stress on a Budget, whether seeking to renovate library space or find resources for programs or special projects. Sharon M. Britton looks at affordable library makeovers, and Barbara Fiehn talks about how to fund your media program during lean times. Stacey R. Ewing and Janelle West offer advice on dealing with budgetary and staff cuts, and Jeffrey DiScala and Sheri Anita Massey promote the effective use of volunteer labor.

We all face unique circumstances in our lives and in our jobs and Part VII, Overcoming Challenges, offers insight in how to rise to any occasion. Charlcie K. Pettway Vann describes the difficulties of being the only minority on staff and emphasizes that diversity makes a community stronger, Kimberly Swanson provides pointers to help with the stress of moving to follow a spouse's career and Lara Frater gives us tips for surviving the scariest challenge of all: being laid off.

The collection ends with Part VIII, Navigating Career Transitions, where Zara T. Wilkinson describes the stress of working multiple part-time jobs in the absence of full-time openings, Beth Evans empathizes with and offers strategies for overcoming the mid-career frustrations of the tenured academic librarian, and finally, Aline D. Wilson takes us full-circle as we prepare to retire by doing our research and setting realistic goals for our lifestyle and finances.

Human beings are quite adept at adapting to difficult circumstances using a host of coping strategies. Within the covers of this book is a treasure trove of useful ideas and counsel from our librarian colleagues for dealing with stress. This book is essential reading for anyone in any stressful job for, while these articles are written by library professionals for library professionals, the approaches for dealing with stress described herein are applicable to any line of work.

Julia L. Eisenstein received her MLIS from Wayne State University and her MA in psychology from Boston University where her research interests included the effects of stress on children and the eating disorders. In 2008, she joined the University of Detroit Mercy (UDM) as a reference librarian. and is a member of the American Library Association, the Association of College and Research Libraries, and the Michigan Library Association.

Introduction

CAROL SMALLWOOD *and* LINDA WADE

Chapters were sought for *Job Stress and the Librarian: Coping Strategies from the Professionals* from practicing academic, public, school, special librarians, and LIS faculty in the United States to share practical how-to chapters on managing stress as working librarians. Creative methods of diffusing stress were selected that were adaptive to various types of libraries and job descriptions: twenty-six chapters written by one or two authors: one chapter of 2,500–3500 words or two shorter chapters equaling 2,500–3,500 were compiled from thirty-one contributors.

The anthology is divided as follows:

Part I : Defusing and Reducing Conflict at Work

Part II: Stress Management

Part III: Library Programs for Patrons and Staff

Part IV: Balancing the Professional and the Personal

Part V: Juggling Responsibilities

Part VI: Easing Stress on a Budget

Part VII: Overcoming Challenges

Part VIII: Navigating Career Transitions

The foreword writer, practicing librarian Julia L. Eisenstein, with an MA in psychology as well as a MLIS, notes: "Human beings are quite adept at adopting to difficult circumstances using a host of coping strategies." The following pages provide a wide variety of tips on ways to reduce stress and help co-workers reduce theirs. With budget and staff cuts, increasingly diverse patrons, rapidly changing technology, librarians have stressful jobs and it is hoped this anthology helps meet the current gap in the literature on the topic.

I. Defusing and Reducing Conflict at Work

Dealing with Impossible Co-Workers

Kathleen Clauson

Difficult people exist in every workplace, in every walk of life. When they are your co-workers, "difficult" is hard to tolerate; but when they reach the level of "impossible," it's almost too much to handle. Nearly everyone can recall horrible life-changing stories about impossible people with whom they have worked. When I think of difficult people I compare them to a challenging math problem requiring a great deal of effort; it may take a lot of work but there is a solution. Impossible people are econometrics to me; no matter how much mastery and tenacity you have, there is one variable that throws everything off; after staring at the problem it seems there is a no solution and much later, hidden in the scribbles on your paper, you realize, a solution has been there all along. Conflict management works the same way.

Despite the conventional image of libraries as quiet, peaceful, stress-free, and friendly places, libraries are not immune from problems with individuals who create a stressful and hostile work environment. My own family is puzzled when I arrive home, exhausted and frustrated at times. Sometimes it feels like I just left a combat zone. The behind-the-scenes-drama gets to me, the gossiping, the bullying, the back-stabbing, the endless attempts to get someone in trouble, the favoritism, punishing the creative, and promoting the incompetent.

Everyone who loves their job has something special for which they can take ownership. I am not alone in what I call the "library paradox." I am among the thousands of library workers who genuinely love their jobs but are affected by uncontrollable conflicts which constantly rain on their parades, and drown out their enthusiasm. Issues with impossible people are everywhere, causing unnecessary stress, feelings of frustration, disappointment, and pessimism.

This essay is intended to help you understand what makes some people impossible to work with and how to deal with them. Also included are major causes of stress among library workers; current data on job satisfaction; conflict management in libraries; forces that compel people to act and make them *become* the impossible co-worker. Included are: two brief impossible library worker scenarios and suggestions for dealing with them; and tips for getting along with co-workers. By understanding what makes them tick, you can better prepare and cope with your impossible people. Perhaps they will become less "impossible" in your eyes.

Labels Hurt More Than They Help

Because of the high incidence of workplace conflict, cynical labels describing the personality types of the most difficult people are common. The Vampire, the Whiner, the Control Freak, the Sniper, may seem entertaining but are not recommended. According to Montgomery and Cook in their book *Conflict Management for Libraries* labeling does not improve effective communication and it is considered counter-productive (2005, 15–16). Avoid the temptation to chuckle; workplace conflict is a serious issue.

Those dealing everyday with difficult people are not laughing. Considering the library's importance in the world, it is especially disheartening to imagine the conflict simmering among the ranks. The library is the highway to knowledge and difficult library employees are roadblocks who affect morale, job satisfaction and commitment, attendance, professional standing, and health. Impossible co-workers add more costs to already over-burdened budgets.

Stress is a necessary part of daily life, but can be a lifesaver, signaling your body in dangerous situations. For short periods of time, stress reportedly boosts the immune system. However, those with chronic stress are more prone to viral infections such as common colds and flu; in some cases vaccines are less effective. Stress affects everyone in different ways, depending on whether it is routine, everyday stress; stress brought on by sudden conflict; or traumatic stress resulting from accidents, war, assaults, tragedy, and natural disasters (National Institute for Mental Health 2012).

Stressing Out Because of the Economy

The crippling recession has had a major impact on the American workforce, compounded by problems with state funding. Because of the nature of the services, a large workforce and subsequently a large budget are necessary to keep up with demands from patrons. Often library budgets are among the largest and among the first to be cut (Siggins 1992, 299). In recent years operating budgets have been shrinking dramatically, resulting in frozen book budgets and cancelled journal and database subscriptions. When library workers retire, their positions often remain unfilled, forcing others to absorb their duties. Raises and promotions are also in limbo and whenever they are granted, the pay increases seldom cover cost of living increases.

Another added stress is the fear of losing healthcare benefits or being forced to pay premiums they can't afford. Performance anxiety, information overload, and techno-stress have crept into the consciousness of library workers (Van Fleet and Wallace 2003, 188–189). Stress in the workplace brought on by impossible coworkers, causes anxiety and depression.

In addition, its' effects on workers include changes in attitudes, beliefs, and behaviors among employees in every type of library. After lengthy exposure to these combined pressures some people exhibit out-of-character behaviors. Eventually, workers who may have been unhappy over an office incident may become chronic impossible co-workers

(Brinkman and Kirschner 2002, 24). To provide more insight into the issues faced by today's library workers, various studies reporting job satisfaction, salaries, and common complaints have been launched.

To Be Satisfied or Not Satisfied, That Is the Question

A job satisfaction survey conducted by Rebecca Miller, the Executive Editor of *Library Journal*, helped identify three of the top reasons for job dissatisfaction. Miller e-mailed the survey to approximately thirty-three thousand print and newsletter subscribers in February 2011, yielding a response rate of 11 percent. Of the 3,612 library workers who responded, 52 percent represented the public library spectrum; 26 percent, academic libraries; 16 percent, school libraries, 4 percent, corporate and/or special libraries; and 2 percent other types of libraries. Twenty-three percent cited low pay as their top reason for dissatisfaction with their jobs; 16 percent named poor management and administration; and budget concerns, 16 percent. Personal comments were included, capturing the pulse of the libraries. Mentioned problems included workload, burn-out, red-tape and bureaucracy, disappointing, unresponsive, and out-of-touch leadership (52–55).

When asked what measures were being taken to improve the situation, 34 percent indicated their library administrators or managers were doing little, if anything. Forty-seven percent felt there were very poor chances for advancement on the horizon. Seventy percent of the total respondents said they were satisfied with their jobs, but 31 percent were actively job searching. Six percent said they were looking for non-library jobs. Among those who indicated they were not at all satisfied with their current library jobs, 66 percent are job searching and 21 percent are leaving library service altogether (54). Miller's survey reports data very similar to the 2007 *Library Journal's* job satisfaction survey (Berry III, 26–29). Although data regarding difficult workers and workplace conflict were not part of neither Miller's nor Berry's surveys, the reasons mentioned for dissatisfaction strengthen our understanding of why library workers, out of frustration, have joined the ranks among the "difficult" or "impossible" in their workplaces.

Conflict Management in Libraries

Even though libraries do not exactly fit the traditional business model, there are many similarities—a library's products are the service they "sell." Libraries also have fixed operational budgets, management structures, a human resource department, and a team of professionals. Conflict management has not traditionally been included in the curriculum at library schools (Kathman and Kathman 1990, 145). In the 1920s and 1930s, businesses recognized the correlation between productivity and motivation and this was the beginning of management practices. Although libraries had begun to follow these trends, directors and administrators were often hired without relevant management experience, sometimes chosen for their social connections. Unfamiliar with teamwork, many library directors were not receptive to creative individuals and their ideas. The proper way to deal with conflict was to simply avoid it. (Montgomery and Cook 2005, 3–4).

You may think that things have improved during the last eighty years, but unfortunately, as revealed in a study by Montgomery and Cook the mentality regarding conflict still exists in some libraries today (2005, 4). Librarians have demonstrated tolerance for any type of conflict. When managers do nothing about problem employees, generally the problems worsen. Miriam Pollack, in her article "Cruel to Be Kind," maintains that libraries enable incompetence by allowing an environment with conflict to thrive (2008, 49). As library trends evolve to meet new demands of students who grow up tech-savvy, business management has become an important part of new library service models.

The Birth of the Impossible Co-Worker

Brinkman and Kirshner, in their 2002 book, *Dealing with People You Can't Stand*, explain that a person's behavior is based on their intent, whatever seems most important, and dictates how they behave (13–16). People will either focus on tasks or people. There are four main areas of focus: they may be driven by a task they need to get done; getting the task right may be the most important; being liked by others and getting along may be their focus; or their behavior is intended to be appreciated and get more appreciation from others.

If, in the course of action, a person fears that something they want isn't going to actually happen, or conversely, that something they were hoping wouldn't happen, is happening, their behavior may take a turn for the worse. The greater the threat perceived, the worse they will act. Sometimes their behavior can spiral out of control in a split second. Extreme behaviors are an attempt to control the situation and get things back on track. However when this happens to one of your co-workers, they may transform into your worst nightmare, the impossible co-worker.

Task-oriented workers focused on something important they intend to finish, may easily become extremely time-conscious and anxious, especially if the deadline is fast approaching. Sometimes they make mountains out of a molehill, irritated by distractions, with a low tolerance for questions and for workers who can't seem to follow directions.

When accuracy and precision are crucial, it is not uncommon to worry about mistakes and errors. Coupled with the pressure to complete the task, those concerned with getting it done right often feel they have to do everything themselves. They worry so much about getting things done correctly, they find themselves always on the look-out for mistakes, becoming hyper-critical, anticipating that everyone else's work will be inadequate.

Workers who are people oriented may be most concerned with getting along with others. The fear of being left out, of not being liked, of not fitting in cause them great anxiety, so they will constantly do things to seek approval from others, thinking that if someone approves of them, they'll like them. They often push aside what their own needs, just to please others (25–28).

When someone does things just to get noticed, they want people to see all the great things they do, in hopes co-workers will pay more attention to them, appreciate them more, and give them the reinforcement they need. Sometimes this stems from personal insecurities and jealousy. In some cases co-workers will opt for negative attention, which in itself can create unwanted conflict. Co-workers focusing on the same purpose are unlikely to have conflicts. According to Brinkman and Kirschner, when something appears to threaten a person's ability to fulfill their intent, their behavior changes, and in extreme cases marks the beginning of the "impossible co-worker" (24, 29).

Sinister Scenarios: Dealing with the Stress of Impossible Co-Workers

The following fictional examples of the impossible co-worker are based on cases studies and stories by Brinkman and Kirschner, Scott, and Montgomery and Cook. They may trigger some memories of your own encounters with difficult people at the workplace.

June's Dilemma

Horace is the circulation supervisor at a university library which includes a wing devoted to a children's book collection and teacher resources. June worked as a temporary part-time replacement while someone was on medical leave. She was a bubbly, friendly young woman and she really loved working with the children. When a position opened up in circulation, she accepted it. Friends told her a few stories about Horace the Horrible. She had a laugh but she wasn't worried. Horace told her they would be very busy working on an important project, which had to be finished in two months. She looked forward to working with Horace and thought maybe she had found her niche.

By the end of her second day, those illusions were shattered. June was working at the front desk when a young mother and her daughter came up to the counter. June stopped to visit with them for a moment and the little girl showed her a new book she had checked out. Horace appeared from nowhere. He started ranting in front of everyone. "We have a deadline but nothing is getting done because YOU are chatting up customers!" June couldn't believe her eyes or ears. His face was so red she thought he would burst into flames. "If you would let me explain, she is the director's..." June said to him, almost in tears. Before she could finish he interrupted her. "Bore someone else with your flimsy explanations," he snapped. "Get back to work, NOW!" She wanted to tell him they are the library director's daughter and granddaughter.

Luckily the mother and her little girl had not heard him. June had spoken just to be polite. Didn't he recognize them? They visit often. June wanted to tell him off, but she went back to her work. She wanted to explain. She considered going home sick. When Horace went to lunch she even called Human Resources to ask if there were other openings in the library. If Horace was going to act like this, she didn't think she could stand it.

What Should June Do?

Horace is a task-oriented person. His only focus is the end result. His verbal slam on June was motivated by his drive to finish the project. When he sees June wasting time, he loses it, becoming more controlling, because he fears they won't finish by the deadline. If she counterattacks, it will make things worse. Trying to explain is also in vain at this point because Horace is not interested in any explanations, excuses, or justifications. If she cowers, she'll lose the chance of getting his respect. The only thing that works with aggressive people is an assertive response. June needs to command respect and send a clear message showing her strength by holding her ground, looking him straight in the eye. If he starts in again, she should repeat his name calmly and assertively over and over until he stops. When he stopped snarling the first time, she could have asked, "Anything else?" followed by telling him "I'm going back to work because I want to finish this part today." At some point she may be able to gently tell him she knows how important this project is, but knew he would have greeted the director's daughter and granddaughter himself if he had been standing there.

Cora's Dilemma

Cora had been working in Library Tech Support for three years. Morgan her supervisor retired and as expected, Macklin the assistant supervisor was promoted. Cora and a woman named Sally, who had worked in the department only two months, interviewed for Macklin's position. A few days later Cora received the good news she was selected. From that moment on, Sally became a demon. She started gossiping about Cora, claiming Cora and Macklin were having an affair. Sally tried to be stealthy and anonymous when she called Cora's husband to ask him how he felt about her affair. Cora wondered what she had done to deserve this treatment. She tried ignoring Sally but it didn't help. One day, Macklin was out of the office and Cora had problems with her computer. She ran a couple of programs on it, but nothing worked so she sat at another computer for work. The next day when Cora walked in, Sally and several other women from the library were standing outside the office. As Cora approached, Sally pretended to lower her voice and then cackled "Hey, she's such a useless computer tech, she couldn't get her own computer to work." Everyone laughed and split up to go to their offices. Cora felt like crying but when she calmed down she felt like knocking Sally's head off.

What Should Cora Do?

Sally's main motive for her inexcusable behavior can be traced to her own insecurities and self-anger for not getting the job, but she blames Cora because she was the one promoted. Sally now has a grudge against Cora. Sally depends on her covert and devious techniques, knowing it will be hard to prove if Cora complains to Macklin. Sally's other motive is to get attention from her friends and to be liked. It won't help Cora if she retaliates, gets mad, or tried to get even with Sally. By calmly asking Sally about what she said, she can't hide her actions and she will lose her power. Cora should document everything that happened in case she needs it. When Cora approached and Sally was making fun of her, Cora could have asked Sally to step aside for a moment and she could ask Sally to explain what she should have done to fix her own computer. This would put Sally on the spot because it is doubtful she herself knew how to fix it. Eventually Cora should sit down with Sally and talk about the real reasons she is acting that way, listening carefully to everything Sally says. If that doesn't work it may become necessary to involve Macklin and ask that they all sit down together.

Finally, when trying to deal with the stress of impossible co-workers, it is important to remember there is no magic wand that will change them. Has making a Voodoo Doll and giving them some of their own medicine crossed your mind? Sorry, that won't work either because revenge usually backfires. People have to change on their own. Perhaps you have even considered quitting your job. Allowing others push you out is unacceptable.

Tips for Getting Along with Co-Workers

- Lock your lips—listen first, talk later
- Remember body language can speak volumes, sometimes more than words
- Focus on your own work and be the best you can be
- Avoid the blame-game; take responsibility for your own actions
- Watch for behavior patterns, adjusting your own attitude accordingly
- Look for the silver lining of every cloud ... or of every co-worker
- Command respect by being calm and taking the high road.
- Remember that loose lips sink ships; avoid gossip like the plague
- Blindsiding co-workers will bite you in the end
- Avoid adding fuel to the fire, i.e., counterattacks and revenge

In spite of the volumes of research on stress and managing conflict in the workplace, I think my mother had the right idea. She believes you should keep smiling; not even the grumpiest person can dislike a happy face. With impossible people, kill them with kindness. Treat others how you wish to be treated. If you can't say something nice, then don't say anything at all. And finally, if you don't know what to say, restrict your comments to the weather.

References

Berry, John N., III. "Great Work, Genuine Problems," *Library Journal* 132.16 (October 1, 2007):26–29.

Brinkman, Rick, and Rick Kirschner. *Dealing with People You Can't Stand: How to Bring Out the Best in People at Their Worst.* New York: McGraw-Hill, 2002.

Kathman, Jane McGurn, and Michael D. Kathman, *Journal of Academic Librarianship*, 16.3 (1990): 145–149.

Miller, Rebecca. "Rocked by Recession, Buoyed by Service: Braced to Meet the Tension of the Times, Most Still Feel Happy to Work in Libraries," Library Journal 136.10 (June 1, 2011): 52–55.

Montgomery, Jack G., and Eleanor I. Cook. *Conflict Management for Libraries: Strategies for a Positive, Productive Workplace.* Chicago: American Library Association, 2005.

National Institute of Mental Health, "Adult Stress—Frequently Asked Questions." Accessed July 26, 2012. http://www.nimh.nih.gov/health/publications/stress/stress_factsheet_ln.pdf.

Pantry, Sheila. *Managing Stress and Conflict in Libraries*. London: Facet Publishing, 2007.

Pollack, Miriam. "Cruel to Be Kind: Why Do We Keep Unproductive Employees?" *American Libraries* (October 2008): 48–50.

Scott, Gini Graham. *A Survival Guide for Working with Humans: Dealing with Whiners, Back-Stabbers, Know-It-Alls, and Other Difficult People*. New York: American Management Association, 2004.

Siggins, Jack A. "Job Satisfaction and Performance in a Changing Environment," *Library Trends* 41, no. 2 (Fall 1992): 299–315.

Van Fleet, Connie, and Danny P. Wallace. "Virtual Libraries—Real Threats: Technostress and Virtual Reference," *Reference & User Services Quarterly* (Spring 2003): 188–191.

Let's Work it Out: Managing Conflict in Libraries

Lisa A. Forrest

One of the more common perceptions of libraries is that they are quiet sanctuaries filled with books and tranquility. Based on this perception, it's understandable when others exclaim "You work in a library? That must be so relaxing!" Most of us who call the library our workplace know this perception can be a bit far from the truth. As library personnel struggle with the pressures of learning unfamiliar technologies, dealing with limited resources, and adjusting to new responsibilities, the library can be a stressful work environment. Some form of conflict between co-workers is inevitable. Conflict in the library is taxing for everyone involved, but if handled effectively, can be a creative force leading to improved communication and a stronger sense of workplace unity.

If you stop and add up the hours, most of us spend more waking hours at work than with our own families. And just as each family system is unique, individuals arrive to work each day with different life experiences and ways of dealing with stressful situations and conflict. Whether you were raised to openly confront others, be more passive-aggressive, or to run from conflict, chances are you'll do the same at the office. These learned behavioral scripts can have a huge impact on how we work with others, what bothers us, and whether or not we choose to openly address conflict. Distrust, workplace incivility, differing priorities, goal incompatibilities, apathy, and power struggles are just a few of the common causes of conflict. What these seemingly disparate causes all share is of high cost to the organization, as employees demonstrate a decrease in job involvement, commitment, and satisfaction. For the health of the organization, it's important that the causes of conflict be addressed quickly and directly. But where do we begin?

Often times, it seems so much easier to simply ignore the issues underlying conflict. In reality, ignoring these issues can only make things worse. Most of us have experienced how conflict can affect team efforts, lead to unprofessional behaviors, and divert people's attention from their work. If co-workers learn to confront each other with mutual respect and cooperation, healthy conflict can actually result in better decision making, improved motivation, decreased stress, and increased respect for one another's opinions. You don't have to be in an official position of management to serve as an emotionally intelligent leader who encourages healthy ways of dealing with conflict. Here are a few communication tips and tools, based upon the theories of emotional intelligence, which anyone can use to help improve a stressful environment and decrease conflict in the workplace.

Be a Good Role Model

One of the easiest ways to encourage better relations in the workplace is to model healthy ways of communicating. When engaging in stressful conversation, you'll be surprised how much influence your own, non-defensive reactions can have on others. When approaching a stressful topic, it always helps to practice what you will say before you say it, and stick to the topic at hand. Improving your own communication skills can make a huge difference in situations of conflict at work or home. Need a little guidance? Check with your Human Resources department for upcoming seminars on healthy workplace communication. There are a multitude of books out there which focus on communicating effectively in the workplace. One idea to encourage healthy communication is to start a lunch-time book club focusing on popular leadership books such as *Crucial Conversations: Tools for Talking When Stakes Are High* (Patterson et al., 2002). Take a leadership role by promoting relevant books, media, and continuing education opportunities to your colleagues.

Are You Listening?

When it comes to communication skills, listening is just as important as to what is being said. Although it seems like a passive activity, good listening actually takes a lot of self-control. As a listener, whenever we react by diagnosing, criticizing, advising, questioning, joking, or changing the subject, we have stopped listening. Be aware of any tendencies you have to interrupt, and try incorporating better listening skills into your daily exchanges with family, friends, and colleagues. Keep in mind when someone tells you about an issue, your job is not to "fix" or diagnose any problem. What are the feelings behind what is being said? Try to just listen and reflect back what you think the speaker is saying to you (i.e., "I can tell this situation is really upsetting you.") In times of conflict, skilled, reflective listening can help diffuse a stressful situation by validating the other person's feelings. (Goleman 1995, 145–146).

Tell It Like It Is

How do you communicate negative feelings in a productive manner, especially when you are in the midst of intense emotions? If you're like most people, it can be a real challenge to get an accurate message across when you are upset. Try dividing up your communication into three parts. First, describe the problem behavior that is occurring, such as, "When you are late for your Reference Desk shift." Next, describe how this makes you feel, "When you are late for your Reference Desk shift, I feel anxious." Then state how this behavior ultimately affects you, "When you are late for your Reference Desk shift, I feel anxious because it makes me late for my next meeting" (Bocchino 1999, 96–101). These steps can help to clarify the issue at hand, and allow the other person to become more aware of how their actions affect others. Ultimately, this can lead to changed patterns of behavior (and perhaps an apology if needed). It can also help you to assess whether or not your own reactions are appropriate to the situation. Don't make the all-too-common mistake of using e-mail to discuss important topics. The tone of your message can become entirely misconstrued, leading to confusion and more conflict. Face-to-face interactions can allow for reflective listening and immediate clarification of each other's thoughts and ideas.

Keep Your Emotions in Check

When you are angry or stressed, it's easy to become over emotional, which can lead to unhealthy ways of communicating. One of the key components of emotional intelligence is knowing yourself and how you react in stressful situations (Goleman 1995, 46–55). This knowledge can help you make good choices with regards to your reactions. You become aware of your feelings (i.e., "I'm mad"), but not lost in the emotions (i.e., you storm out of the room). How does one work on self-awareness? Try saying "I think" or "I feel" before making a statement to others. When you are calm, reflect on past encounters and don't be afraid to ask others for their opinion on how you reacted. Keep a journal of how a certain situation made you feel and how you expressed these feelings. When paying attention to your own inner thoughts, stay positive and be aware of any negative scripts (i.e., "She is always so bossy.") that may be replaying in your head. If do you feel yourself losing control in a situation, it's okay to excuse yourself and explain you need a few minutes to regain your composure.

Try on a New Pair of Shoes

Empathy, or being able to recognize emotions in others, is one of the most important social skills we can foster within ourselves (Goleman 1995, 96–110). Being able to accurately observe facial expressions, body posture, and tone of voice, can help you to make smart decisions when relating to others. The more we are aware of our own feelings, the better we are at reading the feelings of others. When working on empathy, ask yourself questions such as, "How would I respond in this situation" or "What would be the best way for me to be told this"? When reflecting on an experience, try imagining different reactions from varying viewpoints (this can be a useful journal activity). For example, how would extending library hours affect the Circulation staff differently from the Reference Librarians? Fine tuning your empathy skills can help to make you a more sensitive, understanding, and caring colleague.

Manage Yourself

Are you constantly battling feelings of distress and anxiety? Or are you able to brush off difficulty and get on with your day? The easiest remedies for negative energy include deep breathing, exercising, journal writing, and laughing! When dealing with others, try not to be a mind reader; chances are, the other person is thinking something completely different. Remind yourself you work in a library, not an emergency room. As hard as it can be, don't inflate everyday events to total catastrophes. Pause and ask yourself, "What is the worst that can happen in this situation?" When life in the library gets a little too dramatic, answering this question can be a great way to bring inflated situations back down to reality. Again, your positive thinking and good role modeling can help set the tone for how others react to stressful situations.

Don't Be a Gossip Girl

There's little else more damaging to an organization than gossip. It corrodes trust, the basis for all good relationships, and can contribute to stress and conflict. How does one stop the gossip? Simply do not participate in the rumor mill. You can set a good example by being explicit with your own personal guidelines. When someone attempts to rope you into a "juicy story," tell them that you prefer not to talk about the personal issues of your co-workers and walk away. Encourage your close friends at work to do the same. Avoid having to learn things the hard way by keeping your own personal issues private.

Abolish Silent Rules

How many times have you secretly resented someone because they didn't behave as you would have in the same situation? Remember people often don't behave the way we want them to act, so don't set yourself up for disappointment by creating silent rules of how you think others should behave (Montgomery et al., 2005, 155). It's not fair to you or your colleagues. If you feel your silent rule should be made public, now is the time to put your communication skills into high gear and call a meeting to discuss it!

When the Going Gets Tough

In times of stress and conflict, it can be hard to stay focused and address the issue at hand. It's so easy to bring up past grudges or personal attacks when you are feeling upset, but doing so can only complicate matters. When speaking, remember to clearly define what has upset you and why. If you start to bring in other issues or feel like you are losing control, it's best to excuse yourself and approach the situation again with a clearer head (just don't storm out of the room!). When excusing yourself to clarify your thoughts, what are your own intentions? Does your assessment of the situation change if looked at from a different perspective with more empathy? Are there alternatives to solving the problem? How might you accomplish your objectives in a cooperative manner? Do you need to involve management in order to come to a resolution? Once you are able to answer these questions, approach the issue with your colleague again.

Are You Motivated?

Behind every productive person is a lot of motivation. But in stressful environments, it can be incredibly difficult to maintain the level of motivation needed for creativity and mastery. To stay motivated, start by imagining yourself successful and then assign yourself meaningful, achievable goals (Montgomery 2005, 156). You can truly help set the tone of how others act by staying optimistic. Surround yourself with like-minded, positive thinking friends and co-workers. Control your own office space, fill it with things to motivate and inspire you such as photos of loved ones, favorite books, and images. Arrange social events or team building activities with your cohorts, and help to make your work environment a little more fun!

Job Well Done

We all like to hear positive feedback from others. Whether you are a manager or a co-worker, knowing how to carefully critique another's work is a skill worth honing and can help to improve workplace morale. When discussing someone else's work, focus on the specifics of what the person has done and is capable of doing, not what is lacking. If there are things that you think could be done better, offer possible solutions for improvement. Your colleagues will appreciate the thoughtfulness you gave to the project, and can learn how to better communicate from your good example.

Imagine

Conflict in the workplace can be very stressful and greatly affect job satisfaction. One technique often used in managing stress is visualization. When you are feeling most stressed, imagine yourself in a peaceful place where all anxieties and tensions disappear. Whether a tropical island or the comfort of your living room — recall the sights, sounds, and smells and let yourself relax a bit. On your work break, take a walk outside of the building and give yourself time and space to re-energize. Learn how to incorporate simple yoga exercises, such as chair stretches and breathing exercises, into your work day. Find solitude by escaping to a sunny corner of the library to work on reading or writing projects. You only have one life, so you might as well start finding ways to improve the everyday quality of it. Simple stress relieving techniques like visualization and meditation can have a huge effect on how you feel about your day and your job!

Librarians, despite their amicable reputations, are not invulnerable to the effects of stress and conflict. All too often, the stress of the workplace prohibits employees from being able to fully appreciate the positive aspects of their jobs. Learning how to better communicate with co-workers, especially during times of stress, can lead to a happier, more productive workplace environment. No matter your position within the library, you can have a huge influence on how others react to situations of conflict. Things you can do to reduce stress and conflict at work:

- Model healthy communication
- Be a good listener
- Describe the problem, how it makes you feel and affects you
- Don't let emotions rule your communications
- Emphasize and recognize emotions in others
- Manage your negative energy
- Don't participate in gossip or give co-workers the silent treatment
- Be optimistic and positive
- Make work fun
- Complement others with positive feedback

Through modeling good communication skills, encouraging team building, and utilizing stress management techniques, you can be a positive force in making the library a peaceful and satisfying place to work.

References

Bocchino, Rob. *Emotional Literacy: To Be a Different Kind of Smart.* California: Corwin Press, 1999.

Goleman, Daniel. *Emotional Intelligence.* New York: Bantam Books, 1995.

Montgomery, Jack G., Eleanor I. Cook, Patricia Jean Wagner, and Glenda T. Hubbard. *Conflict Management for Libraries: Strategies for a Positive, Productive Workplace.* Illinois: ALA, 2005.

Patterson, Kerry, Joseph Grenny, Ron McMillan, and Al Switzler. *Crucial Conversations: Tools for Talking When Stakes Are High.* New York: McGraw-Hill, 2002.

Gender Specific Stress Management Strategies

Leigh A. Woznick

Men and women tend to cope differently with stress. Simply broaching the subject invites debate. Not everyone fits into socio-political stereotypes of gender, and there can be more variety within a gender than between them (Stanton 2004). Any person can choose from a range of coping strategies. There is a host of other factors that affect one's coping style, including: age, education level, ethnicity or culture, past experiences, personality traits, job characteristics, and many more. My purpose is not to condemn or condone any one particular style. It is simply to recognize tendencies and explore strategies as models for stressed out librarians. Numerous research studies have shown that certain coping styles tend to be used by men, and others by women. Recognizing what stresses you out, and how you cope, can reduce the effects of stress (Kirk 2011). Since we all interact with numerous colleagues, patrons and administrators, understanding how others cope can reduce the effects of their behavior on you as well.

What Are We Dealing With?

Librarians face the same job stresses as men and women in other occupations: interpersonal conflicts, overworked, understaffed, wasted time/effort, lack of recognition, reduced funding, organizational constraints and job insecurity (Mazzola 2011). The nature of the profession brings specific stresses: frequent and varied interactions with students or patrons (some of whom are difficult), keeping up with new technology, changing roles or job responsibilities, challenges to materials, time constraints, and low salaries. Chronic or long-term stresses on top of the little daily ones or feeling that we have no control over circumstances can make things worse (Kemeny 2003). If we let it get to us, we may find ourselves burned-out, exhausted, cynical, and doubtful of our ability to make a difference (Attafar 2011). The stereotypical image of libraries as calm, quiet, peaceful places belies the bustling reality. Like everyone else, we also have stresses off the job, including financial concerns, caring for children or family members, personal health, family or partner relationships, community responsibilities, and so on. This pile-up of stress can have significant effects on our bodies, minds, and emotions.

How to Deal

Coping strategies are "specific efforts, both behavioural and psychological, that people employ to master, tolerate, eliminate or minimize stressful events or their impact" (Mazzola 2011). These can be long or short-term strategies, and are commonly grouped into two categories: problem-focused, or active strategies, which focus on a specific problem and involve action to directly address it; and emotion-focused, or reaction strategies, which focus on emotions, are usually used in situations that can't be changed, and influence how you perceive or handle the stress (Bennett 2006; Kirk 2011; Mazzola 2011; Krajewski 2005; Torkelson 2004; Woznick 2002). Researchers differ on which is more effective.

Common Coping Strategies

Problem-focused strategies:

- Take direct action
- Confront/address a person or situation
- Gather information, take stock of the situation, planning
- Learn/practice new skills, professional development
- Change something about yourself
- Time management, reduce responsibilities, refuse to take on new ones
- Prioritize, handle things one at a time
- Let go of things you can't do; delegate; ask for help, mobilize resources

Emotion-focused strategies:

- Seek emotional, collegial and/or spiritual support; talk to others, vent
- Release tension/do something physical: exercise, dance, gardening, sports, yell, cry
- Relaxation exercises, meditation, positive imagery, self-talk
- Take care of yourself, "me-time," hobbies, maintain a sense of personal worth
- Withdrawal: listen to music; being passive, put up emotional barriers
- Avoidance; denial
- Escape: movies, driving, shopping, reading
- Look at it a different way, wishful thinking, look on the bright side, focus on positive, search for personal meaning, compare self to others
- Quick coping strategies: count to 10, deep breath, remove yourself from scene to regroup
- Acceptance, hardening your heart
- Seek professional counseling

Depending on the situation, strategies can move between the two categories. For example, purposefully setting aside work stresses to focus on responsibilities at home or give yourself time to see a problem in light of a new day could be considered an active strategy. Prioritizing can be a way to reframe what's important in your life. While the division does not show the whole picture by any means, it is a common conception that men draw primarily from problem-focused strategies, and women primarily from emotion-focused strategies.

Men

Although they may loathe admitting it, men suffer from stress as much as women do. They report it less. They say they're doing enough to manage it. While they aren't likely to claim excellent relationship skills or healthy lifestyle habits, they probably won't change their behavior, either. Men have fewer friendships, smaller social networks, and aren't likely to seek professional counseling, effectively cutting themselves off from good sources of support. They are reluctant to admit the impact of stress on their physical or mental health. Yet they are more often diagnosed with chronic stress-related health problems such as high blood pressure, type 2 diabetes, or heart disease (American Psychological Association 2012; Stanton 2004). This all sounds pretty grim. In fact, however, men do use a variety of coping strategies (APA 2012; Levant 2011; Mazzola 2011; Stanton 2004; Torkelson 2004).

COPING STRATEGIES COMMONLY EMPLOYED BY MEN

- Take direct action
- Make a plan, set goals
- Intellectual, logical, rational problem-solving
- Rely on themselves, highlight their strengths
- Unwind physically after work, play sports to release tension
- Withdraw socially
- Denial, distraction, talk themselves out of it
- Channel vulnerable emotions into anger and aggression, and caring emotions through sex
- Use of alcohol or drugs
- Less likely to confide in friends, disclose problems, ask for help
- Less likely to focus on or vent emotions

Society pressures men to be strong, in control, knowledgeable, assertive, aggressive, competitive, independent, professionally successful, self-reliant and stoic; being vulnerable, emotional, passive, and asking for help are frowned upon (Levant 2011; Stanton 2004; Woznick 2002).

Traditional male tendencies to bottle up emotions and a reluctance to reach out to support, can lead some men to less helpful coping strategies, such as avoidance, denial, social withdrawal, or the use of alcohol or drugs. According to Stanton (2004), men don't respond to stress in healthy ways, have more physical symptoms of stress, and recover more slowly from stress. This results in more anxiety, depression and psychological stress (Levant 2011). Attafar reports that male librarians in Iran suffer more emotional exhaustion (lack of energy and emotional resources, fatigue), and depersonalization (cynicism toward organization and patrons) than their female counterparts (2011).

Other traditional male traits, being self-sufficient, assertive, and knowledgeable, lead to positive coping, such as planning, problem-solving, highlighting strengths and releasing tension. The stereotypical take-charge guy doesn't focus on the stress, though he certainly feels it; he gets the job done. For example, David, a MS/HS librarian, told me, "I turned in three book orders totaling about $4500. I expected to find boxes of new books when I returned [in the fall]. Instead, the principal brought my POs back and told me that I had only $2000 to spend. I revised the purchase orders and turned them back in." Men are also good at compartmentalizing. David continued, "I pray about problems, then stop worrying about them…. I also try to keep various parts of my life separate from each other, so that school problems don't carry over to church, church problems don't carry over to school, and neither carries over to home."

Women

Women report higher levels of stress, and experience it more intensely. They report more interpersonal conflict. Instead of winding down after work, they tend to gear up for home obligations. Women perceive less control over stressful situations than men do. They know how important it is to manage stress, but unlike men, are more critical of how they are handling it. Like men, they suffer from stress-related health problems, but they tend to have better long-term psychological and physical health than men. Perhaps because of their sensitivity to stress, women use multiple strategies, and employ them more often. (APA, 2012; Bennett, 2006; Kirk 2011; Krajewski, 2005; Stanton, 2004; Mazzola, 2011; Torkelson, 2004).

Coping Strategies Commonly Employed by Women

- Talk to co-workers and family, vent emotions
- Ask a colleague or boss for help
- Spend time with family/friends
- Pray/go to religious services; spiritual support
- Escapes: shop, get a massage, read
- Seek professional mental help

Like men, some stereotypical traits lead to positive coping skills, including seeking emotional support, asking for help, and controlling negative emotions. The predominance of women in the workplace can give them an advantage, in that there is a built-in support system. Psychologist Shelley Taylor proposed a new term for this factor that affects how women cope with stress, with a possibly evolutionary biological basis. She says that under stress, instead of the traditional "fight-or-flight" reaction, women "tend-and-befriend," by nurturing themselves and others and building social networks (2000). One school librarian explained, "My fellow teachers, my friends, get me through so many days! It can be so lonely when you are the only one of you on a campus ... my friends are there to listen. Even if they (and I) can't change anything, it is good to have shoulders upon which to cry!" This could partially explain why women use more emotion-focused strategies: because they involve attachment to others and engaging social networks (Bennett 2006).

That same trait can become a source of stress. Because interpersonal relationships are so important to women, social conflicts are far more stressful than they are for men (Krajewski 2005). A school librarian tells how she coped with one such situation: "I had a principal who was picking on me and I resolved to 'stick it out.' I just did the best job I could and proved him wrong every time he tried to get me fired. He put me on a plan for improvement and I showed him just how good I was. He was transferred 5 years later to a job where he was not over teachers after numerous complaints."

Putting too much importance on relationships can make it hard for a woman to ignore advice, pleasing others instead of doing what's best for herself, giving up her own needs for those of others (Bennett 2006). Women worry about what others think of them, and put pressure on themselves to do it all, feeling guilty when they can't. Another librarian told me: "I am working hard not to apologize for what is not my fault. For example, the library printer broke. I didn't break it, so I altered my e-mail warning of the problem three times until I was not the one saying sorry. I think when I take ownership of issues that aren't mine it makes me feel worse and others view it as a situation I can control when I cannot." This seemingly small strategy reframed her own and others' perceptions and expectations of herself. I recently did something similar myself, changing my explanation for not reserving books. Instead of saying, "I just can't, it's too much," I now say, "we don't have sufficient staff to provide that service." Not only does it stop me from being a doormat, but it gets the message across that we are understaffed.

Women often have the additional role of primary caregiver for children and family members, emotional caretaker of the family, and still do the bulk of daily housework and childcare, with less leisure time than men (Bennett 2006, Crosby 2006). This can add to their strain. This strain is mitigated by the sense of achievement women gain in each role. Satisfaction and balance between work and home provides a core of strength, for both men and women. If something goes wrong in one, you can focus on success in the other, at least temporarily (Betz 2006). Then again, the combination of low pay, lack of autonomy, job insecurity and the current climate of devaluation of librarians no doubt dampens that sense of achievement, for men and women.

Librarians

I conducted a small, admittedly unscientific survey of coping strategies on LM-NET. All but one who responded were women. I have already shared some of their thoughtful responses. My observations from that survey, and from my experience, are that librarians are generally able to handle their job stresses. They acknowledge them, accept that certain stresses go with the job, and generally use good strategies to alleviate it. Only a few stressors were rated high, including, as you might expect: work overload, understaffing, and extreme situations (difficult co-worker/boss, library fire, additional or unreasonable expectations, and job insecurity). It's pure speculation, but one might wonder whether the very traits that make them good librarians also function as good coping strategies, such as being intelligent, organized, gatherers of information and considerate of multiple points of view.

Farler found that librarians often use humor to help them deal with difficult patrons. I remember an incident in my own library, when two students were trying to explain what they wanted. Because they didn't quite know themselves, and used terminology given them by their Chinese language teacher, I could not understand them. It took a few minutes of laughing and redirecting, but we finally figured it out. An aide, who had been watching the interaction, expressed amazement at the way I handled it, as she had been stressed by the situation. Like most librarians, I have interactions like that every day. Someone needs something from me, and I have to figure out how to give it to them. Stress can be positive, for example, when it encourages connections (Farler 2012).

The majority of the female librarians who responded to my survey rated interpersonal relationships with coworkers as not stressful, contrary to Mazzola's 2011 findings that women report interpersonal conflicts as highly stressful. The two that reported high stress were extreme cases involving a difficult administrator and a clerk with a mental illness, which would be highly stressful to anyone. Most reported that co-workers were a source of support. They also rarely delegated to others. Librarians are a self-sufficient bunch, overall, but due to understaffing, there may be no one to delegate to, at least on the job. Talking to an administrator or supervisor was used in governance situations where the boss' intervention was absolutely necessary (staffing issues, questions of responsibilities), which is in line with Farler's 2012 findings.

The female responses did show a typical tendency for using a variety of coping strategies, including both those traditionally associated with men and those with women. The problem-focused and emotional—focused coping strategies reported were:

- Ask for help
- Venting to coworkers
- Ask for others' opinions or advice; change my mind
- Take it one day at a time
- Time alone; take care of myself
- Sleep on it or pray
- Spend time with friends and family
- Solve the problem myself; don't let the problem fester
- Approach people directly
- Stand up for myself

- Gather information
- Document what I do; get assistance from a union representative
- Prioritize
- Refuse to take on additional tasks
- Work on activities such as gardening or crafts
- Exercise such as bike rides, swimming, or dancing
- Listen to music; surfing the Internet and social networking web sites
- Stay busy and tough it out

These are in line with the styles previously mentioned, which are that women use multiple strategies, and when they use problem-focused strategies, they add emotion-focused strategies, as well (Torkelson 2004).

My one male respondent reported predominantly traditional male problem-focused coping strategies, with the exception of also asking for help sometimes, and rarely using avoidance, alcohol/drugs or bottling up anger. He also, typically, reported far fewer symptoms of stress. A survey of more male librarians could be more revealing of their characteristics. All responses reported rarely or never using: denial, avoiding the problem or person, getting revenge, seeking counseling, letting out anger, and alcohol or drugs. It seems we have a healthy coping group on LM-NET, at least in the small group that responded.

Why Look at Gender?

According to the most recent ALA survey (2012), our membership is still predominantly female (more than 80 percent). It is traditionally a female occupation, but that does not necessarily mean those who take the job have traditional views on gender roles. Our own upbringings have socialized us in certain ways, although we tend to be a liberal bunch. Another factor to consider is that more administrators and supervisors are men, including in business and education (Betz 2006). Principals and library administrators may more often be men. While administrative jobs may be changing over to include more women, new technical library positions are more often filled with men (Edge 2011). People in managerial or administrative positions have more power and resources, and tend to use direct action coping, whether they are men or women, but those that are women also look for emotional or social support. Men and women in non-managerial positions follow along more traditional lines (Torkelson 2004). Interactions between managers or administrators and employees who are of different genders can have associated conflicts or misunderstandings.

Librarians don't always easily fit into either of those two slots. They are highly educated (at all levels), but their job descriptions, power structure, and levels of autonomy differ widely, not only between school, public and special libraries, but also within each category. This makes it difficult to account for job status as a factor. I reviewed several valid psychological research articles on occupational stress and gender coping, as well as articles on librarian stress, but haven't found any studies that deal specifically with librarians with regard to gender. It hardly seems necessary, given the demographics of our profession. I conducted my own survey because I wondered whether librarians would break the mold, so to speak, on traditional gender coping styles. The results were inconclusive.

It's not simply a question of whether librarians fit the stereotypical gender mold. They may or may not. The fact is most of us interact with a wide range of other people, on and off the job. In a stressful situation, evaluating the behavior of yourself and the other person, as either a signal of stress or as a coping strategy (positive or negative), and pinpointing triggers that set them off, can help you better understand the situation, react more calmly and appropriately, and perhaps avoid the situation in the future.

Remember that men and women can react differently, even in the same situation. According to Stanton (2004), "learning patterns and conversational styles of women and men in this society differ distinctively, because women and men respond to and accept information differently." Men report less stress and women report more, but their perceptions are subjective and personal. The point is not to compare apples and oranges, but to appreciate what a person is experiencing, taking into account the "glasses" they are looking through.

References

American Library Association Office for Research & Statistics. "ALA Demographics Studies." *American Library Association.* March, 2012. http://www.ala.org/research/initiatives/membershipsurveys.

American Psychological Association. "Stress in America." *American Psychological Association.* January 11, 2012. http://www.apa.org/news/press/releases/stress/2011/gender.aspx.

Attafar, Ali, Simar Asl Nastaran, and Arash Shahin. "Effects of Demographic and Personal Factors on Job Burnout: An Empirical Study in Iran." *International Journal of Management* 28, no. 4 (Dec 2011): 275–286.

Bennett, Patricia A., and Susan H. McDaniel. "Coping in adolescent girls and women." In *Handbook of Girls' and Women's Psychological Health: Gender Well-Being Across the Life Span*" edited by Judith Worell and Carol D. Goodheart, 138–148. New York: Oxford, 2006.

Betz, Nancy E. "Women's Career Development." In *Handbook of Girls' and Women's Psychological Health: Gender Well-Being Across the Life Span*" edited by Judith Worell and Carol D. Goodheart, 312–320. New York: Oxford, 2006.

Crosby, Faye J., and Laura Sabbatini. "Family and Work Balance." In *Handbook of Girls' and Women's Psychological Health: Gender Well-Being Across the Life Span*" edited by Judith Worell and Carol D. Goodheart, 350–358. New York: Oxford, 2006.

Edge, John M. "Growing Pains: How Technology Is Influencing Human Resources in Academic Libraries." *Library Student Journal.* June 2011. http://www.librarystudentjournal.org/index.php/lsj/article/view/199/306#lamont.

Farler, Liz, and Judith Broady-Preston. *Aslib Proceedings,* 64, no. 3 (2012): 225–240.

Kemeny, Margaret E. "The Psychobiology of Stress." *Current Directions in Psychological Science* 12, no. 4 (Aug, 2003): 124–129.

Kirk, Chang. "Less Stressed at Work: Research on the Efficacy of Job Stress Coping Strategies." *Advances in Management* 4, no. 11 (2011): 31–40.

Krajewski, Henryk T., and Richard D. Goffin. "Predicting Occupational Coping Responses: The Interactive Effect of Gender and Work Stressor Context." *Journal of Occupational Health Psychology* 10, no. 1 (2005): 44–53.

Levant, Ronald F. "Research in the Psychology of Men and Masculinity Using the Gender Role Strain Paradigm as a Framework." *American Psychologist* (Nov. 2011): 765–776.

Mazzola, Joseph J., Irvin Sam Schonfeld, and Paul E. Spector. "What Qualitative Research Has Taught Us About Occupational Stress." *Stress and Health* 27 (2011): 93–110.

Stanton, Annette L., and Will Courtenay. "Gender, Stress and Health." In *Psychology Builds a Healthy World: Opportunities for Research and Practice*, edited by Ronald H. Rozensky, Norine G. Johnson, Carol D. Goodheart, and W. Rodney Hammond, 105–135. Washington, DC: American Psychological Association, 2004.

Taylor, Shelley, et al. "Biobehavioral Responses to Stress in Females: Tend-and-befriend, not Fight-or-flight." *Psychological Review* 107, no. 3 (2000): 411–429.

Torkelson, Eva, and Tuija Muhonen. "The Role of Gender and Job Level in Coping with Occupational Stress." *Work & Stress* 18, no. 3 (2004): 267–274.

Woznick, Leigh A., and Carol D. Goodheart. *Living with Childhood Cancer: A Practical Guide to Help Families Cope.* Washington, DC. American Psychological Association, 2002.

Laughter in the Library

SU EPSTEIN

Laughter and play in the library may seem almost antithetical. Even with our new friendlier image as the abandoned "shusher," a library is still a place of intellect, knowledge, learning, and literacy. Librarians hope we can accomplish these things with an element of fun, but the idea of guffaws ringing through the stack, would still make many of us shudder. Although many view libraries as tranquil work environments, those who have worked in these locations know this to be anything but true.

Libraries can be stressful places. In 2006, the BBC reported librarianship as one of the most stressful jobs. While there are many things we cannot change in the library, laughter and play can help alleviate stress and make our work environment more pleasant.

The idea that laughter is the best medicine is nothing new or original. Everyone from Oprah to the Mayo Clinic has purported this idea. Medical research has suggested that laughter not only relieves tension in the short term, but can have long term medical benefits such as improving one's immune system and relieving pain. Psychologically, it makes you feel good. Laughter and play are believed to increase personal satisfaction, help you cope with difficult situations, and connect with others.

Librarians often forget that humor can take many forms, as can laughter. One does not have to roll on the floor with tear flooded eyes to benefit. Likewise, if you've ever been an adult who has dined with a handful of pre-teen girls, you know first-hand what is hilarious to some is completely baffling to others. What makes something funny is difficult. Academic studies have suggested humor comes from harmless criticism of the way the world ought to be. I would suggest this could go a step further. Humor not only includes things that go against the way things should be, but some humor points out the ridiculousness of the way things are. Likewise, while a deep belly laugh feels good, sometimes all we need is a small smile or chuckle. Humor can defuse the tensest situations, save the day, our health and our sanity. It can bring diverse and conflicting parties together and most important, it makes us human. So how can we use humor and play in the library, relieve stress, keep our decorum, and stay within the library's mission? Some librarians and customers would say, "We can't." I would say, let me tell you how.

A Time and a Place Do No Harm

No doubt, at some point growing up you heard, "there is a time and a place for everything." At least for me, this was often followed by "and this is not it." Some librarians or customers might argue working in the library is not the time or place for humor. There are certainly situations when working that humor would be uncalled for, but not always. Having found myself in the unfortunate position of cleaning up a young person's "accident," humor was about the only way through it. ("They didn't teach this in Library School!")

To utilize humor at work one has to be a thoughtful and considerate person. First and foremost, we should borrow an idea from the medical profession: do no harm. Work place humor should never offend, threaten, or make anyone uncomfortable. As professionals, being humorous or not, we should be aware of where we are and what we are saying. Therefore, I believe a good administrator, be it a director, a manger or supervisor needs to know their staff. Likewise, a good staff knows their patrons. The use of humor in the work place requires sensitivity and not being rude or hurtful. It also requires the strength to set boundaries. If you use humor all of the time, in all situations, you very likely will be voted the class clown and not taken seriously as a librarian. Humor is great for easing tension, relieving stress and bridging gaps. It is not for cajoling favors, or asserting power. Do not confuse humor as a means of winning friends or influencing people.

In fact, for those who allow or even encourage humor in the work place, you must be willing and able to compassionately say no. Depending on the size of one's work place, the odds are very good that eventually you will be working with a co-worker who has no sense of humor. Sometimes jokes have to be explained to them; this is not an easy task, but something you need to be prepared to do. Honest, straightforward, thoughtful explanations are always best.

When I worked in a school library, my sense of humor quickly became known. Students learned I appreciated a good joke and there were little harmless pranks I would chuckle at and not pursue. However, there was always a student who did not recognize the difference between a harmless prank and an inappropriate act: the joke gone too far or the unintentional painful comment. To use humor, know the boundaries and be ready and willing to explain them. Remember the context. Dirty jokes are not appropriate. However, bad library puns are often appreciated.

Laugh With, Not At

Work place humor should never be directed AT a colleague or patron. Again, this takes a considered and conscious effect. If something would offend you, don't say it about another! Respect is the key.

For instance, I shamefully admit I am a fan of "blonde jokes." This reflects my personal sense of humor and not my belief about the abilities of one whose hair is a particular color. I will not share my blonde jokes with my colleagues, because, not being blonde myself, I do not want them to misconstrue my intentions. I will, however, since I am of short statue, happily make jokes at my own vertically challenged expense.

A distinction should always be made between childlike and childish. For some this can be a difficult division, and so I have come to use what I think of as the "Halloween Explanation." Many dress up in fanciful things for Halloween, but we do not change our behavior. Dressing up is childlike and behaving as the character we appear as maybe childish. This explanation shifted, of course with the age of the person with whom I was having the discussion. Kindergartners responded well to a tiger as an example, while I might reference vampires or horror movie characters with older individuals.

Be Willing to Laugh at Yourself

Laughing at yourself can ease a lot of tension. It can make you seem human, more "real" and less intimidating. Also it shows a confidence most people in the work place respect. Imagine you have just said or done a most ridiculous thing, as we all at some point do. Your colleagues are standing around you — now wondering if you realize this was ridiculous. Should they take a risk and point this out? Stress is building. There is nothing that will relieve tension as much as your saying, "Duh? What was I just thinking?" and being willing to laugh at yourself.

In every position and location I have worked, there has been the need to brainstorm: what do we do for programming? What will be our next display? How can we communicate this new service or updated program? How do we apply for this grant? We sit and generate ideas. This is work, and we get silly.

I have sat in many of these sessions in which the library staff generated wording that definitely was not for public display, but was very funny. Sometimes these moments happen naturally when everyone is willing to let themselves go. While trying to come up with a Valentine's Day program for children, I once innocently turned to the Children's Librarian and said, "What about speed dating for toddlers?" In my mind I was innocently thinking, how do we capitalize on play dates? There was a moment of silence, and I registered what seemed to be a look of panic on my colleague's face. Then, I realized the ridiculousness of what I had just said, rolled my eyes and laughed, apologizing and explaining.

This exchange became a classic moment. From that point on, whenever anyone started to have a crazy idea we'd say, "Speed dating for toddlers?" The phrase would preface things being offered as humor, knowing they were not appropriate or things that might be too out there like speed dating for toddlers, but it always made us chuckle.

Remembering to Play

In 2009, *Scientific America* devoted its cover to play and proclaimed play was crucial for normalcy. As something imperative for social, emotional and cognitive development, the article claimed it made us better adjusted, smarter, and of course ... less stressed. We have heard this from many sources, but how many of us include play regularly in our daily routine?

Likewise, many librarians and customers conceptualize "play" as the opposite of "work." Most librarians "play" over the weekend by taking a skiing trip, going to a movie or engaging in a hobby. Other forms of "play" include video or board games, but for most of us, playing at work is unheard of. However, as humor takes many forms and mirth has many levels, work and play can coexist.

At one university library, the top of the file cabinets in technical services is covered with toys: old action figures, dinosaurs, toy cars. This collection has been acquired over the years as various staff contributed. There is no theme or coordination of scale; it is simply a collection of toys. Not only does the collection make people smile, but frequently objects get arranged in unique ways. One afternoon Spock might appear to be having a serious discussion with a Tyrannosaurus Rex. A few weeks later, a different figure might be appearing to nibble on a piece of giant fruit. At some point Barbie could be found intently reading a withdrawn copy of D.H. Lawrence. When the library staff noticed the scene, they would smile. They might add something to the vignette, and they would play.

Usually on my desk I have a slinky or snow globe. Everyone notices it and sometimes they ask about the items. When I need a minute to think or I've reached a frustration point, taking a minute to play with these items breaks the tension and sets me back on course.

All these examples of play in the work place serve several functions. First, they are fun. Second, they make people laugh. Additionally, they increase creativity, allowing workers to let their minds go for a few minutes. Play allows people to take a quick break, switch gears, de-stress and the result is often better productivity.

Don't Forget the Furry Friends

A furry animal can add a calming effect and fun to the work place. The act of petting something is soothing, and the therapeutic value of pets is well documented. I am green with envy over Dewey, the library cat at the Spencer Public Library in Iowa. I have always wanted to work in a library with a pet: cat, hamster, even a rat would be fine. Unfortunately logistics, costs, allergies and fears have always prevented this option. But that does not mean librarians cannot still utilize the benefits of furry friends.

One day, having come across a stuffed tiger in a local dollar store, I brought it to the high school library where I then worked, which was an academically challenging, private institution. The tiger was soft and cuddly and I just liked him. Faculty and administration gave me all kinds of grief about the tiger. "Didn't I realize this was a *high school*?" They warned students would rebel at such a childish addition! I shrugged, petted my tiger and put him on a shelf. It did not take long for me to notice my tiger got around. He was never in the same place twice. One day I arrived to find him "reading" a reference book in a corner. By midterms, students were sitting with the tiger in their lap, petting him absently while they studied. Eventually the tiger needed a signup sheet, and I had to get more animals for the library.

A few years later, I found myself as department head in an extremely stressful public library. Like many places, the department was understaffed and consequently overworked. In this particular circumstance, the administration was terrorizing its employees with various threats. Morale was low and there was a culture of fear. One of my staff members was having a difficult time adjusting. She was a naturally high strung and volatile personality. In the best of circumstances, she was described as "difficult." With the institutional problems, her stress was palpable and contagious.

One day I decided to bring my tiger to work. I admit I was a little nervous at first to approach a woman old enough to be my mother and say, "I think petting this stuffed animal might help you." Instead, I caressed the tiger; it helped me. The staff talked about how soft and cuddly he was. Everyone at some point then hugged the tiger. Finally, I suggested to this woman when she was ready to scream and possibly kill someone to sit for a minute and pet the tiger.

This simple action of petting the tiger did not change our situation, but it did shift the level of tension. Plus, it gave us something to joke about, "Oohhh I'm so upset, where's the tiger?" It gave a means to calm down; a way to refocus and it changed the tone of the environment.

Because of its nature and mission, the library is actually a wonderful place for humor and play. They provide a mini-break and help dilute tension in the workplace. Humor can be utilized in library signage, policies, displays, programming, and communications.

Styles and context will influence the manifestation of humor and play in any institution, as will the culture of the particular library. No one can easily tell another how to be funny in the library, but there are several points to use as guide:

- Do no harm and be considerate.
- Know the boundaries and be able to explain them.
- Always be respectful.
- Develop a willingness to be silly and child-like in front of others.
- Remember laughter, play and toys are not only for children.

The key to successfully play and laugh in the library is to consider context and shared experience. What generally makes something funny to people is they recognize themselves or the inherent silliness in the presentation. Remember the context, respect others, and most importantly to laugh at yourself and have fun!

References

Force, Nichole. *Humor's Hidden Power: Weapon, Shield and Psychological Salve.* Braeden Press, 2011.
Jacobson, David M. *The 7½ Habits of Highly Humorous People.* Texas: Virtualbookworm.com Publishing, 2007.
Romero, Eric J., and Kevin Cruthirds, "The Use of Humor in the Workplace." *Academy of Management Perspectives* (May 2006): 58–69.
Sathyanarayana, K. *The Power of Humor at the Workplace.* California: Sage Publications, 2007.

Shelving Stress Through Self-Care and Nutrition

Amy Bodine *and* Kim Rush Lynch

The Centers for Disease Control and Prevention (CDC) and National Institute of Occupational Safety and Health (NIOSH) defines job stress "as the harmful physical and emotional responses that occur when the requirements of the job do not match the capabilities, resources, or needs of the worker. [And continues to add,] job stress can lead to poor health and even injury" (NIOSH 1999, 6).

As the Technical Services Librarian working for a small two person library at the Office of Minority Health Resource Center's Knowledge Center, I am very familiar with stress as it is defined by the CDC/NIOSH. During this time of slimming budgets, staff reductions, and new technologies, you, fellow librarians, are all too familiar with job stress as well. Librarians, despite our changing work environments, still provide the highest level of quality service to our patrons and clients. And in the frenzy of a work day, we lose track of the physical and emotional toll our work has on us. Before I enlisted the help of Kim Rush Lynch, coauthor and nutritional consultant, I felt tired and drained, regularly experiencing headaches, painful acne breakouts, and anxiety attacks. Through working with Kim, I discovered food is an integral part to a less stressful life.

In the following sections, we explain how food choices impact our bodies, how to nourish our bodies, and provide tips for successful, healthy, and carefree meal times and a less stressful work day.

The Basics: Nourishing Our Bodies

The food we choose to consume can enrich our lives or further exacerbate the stress we already experience. (We are using the terminology "nourish" instead of "feed" because of the important distinction that one can feed his or her body without providing it the substance and nutrition needed to function properly.) If we choose foods that create an unhappy internal environment and wreak havoc on our digestive tract, we will in turn suffer. The health of the gut is directly related to the health of the immune system. The gut, often referred to as the second brain, has one hundred million neurons or nerve cells embedded in the gut lining, and the gut lining contains a large portion of the body's serotonin. If your gut lining isn't healthy due to illness, stress, or poor food choices, your nervous system is affected. Every cell, organ and hormone is integrated into the overall body, so you can't affect one part of the body without affecting the others. This is why it's so important to do your part through self-care and proper nourishment! This may be one of those "duh" statements, but we so often forget how important it is and instead, treat our bodies like indestructible machines.

To nourish your body, four main macro-nutrients are needed: carbohydrates, fats, protein and perhaps the most important one most often overlooked is water.

CARBOHYDRATES

Carbohydrates are the body's main source of energy and the only source of energy for the brain and red blood cells. Consuming the right kinds is important. (In this instance, "diet" refers to what one eats as opposed to a modified eating regimen for weight loss and other health purposes.) Your diet should focus on whole food sources, removing food artifacts such as refined flours and sweeteners.

Too many refined carbohydrates and sugars can stress the body and cause an imbalance on the gut flora that feeds on them. Additionally, refined carbohydrates and sugars stress the adrenal glands and in time, cause a variety of stress symptoms including fatigue, hypoglycemia, low sex drive, muscle breakdown, weight gain or weight loss, allergies and a compromised immune system. Excessive refined carbohydrates and flours in the diet are responsible for numerous health conditions including arteriosclerosis, *Candida* overgrowth, chronic constipation, gout, obesity, peptic ulcers, thyroid weaknesses, sinus problems, bladder infections, osteoporosis, kidney stones, gallstones, cancer, nerve damage and even behavioral disorders. Consuming carbohydrates in their whole food form will assist with prevention and in some cases, elimination of these issues. *We are providing this information based on Kim's expertise and my personal experience. We are not doctors or medical practitioners, please consult a doctor or experienced medical professional if you are experiencing medical issues.* Following are some carbohydrate tips:

- Stop by your local farmer's market or stand, and pick up fresh fruits and vegetables for the week. You can plan meals in advance or select what speaks to you and then find recipes when you are at home.
- Eat whole grains, such as amaranth, buckwheat, millet, barley, steel cut oats, brown rice and quinoa. *Some individuals have a grain intolerance, regardless if the grain is gluten-free or not. So talk with a nutritionist or nutritional consultant if you suspect an issue.*
- Eat pasta and bread in small infrequent doses. When possible, choose a whole grain pasta or eat whole grain breads. Pastas, breads and crackers made from sprouted whole grains are best.
- Use fresh and dried herbs with abandon, and consider growing your own. Not only will you have your own fresh herbs, but gardening is a great stress reliever.
- Pre-wash and cut fresh vegetables for quick snacks.

FATS

Fats are vital to human health. About 30 percent of your diet should be a mixture of saturated, polyunsaturated and monounsaturated fats. Saturated fats are essential to good health, but often receive bad press. As a result, most people eat too many processed polyunsaturated fats, such as vegetable seed, corn, soybean, safflower, and cottonseed oils. Polyunsaturated fats are healthful in their whole food forms and include the special kind of fats known as omega 3 and 6 essential fatty acids that assist with healthy skin and hair, a strong immune system and healthy blood, nerves and arteries. In particular, omega 3 fatty acids help counteract inflammation in the body and are vital to brain development and *the health of the nervous system, which is imperative when you want your body to adapt to or counteract stress.* Fish, walnuts, Brazil nuts and seeds, such as flax, sunflower, sesame, poppy and pumpkin are good sources of polyunsaturated fats. On the other hand, "demonized" saturated fats are vital for organ, cell membrane, and nervous system health. Healthy sources of saturated fats include old fashioned, pastured butter, beef, pork, poultry and wild game, dairy, eggs, coconut oil and palm oil. Finally, heart healthy monounsaturated fats lower cholesterol and include olive oil, peanut oil, peanuts, hazelnuts, cashews, almonds and avocados. Following are tips for you when consuming fats:

- Consume healthy oils such as olive and coconut oil. You may also incorporate oils such as flax, sesame, and peanut in small amounts. Never heat flax oil. Remember, butter is your friend.
- Eat wild-caught fish from clean waters. Look for the MSC (Marine Stewardship Council) certification.
- Eat raw nuts such as almonds, walnuts and Brazil nuts, especially during the afternoon munchies.
- Keep seeds such as flax, sesame, poppy, and pumpkin on hand and toss them in with your morning oatmeal, your chop suey dishes, or help season whatever you are making for dinner.
- Enjoy avocados on salads, sandwiches or sliced up with a little sea salt and olive oil as a snack. You can even stuff avocado halves with egg, tuna, chicken, quinoa or bean salads.
- Remember the adage, "You are what you eat!" If you consume animal protein, make sure it's from clean, hormone and antibiotic-free, organic, pasture raised sources, which contain less saturated fat and higher levels of omega 3s and vitamin E than their non-pastured counter parts.
- Use your more expensive meat purchases as a condiment or side rather than as the main constituent of your meal.

PROTEINS

Meat not only serves as a good source of fats, but also of proteins, an integral part of a healthy body. Proteins play a role in our hormones, nerve structures, neurotransmitters, cell membranes, bones, muscles, and enzymes. If our bodies don't get the protein they need, we can experience a variety of symptoms including fatigue, edema, depression, poor wound healing, sugar cravings (also caused by too much protein), weight loss, dry skin and hair and damage to the kidneys and other organs. Conversely, too much protein can cause osteoporosis, arteriosclerosis, kidney stones and even bowel disorders. Good protein sources include organic, pasture raised animal products such as beef or poultry as well as plant based sources including legumes and whole grains. Vegetarians and vegans should consume a variety of plant based proteins including nuts, seeds, legumes, whole grains, sea vegetables and algae. Note additional supplementation may be required for some vegetarians or vegans to ensure that they receive a full complement of nutrients. Here are some tips when consuming proteins to reduce stress and stay healthy:

- Be prepared to pay more for your animal protein. Only purchase organic, pasture-raised beef, bison, poultry, eggs, pork, lamb, and diary. You can often find this type of meat at your local farmers market or health food store.
- Wild game can be a healthful alternative to commercial animal products. Befriend a hunter and check out Hunter Angler Gardener Cook's blog for great recipes, written by Hank Shaw located at http://honest-food.net/
- Consume wild fish from clean waters.
- Consume a variety of whole grains, legumes, nuts and seeds. Combine them to create complete proteins with all of the essential amino acids (i.e., brown rice and lentils).
- Balance your animal and plant sources for best nutritional coverage and benefits.

WATER

How do we transport vitamins and minerals found in carbohydrates, proteins and fats to the cells that need it? Let's take a look at the most important macronutrient, water. Dehydration equals stress! About 60 percent of the human body is made of water, give or take 5–10 percent depending on one's age, gender and body structure. Regardless, most of the human body is water. Water is responsible for the movement of essential nutrients from the gut into the bloodstream and cells. It protects our joints and major organs, and prevents inflammation through the removal of waste from our bodies. When our bodies are not properly hydrated, we risk heartburn, gas, weak digestive juices, arthritis and joint pain, back pain, migraines, constipation, muscle cramps, high cholesterol, high blood pressure, and inflammation in the stomach and gut due to a compromised mucosal lining. Following are some tips to help you consume more water:

- Head to bed with a glass of water and keep it on your nightstand.
- Drink that glass of water on your nightstand just after you shut off your alarm clock in the morning.
- Drink half your body weight in ounces each day. Carry a water bottle around with you so you can keep track of how much you drink.

- Concentrate most of your water intake before dinner so you don't waste precious sleeping hours in the bathroom.
- Add a pinch of a high mineral sea salt, such as Celtic Sea Salt, to your water. Your body hydrates best when there are minerals present.
- Don't drink during meals. If you absolutely need to, take small sips of warm or room temperature water.
- Add a little punch to plain water with some cut up lemon, cucumber or mint.

Breakfast and Meal Planning

Now that we have a better understanding of macro-nutrients and their importance to nourishing our bodies, let's examine how we can build our meals around them. While allowing yourself the time to eat and plan meals may seem like a stress inducer, this practice can give you brief moments of serenity and the chance to charge up before diving into your next task or activity. Meal time is your time.

BREAKFAST

Breakfast is the most important meal of the day. Often, we neglect it, either to get an extra 10 minutes of sleep or because we have pets and family needing our time and attention in the morning. If we do eat, we reach for a cup of coffee and a bagel, muffin, or donut. By the time, we arrive at work, we are hungry, dehydrated, and quite possibly suffering from a sugar crash. Caffeine and sugar-laden breakfast treats can further tax the adrenal glands creating blood sugar fluctuations which make people tired and causes them to reach for more stimulants. This vicious cycle continues through the rest of the day leaving us feeling exhausted and moody. Endless possibilities of better more nourishing breakfast food choices are at your disposal and listed next are just a few:

- Build up your breakfast repertoire. If you are not used to eating breakfast, start with a piece of fruit and your favorite nut butter or a slice of sprouted whole grain toast spread with butter. Use a nut butter such as almond, peanut, or coconut oil.
- Eat something with protein. It will sustain your energy levels and stabilize your blood sugar levels during the early morning and afternoon.
- Include all four macro-nutrients in your breakfast. This is accomplished easily by having a plethora of oils and other fats, fruits or vegetables, seeds, and nuts on hand.
- Prepare whole grain porridge the night before in a slow cooker and add walnuts, butter, flaxseed, blueberries, and/or honey to the dish.
- Eat eggs with dark leafy greens, smoked salmon with a side salad, yogurt or cottage cheese with fruit, muesli or granola with almond milk or yogurt and green smoothies. All these items require limited preparation.
- Eat dinner left-overs from the night before, saving you the time and aggravation involved in morning meal preparations. Dinner for breakfast is common and healthy

practice in Asian cultures. Soup is one of our favorite "dinner" breakfast foods. They can be heated or chilled depending on the season.

MEAL PLANNING

The keys to a healthy, stress-free breakfast is meal planning. A little up front work can save you a world of aggravation and poor food choices later. One of the biggest hurdles with eating healthy is meal planning. Many of us don't feel we have the time or simply don't know where to begin. Trust us. Taking just 15 to 20 minutes to plan will help take the stress out of cooking, because you won't be faced with the in-famous question, "What's for dinner?"

When planning meals, you should be planning for breakfast, lunch, and dinner with a few snacks planned for in-between meals. You may decide to eat out, but it is better to have a little too much healthy food in the fridge than to grab that frozen pizza. While we have thoroughly impressed upon you the importance of breakfast by giving the meal its own section, you should not infer that lunch and dinner are optional as long as you had a good breakfast. A nourishing lunch focuses on vegetables with a protein source. For a healthy dinner, prepare steamed or sautéed dark leafy greens mixed with other brightly colored vegetables, and add a starch: brown rice or lentils, or a protein such as chicken or fish for a complete meal. A successful meal plan uses seasonal vegetables of multiple colors, fresh and dried herbs and continually rotates through different vegetables, grains and protein options. Snacks can be quick easy proteins and carbohydrates like celery or apples with almond butter, or hummus with a whole grain cracker or sliced red pepper. Next are some meal planning tips to help reduce your stress:

- Plan a weekly meal planning and shopping date. A key to healthy eating is to maintain a well-stocked and organized kitchen.

- Organize foods when you purchase them. Each type of food should have a special location in your kitchen and be arranged for your ease of use. Develop a system for your fridge, too.

- Find a few favorite cooking magazines, cookbooks or recipe search engines. A couple of our favorite examples include *Eating Well* magazine, *The Healthy Hedonist* by Myra Kornfeld and Foodily.com.

- Devise a menu plan tracking system whether it's a physical-based or virtual system, such as a chalkboard, binder, or an on-line meal planning system. Many health sites and recipe websites offer meal planning tools.

- Be detailed and use colors or icons to highlight special preparation considerations when planning. For example, you may need to make a note about soaking brown rice or thawing chicken.

- Cook once and eat twice! Set aside time each week to cook staples such as whole grains, legumes and stock, and then personalize these items for each meal by adding vegetables, herbs, nuts and seeds, or meat to them.

- Put LOVE into your meal. Like Carla Hall from Alchemy Caterers (and Top Chef finalist) says, "If you're not in a good mood, the only thing you should make is a reservation" (Hall, 2012).
- Choose healthier options if you decide that a reservation is in order. Eat salads and meals that do not have high dairy or meat content and lots of bread. Instead of a fountain soda, order water or hot tea.

As stated, meal planning is your time to care for yourself, and it should be a relaxing and enjoyable experience. The energy you put into your meal times can be just as important as the food itself. Playful meal practices are one method to infuse your meal time with the serenity needed to combat stress.

Playful Eating: Optimizing Digestion

Playful eating practices are tools for mindful eating with a fun and sensual attitude. They allow you to enjoy your food in a positive, relaxed state, allowing you to assimilate more nutrients and have better digestion. In addition, you will eat less, because you will feel more satisfied. On the flip side, when your body is stressed, energy is diverted away from the digestive system to the limbs so that your body can prepare for "fight or flight." Consider some of the following playful eating practices to calm the nervous system and allow for optimal digestion and nutrient assimilation to take place:

- Set the table with your favorite fancy tablecloth or placements and cloth napkins. In other words, take yourself and/or family on a date without leaving the house.
- Involve all family members in the food and ambiance prep process, allowing you and your loved ones quality time. And, as a bonus, the prep process helps everyone relax and take ownership of nourishing their bodies.
- Dim the lights. Light some candles and play some soothing dinner music. A peaceful, grounding ambiance can set the stage for relaxed digestion.
- Bless, meditate on, or simply give thanks for your meals before you eat. Gratitude for your food is another way to eat intentionally and prepare the body for digestion.
- Before you take that first bite, close your eyes and smell your food. Take a few deep breaths. The smell of food tells your gut something is on its way, thus preparing for digestion.
- Slow down when eating. Take one bite of food and put your fork down. Savor the texture, shape and flavors of the food. Chew until liquid before swallowing. Repeat.
- Most importantly, eat with a smile!

Conclusion

Using the tips discussed in this paper, I have personally found my way to a clearer complexion, better health, and much less stress. I now look forward to my lunch break at work and do not view it as a distraction, but rather a rejuvenating experience preparing me for the rest of the work day. And I no longer frantically scrounge for food from my office's vending machines. Kim and I both hope you have found some tips for giving yourself the nourishment you need. With the proper fuel, we can all live a less stressful life.

References

Hall, Carla. 2012. "About Carla Hall." Last modified July 12, 2012. http://www.carlahall.com/blog/.

National Institute of Occupational Safety and Health. "Stress at...Work." CDC Website. NIOSH Publications and Products. DHHS (NIOSH) Publication Number 99-101 (1999). Assessed July 23, 2012. http://www.cdc.gov/niosh/docs/99-101/pdfs/99-101.pdf.

Further Reading

David, Marc. *Nourishing Wisdom: A Mind-Body Approach to Nutrition and Well-Being*. Vermont: Three Rivers Press, 1994.

_____. *The Slow Down Diet: Eating for Pleasure, Energy, and Weight Loss*. Rochester, VT: Healing Arts Press, 2005.

Enig, Sally Fallon, with Mary G. *Nourishing Traditions: The Cookbook That Challenges Politically Correct Nutrition and the Diet Dictocrats*. 2nd ed. Washington, DC: Newtrends Publishing, 1999.

Lair, Cynthia. *Feeding the Whole Family: Whole Foods Recipes for Babies, Young Children and Their Parents*. Seattle: Moon Smile Press, 1997.

Wilson, James L. *Adrenal Fatigue: The 21st Century Stress Syndrome*. California: Smart Publications, 2001.

World's Healthiest Foods. The George Mateljan Foundation. Last modified July 23, 2012. http://www.whfoods.com/.

The Active Librarian:
The Importance of Physical Activity for Mental and Physical Well-Being

JOHN BOYD *and* ELIZABETH CRAMER

Exercise is a stress killer. Studies show exercise builds resilience against stress and improves mood and productivity during the workday (Coulson, McKenna and Field 2008). Yet very few people are motivated to meet their fitness and exercise goals. Even those with the best intentions of exercising experience shortages of time, the inability to motivate themselves sufficiently, or suffer from fatigue or physical restraints. As librarians, too many people in our profession do not commit to exercise as part of their regular routine. Perhaps it is due to the somewhat sedentary nature of our employment or the large percentage (63 percent, 75 percent in technical services) of librarians who are introverted in nature — people that work "best with the reflective world of ideas" (Scherdin and Beaubien 1995). As individuals and as a profession, we would benefit greatly from a commitment to regular exercise.

This essay illustrates the benefits that come with exercise — lower stress levels, increased job satisfaction, improved self-image, and better health. We, the authors, make a commitment to incorporate exercise into our lives through cycling, an activity we love. We realize the benefits regular exercise brings to our lives, our careers, and our ability to handle stress. To help others reach their fitness goals, we suggest creative ways to get motivated when they do not feel like exercising, plus tips for time management. In addition, we discuss various options for exercise. One does not need to be training for a marathon to increase your level of fitness. We suggest exercises one can do at a desk or within the workday, plus more strenuous activities that can be pursued individually or within a group.

We also emphasize the importance of gaining the support of employers in order to create a culture of fitness within the workplace. Both employees and employers benefit from health incentives such as the provision of fitness facilities, organized health promotion activities, and the availability of flexible scheduling. If your institution or library does not provide such incentives, we urge you to become a fitness advocate. Employers should be aware that increasing support of physical activity results in proven benefits—lower costs for healthcare plus a healthier, more productive, and calmer workforce.

Commit to Exercise

You have to make exercise a priority. Discover what time of day works best for you and schedule exercise as part of your daily routine. If you are a morning person, exercise before work can be a great way to begin your day and you only have to shower and dress once. Or try a brisk 30-minute walk around the neighborhood, a less vigorous workout that doesn't leave you covered in sweat and requiring a change of clothes. Many people prefer to exercise in the evening, after work or dinner. However, be aware working out too close to bedtime may affect sleep habits.

There are many ways to seamlessly incorporate exercise into your day. If you drive to work, park in the far end of the parking lot or in the lot of a nearby building. Take the stairs, not the elevator. Instead of e-mailing or phoning your co-workers, go talk to them in person. When you do use the phone, stand up. Consider having meetings (these would likely be small meetings) on the go, outside, if the weather is nice.

During your breaks is a great time to go for short, brisk walks. The U.S. Surgeon General recommends 150 minutes of moderate physical activity per week (U.S. 2010). Three 30 minutes walks over lunch per week, and six, brisk 10 minutes walks over a morning or afternoon break, and you're on your way to a healthier and less stressful life.

Motivators

One of the biggest obstacles to following through with an exercise plan is a lack of motivation. Learn some tricks to self-motivate. Writing out your exercise plans in advance and keeping track of your progress (exercise log) is a good idea for staying on-track. Motivate yourself through visual or mental images. Effective strategies include looking at magazines, searching for images on the web, or imagining yourself faster and sleeker. Share your commitment with others—create a blog announcing your goals and record your progress online. Or read other people's exercise blogs. After reaching specific fitness goals, reward yourself.

If it helps, write a list of health benefits resulting from exercise and post it somewhere in your office. Among the many benefits are: better health (reduced risk of high blood pressure, diabetes, heart disease, and stress), increased self-confidence, potential weight loss, improved sexual performance and satisfaction, and feelings of well-being and relaxation afterwards. Remind yourself the biggest rewards of exercise are results of delayed gratification. At times, it is difficult to start. But you know you will feel better after you exercised and that good feeling will last throughout the day. If it helps, pick an activity that borders on relaxation. On lazy days, we go to the gym armed with iPads, sit on a reclining stationary bicycle set at a low setting, and watch a streaming video.

Create Fitness Goals

Set realistic goals and choose activities that motivate you. Talk to your local doctor or a fitness trainer about your goals. Fitness takes time. Start out slowly to lessen the chance of injury and to "discover" an activity you enjoy. We both spent time running but it proved more work than fun for us. Cycling, on the other hand, we enjoy during rain or cold, and for extended periods of time. It is all about your personal preference. Simply walking more is a great start to becoming a more active person.

As you begin to make exercise part of your daily routine, do not focus on weight loss, which can lead to frustration and even poor eating habits. Early goals should focus on leading a less sedentary life. Look for opportunities. Could you walk instead of drive? Can you find the time to take that yoga class? Whatever exercise activity you choose, your primary goal should be committing to an ongoing active lifestyle.

Find an Exercise Buddy or Group

It can be as easy as sending out an e-mail to your library or asking a friend if they would be interested in heading out for a walk during a break or over lunch. Conversation with an exercise buddy can make time pass faster and they can be your motivation during lazy times. It can also help your motivation to see a friend doing the same activity. But, be sure your exercise buddy is motivated to do the same physical activity you are. If you don't, the relationship could end quickly. An exercise buddy can be an office mate who encourages you to go to the gym, even if they do not accompany you.

If you are a competitive person, you might also consider looking for team sports. Many communities have recreational leagues, ranging from basketball to softball to adult soccer. And in addition to sports, look for other opportunities to increase your activity level. For example, a colleague in our library offers line dancing instruction twice a week during the lunch hour.

You can find additional support within groups that organize activities such as hiking, swimming, trail running, and cycling. Many such groups now have web sites and discussion forums announcing upcoming events. Look for activities in your community matching your interests and fitness level. For cyclists, organized rides exist in many communities. We feel fortunate our small town has a local bike club (Boone Area Cyclists), two bike shops, and a restaurant that sponsors bike rides throughout the week.

Combine Exercise with Helping Others

If the idea of helping a charitable cause while improving your health appeals to you, consider combining exercise with a fundraiser. Library staff at Regent University Library in Virginia Beach raised over $1,000 in pledges for miles walked in order to help the University build a new building (Henkel 2012). Many opportunities exist; popular national exercise-related fundraisers include Relay for Life, Tour de Cure, and Bike MS.

Our University Health Promotion Office sponsored three 5k run/walks last year, two of which raised money for local student scholarships. By committing to participate in such an event, you are making a commitment to train, to run/walk with your friends, and to help others.

Exercise at Your Desk

Many librarians spend the majority of the day sitting in front of a computer screen. Sitting all day is conducive to poor posture, muscle fatigue, stress, and back pain. So is there anything you can do during your workday, even at your desk, to help? Absolutely. When you are sitting at your desk, be aware of your breathing. A few deep breathes can make you feel calmer and slow down your heart rate. You may also need to remind yourself to move. A few simple stretching exercises can help loosen muscles and relieve tension:

- Raise your arms over your head as if you are trying to touch the ceiling. Slowly lower your arms. Rotate your shoulders back and then forward. Repeat in each direction a few times.
- Stretch your legs by extending one leg out in front of you, holding for a few seconds, then raising higher for a few seconds more. Repeat with each leg 10 times.
- Extend your arm in front of you, palms up. With the other hand, grab your fingers and gently stretch your hand down. Repeat with the other arm.
- Keep a stress ball on your desk and squeeze it, working the muscles of your arm and hand. Take the same ball and throw it up in the air and try catching it. This helps to loosen your arms, shoulders and back muscles.

Consider trying a standing desk, preferably one that can be lowered too. And if your library budget does not allow this expense, consider trying an exercise ball in place of your office chair, at least for part of your working day. Other fitness equipment for your office could include small hand weights or resistance bands.

Commit to Scheduled Athletic Events

What keeps us motivated and active is committing to organized events. Each May we schedule a seven to ten day bicycle touring trip. Planning begins in January, and keeps us motivated through the cold winter months. Also, we participate in numerous sponsored one day rides throughout the year. Left to our own means, we may not go for a bike ride after a long day at work, or find the time on the weekend. But if we know we have committed to a bike event, a 5K run, or a hike in the mountains, we are much more likely to maintain an exercise routine to stay in shape.

One library-related scheduled event is the ALA Fun Run (walkers are welcome too) held at the American Library Association (ALA) conferences. The ALA Fun Run was held annually for 21 years, from 1984 to 2005. Due to popular demand, it re-commenced after an eight year hiatus during the 2012 Midwinter conference in Dallas, Texas. If running or walking is not your style, consider renting a bicycle in the ALA host city. We often rent bicycles as part of our ALA conference experience — it's a great way to sightsee, particularly neighborhoods you would not normally visit. Chicago, the home of ALA, and frequent host city for library conferences, has over 110 miles of on-street bike lanes. There are miles of off-street bikeways, including the 18.5 mile Lakefront Trail. Local bike shops will rent you the bikes and are very knowledgeable about where to ride.

Take Advantage of Physical Fitness Facilities or Programs

Many universities and college campuses allow employees to use the athletic facilities for free or for a nominal fee. It is to their advantage to support fitness facilities, since promotion of good nutrition and exercise result in improved employee weight management and overall health (Anderson et al., 2009). Do not use the excuse of not feeling comfortable around younger, perhaps more fit students to avoid going to campus facilities. Remember — anyone that works out deserves the respect of fellow athletes.

Some campuses provide services specifically for staff and faculty. Our Health Promotion Office offers weight training, yoga, Pilates, and spin classes. In addition to indoor classes, our campus Outdoor Programs Office offers hiking, kayaking, skiing, rock climbing for students, staff, and faculty. One of our colleagues went on a first-time kayaking trip (with students) over ten years ago and today is an expert on whitewater.

Create a Work Culture That Values Exercise

Few people would argue about the benefits of exercise in the work environment. Workplaces should find methods to target healthy behaviors such as exercise and healthy eating in order to counter-balance stress (Fernandez et al., 2010). If you are a supervisor, set a good example for workers by taking the time to exercise and encouraging others to do so. To increase participation in a healthy lifestyle, you can organize a library-wide effort to increase physical activity among workers. The Bettendorf Public Library in Iowa combined good health and exercise with promotion of their partner library in Bulgaria through the "Walking to Bulgaria" campaign. Library staff kept track of mileage walked, swam, ran, and biked and celebrated upon reaching a combined mileage goal equivalent to the distance from Bettendorf to Bulgaria (Clow 2006).

Many people get in their daily exercise and help the environment by either walking or biking to work. In many metropolitan areas, the number of bicycle commuters is rapidly increasing. In response, workplaces offer incentives or facilities for those who select an alternative and energy efficient method to arrive at work (Jullian 2008). Incentives include subsidized purchase of bicycles, facilities for a safe place to park your bike, or provision of bikes for local use.

Many workplaces offer health and exercise initiatives created by health insurance providers to encourage a more active lifestyle. Look to see what your institution offers. Our healthcare plan has a 15-week, live, interactive program to encourage smarter eating habits and a more active lifestyle. It allows participants to interact with others in the program, offer encouragement, and adapt the program to their specific needs.

Advocacy

If you feel your library or institution lacks fitness and health initiatives, become an advocate for increased institutional support. Your best plan of action begins with citing the research. Studies show employees that exercise report higher job satisfaction and lower levels of stress (Anderson et al., 2009). When employers realize the high financial cost of poor health, they are more motivated to promote and support healthier lifestyles. In the United States, 75 percent of health care costs go towards treating chronic and mostly preventable diseases. Most of these illnesses, such as heart disease, diabetes, and cancer, are due to poor eating, smoking, and lack of exercise (Centers for Disease Control and Prevention 2002). An abundance of chronic illness adds to the high cost of employee medical insurance and to significant loss of productivity due to sick leave.

If you are a supervisor, allow flexibility in employee's schedules for exercise. Set an example by committing time in your day for exercise. Give up the excuse of being too busy. Even if you are not an administrator, you can work to advance an exercise-friendly work culture. You can campaign for new or improved exercise facilities/equipment or organize a friendly fitness competition. Think about exercise as an opportunity to do something good for yourself and for others—helping to create a more productive and calmer workplace.

Points to remember

- Plan your day to include a commitment to exercise. Do not make the mistake of trying to "find" the time.
- Identify motivational support within your workplace—an exercise buddy.
- Seize all available opportunities for additional exercise throughout the day, no matter how minor. Stretching, taking the stairs, exercises at your desk.
- Set realistic fitness goals.
- Find a scheduled event (a 5k run/walk is a fun event) two months away and start training for it.
- Be an advocate for physical activity. Create a library-wide exercise program or competition campaign for access to exercise facilities.

References

Anderson, Laurie, et al. "The Effectiveness of Worksite Nutrition and Physical Activity Interventions for Controlling Employee Overweight and Obesity: A Systematic Review." *American Journal of Preventive Medicine* 37, no. 4 (October 2009): 340–357.

Centers for Disease Control and Prevention. *The Burden of Chronic Diseases and Their Risk Factors.* Atlanta: Centers for Disease Control and Prevention, 2002. Accessed May 31, 2012. http://perma nent.access.gpo.gov/lps24530/2002/Burden_Book_2002.pdf.

Clow, Faye. "Geo Milev Library, Montana and Bettendorf Public Library, Iowa." *ABLE Newsletter*, 1, no. 3 (2006): 5.

Coulson, Jo, Jim McKenna, and M. Field. "Exercising at Work and Self-Reported Work Performance." *International Journal of Workplace Health Management* 1, no. 3 (2008): 176–197. doi:10.1108/17538 350810926534.

Fernandez, Isabel Diana, Hayan Su, Paul Winters, and Hua Liang. "Association of Workplace Chronic and Acute Stressors with Employee Weight Status: Data from Worksites in Turmoil." *Journal of Occupational & Environmental Medicine* 52, no. 1 (2010): (Supplement): S34–S41.

Henkel, Harold. "Rise Up and Build: Library Faculty and Staff Raise Over $1,000 for Regent Chapel." (2012). Accessed May 8, 2012. http://librarylink.regent.edu/?p=1261.

Jullian, Maité. "Companies Push Biking to Work." *USA Today*, December 1 (2008). Accessed May 8, 2012. http://www.usatoday.com/money/workplace/2008-11-30-bikecommuting_N.htm

Scherdin, Mary Jane, and Anne K. Beaubien. "Shattering Our Stereotype: Librarians' New Image." *Library Journal* 120, no. 12 (1995): 35–38.

U.S. Department of Health and Human Services. "The Surgeon General's Vision for a Healthy and Fit Nation." Maryland: U.S. Department of Health and Human Services, Office of the Surgeon General, 2010.

Leave Me Alone!
The Value of Solitude

JONATHAN FRATER

Stress is the feeling of being pressed upon when you encounter a situation which makes you feel backed into a corner, a situation generally known as "fight or flight." There are other kinds of stress, too: excitement, empowerment, a feeling of self-worth and mastery over one's surroundings, but the first type is what the majority of us deal with most often at work. It's dangerous because it can be harmful. When we evolved this way it was in response to real pressures on our daily lives: being chased by big animals is terrifying. Terror makes your heart race, the hormones surge and your blood fills with adrenaline. Your body essentially squeezes two or three hours of life into about five minutes. For tribal nomads living on the plains of Africa, this was a life-saving development, as it gave our ancestors the energy needed to run away from or combat immediate threats to their lives. For librarians who are living in drastically different surroundings, not so much.

The take away from this: occasional stressors can be beneficial. When your daily life becomes a constant stream of stress, you get sick. According to the 2010 Stress in America Survey, the most common results of being overly stressed include insomnia, weight gain, headaches, stomach upset, poor eating habits and lethargy. Worse, the same report said even stressed individuals who knew their health was being worn down felt it impossible to make any changes (APA 2012, 6).

Coping Mechanisms

The answer to dealing with stress is to find a way to not let it control your waking or sleeping life. Of course, the simplest way to deal with stress is to re-arrange your life to involve less of it, but reality being what it is, that's probably far more easily said than done. You can change certain things about your life. You can change jobs—if you can find a better and more interesting job in one of the worst job markets we've seen in decades. You can change your spouse or partner — if you're willing to initiate a divorce which is far more likely to add stress than eliminate it. You can change your living situation — if you are willing to go through the stress of shopping for a new place then figuring out how you can pay for it, even if you can find a bank you trust enough to go through with a mortgage. Americans are likely to try all kinds of different methods to deal with the stress, including alcohol, exercise, over- or under-eating, or prescription medications. My personal experience has given me an answer of sorts: arranging for a sufficient or minimum time by myself.

The Value of Alone Time

Americans crave privacy more than any other culture (Cain 2012). It's not difficult to understand why: our lives have gotten more hectic in the past thirty years, abetted by the proliferations of gizmos and gadgets which actually suck what little private time we have. We constantly check e-mail on the bus or train, field calls from co-workers, kids, and clients; and check schedules and to-do lists. Who lives without being connected for even a moment? In that context, an hour to yourself is a valuable part of your day.

Some basic arithmetic: How long is your commute? Half an hour? An hour? Chances are you have a forty hour work week too, right? If you're an average American, you spend something like forty-six minutes on the road to and from work, five days a week. (Caroll August 24, 2007). In other words, nearly four hours a week, twenty-eight hours a month, or three hundred, thirty-six hours a year by yourself, on a train, bus, or in a car, waiting to move from home to work or vice versa. This time can be used to evaluate the details of your personal and professional life.

Just to give a bit of perspective I found a few chores to compare your commute to:

- Becoming proficient at a new skill: 10,000 hours (Ericsson 2000)
- Going out on a date: 4 hours
- Cleaning the house: 2–3 hours
- Preparing a meal: 20–45 minutes
- Washing dishes: 20–30 minutes

In this context the two hours a day you have to yourself can be extremely useful, even productive. It's only when we reflect on the trials of our day that we obtain some idea of just how productive being alone can be.

Defining Alone

You're sitting by yourself on a bus, train, or driving in your car, on the way to work or back home. Are you alone? Perhaps. Alone means you are by yourself, having established your own space, and your attention is focused on some activity which does not involve other people. Having a conversation, for example, defies the concept of being alone, even though you might be physically alone, such as talking on the phone.

So let's be clear here: alone means alone. It means creating a mental space around yourself where you engage with no activities, no items, and no people who are not an extension of your own thoughts. No iPod, no radio, no gadgets or games, no conversations. In a word, you have no distractions.

How to Be Alone

One may be the loneliest number, but it's also highly productive. Consider the fact that there are 22.7 million sole proprietorship businesses in the United States alone (Paninos et al., 2009) and you get the idea: people can be extremely resourceful when they must rely on themselves for absolutely everything. Following are 5 steps on how to be alone.

1. Establish your space: The first rule of Productivity 101 is to organize your workspace. In this case, your workspace is primarily inside your head which makes it a little more challenging to follow this bit of common sense.

2. Turn your gadgets off: Your smart phone is making you crazy (Gonzales February 7, 2012). *Turn it off.* The only exception to this rule is if your gadget is essential to carrying out some task. For example, my iPad is mission critical equipment for me, but only because I decided early on it was going to be. I never use it for text messaging or other direct communication. I use a Kindle app to read, Pages to write, and Drop-Box to keep a series of off-site stored articles and electronic documents to use as references as I write. If you are first and foremost a music lover and you decide your morning alone task will be devoted to listing to music, then fine. But listen to the music. Don't try to play games on your iPhone while listening to music and texting your best friends all at the same time.

3. Decide on a task: You get to do one thing. An hour of alone time isn't a lot, so be particularly selective. You can choose from among competing projects or lists of things needing to be done. To maintain the previous example, it's fine to be in the middle of a writing project and swapping between two or three related apps on a single gadget if they are all related to the writing project in question. In other words, I'm writing an article about weeding, and if I need to swap out Pages to look at a PDF on the subject I want to reference, and then swap back to Pages, fine. But if you stop writing after ten minutes to play a few rounds of Angry Birds then swap back to a spreadsheet you were working on for an IT project at work, then swap back to the writing project, you might as well have not done anything. If you want to play Angry Birds or another game, that's perfectly fine: go ahead and play. For an hour.

4. Take Notes: Keep a record of what you are doing. If you decide to read, keep a book mark handy (yes, e-books have bookmarks). If you have a thought about an article you would like to write soon, jot a note of it down so you don't forget it. In a slight contrast to my rule about deciding on a single task I'll make this a blanket statement:

you may always write down a note for future reference. Don't make the notes so brief or obscure you won't remember what you wanted to say in three or four weeks. Even computer programmers stick notes into their programs for other programmers (or themselves) to see what the writer's train of thought was.

5. Wrap-up: Your alone time is going to come to an end. When it does, you will need to get back into your ability to deal with your daily routine. A bit of situational awareness can help. While you are engrossed in your alone-time activity, keep an eye on the time, or the next stop on the train or bus, or on the crush of the crowd around you. Never get so engrossed in your own world that you miss your stop. That's the sort of thing that adds stress, possibly a lot of it depending on how much grief you could catch for being late. This may take a bit of practice to master.

How to Spend Time Alone

Some activities do not lend themselves to a solitary setting: real-time conversations (especially with multiple parties), team sports, and performance evaluations are only a few. However, there are plenty of activities requiring a solitary environment (mentally if not physically) to work. These are only a few suggestions:

Office work: I don't generally suggest librarians who are already stressed out add to their stress by trying to catch up with unfinished tasks at their office on their commute. That's what the library is for. The last thing any stressed human being needs is to bring work home with them, even though we're expected to do so more and more. Chances are you are playing the catch-up game is because you need to plan your daily work routine better. In any case, you're not me and you may have a good reason to work during your morning or evening commute. There is one exception to this rule I've made over the years: making plans to meet up with co-workers. Checking your daily schedule is something we can do with our smart phones, between text messages and e-mails because it can be conveniently done. Figuring out lunch dates can be an excellent use of alone time. A lot of productive work gets done over lunch.

Read: Read for fun. Read for education. Read for a bit of an escape. Read for work. In this case, taking work home with you makes some sense. I have trouble keeping up with my normal RSS feeds, simply because there are so many articles coming down the wire on a regular basis. The commute is a fantastic place to cover as much new material as you can arrange to see.

Write: Writing is a deeply personal act of communication which requires concentration more than anything else. This means removing yourself from all sources of distraction. Not always easy to do in a crowded environment like a bus or train. But I've timed my own writing over the years and I tend to come up with about a page (roughly 300 words) per hour if I truly push myself. If you can set a similar rate for your own writing, then fantastic. If you can eke out a page per hour, that's two pages of writing to and from work. It equals 90,000 words (a novel or the equivalent) in about 300 hours. It's not exactly National Novel Writing Month, but it's an enormously productive time. Even if you're not into writing, fiction- writing is still writing: there are articles to research and submit for publication. For example, there's blogging, drafting e-mails, or even library policies that you may want to get out of the way for discussion at the library later on. Write.

Think: Here's an idea. The next time you have an hour to yourself, do nothing. Just observe your surroundings (all right, that's doing something but you know what I mean). Look at the commuters who share your daily ride, notice what they're wearing, how they hold themselves, what they do in their hour of alone time. Take a look at the ads on the bus or train, study a subway or a bus map if it's nearby. Take a look out the windows and really look at the scenery or new neighborhoods as they pass by on your way through them. All of these things are part of your daily life, even if you've never noticed them before.

Remember: Have an especially irksome problem? Now is the time to replay it inside your head. Think about what's going on and try to analyze the situation in a way you haven't before. Had an argument with someone close to you? Got a sticky problem or an annoying patron? Replay the event a few different ways and try to imagine how it might have gone differently. Imagine new circumstances and solutions to your experience.

Mental Rehearsal: Got a presentation in the morning or afternoon? Take out your notes and polish them. This works for classroom situations as well as presentations at conferences or even in front of your director or coworkers. Nothing encourages solid communication like practicing your speech, mostly because we think of items in practice we often forget when put on the spot. Little details make the difference between maintaining interest from an audience and giving a smooth but slightly dull impression. Practice, as they say, makes perfect or at least interesting.

Checklists: You have a complicated work and personal life. We all do. One way of helping to manage the details is to make checklists. I have three lists I refer to and expand upon on a regular basis which are: daily tasks, weekly tasks, and project-related tasks. Some of the daily and weekly tasks are now automated (i.e., running ILS reports) while the bulk of them are in-person activities. These include things like opening, closing, managing inventory and checking shelf lists, overseeing the circulation and reference desks. Other common tasks include figuring out staffing, sharing process reports with coworkers, and equipment maintenance. Checklists make managing and tracking these tedious tasks easy but essential to completing the chores. Give it a try and make one.

Report: You left work a bit early last night to attend a presentation at your local public library. Was it interesting? (It must have been at least enticing, or you wouldn't have left early to attend, right?) Did you take notes? Great, now spend your hour on the train turning those notes into a short 10-minute presentation for your director and coworkers on the event. Your notes don't have to read like a TED Talk, but they should enable you to discuss essential information such as: What was the event about? Who were the speakers? Which speaker spoke on what subject? Who was your favorite presenter and why; and what kinds of questions did the audience have, if any? What kind of questions did you have and what kinds of answers did you get? Think of it like taking minutes at a library committee meeting. Keep what information you need to explain to the staff what happened. The side-talks and distracting chatter from the audience can be left out.

Evaluate: You've mastered the practice of replaying events in your head during your alone time. Terrific, life is a learning experience. Did you have a particularly good day at work? An especially bad one? Or did you have a thrilling success with a patron or a painful disaster with a co-worker? Evaluate it in your alone time. Note that evaluation is different from a judgment. Whether we are aware of it or not, we constantly judge events, people, and situations. There is no reason you can't spend an hour to make your own observations. Evaluations are a bit more in-depth and carefully reasoned; however, during your hour of alone time, clear your mind and try to imagine the answer to the questions: What happened? Why did it happen? What were each party's expectations (real or implied)? What could have gone differently for a different outcome to be created? Write these answers down and talk about them with a coworker when you get to the library. Chances are you aren't the only one who had these questions.

What Not to Do: Procrastination

I've given you a few suggestions about how to spend your alone time; surely you will come up with many others on your own. And because it's your time, you get to spend it any way you like. One word of caution, don't attempt to create alone time for the sole purpose of avoiding your normal responsibilities. Down time is good and absolutely necessary to maintain a balance between our work and personal lives. An hour of work on a project that is near and dear to you personally or even a bit of mindless stupidity here and there is your business. Don't avoid your daily work in favor of it, is all I'm saying.

To recap, remember these points in planning your commute:

- Alone time is good for you.
- Set your space away from distractions.
- Gadgets are distracting, so turn them off.
- Focus on one task for an hour.
- Watch the clock. Don't miss your stop.

As a final word, remember that spent time is something you never get back. You have a brief window each day to get some project accomplished, be it a plan to improve your work or personal life, a bit of art to create, or a chance to reflect on how to make better choices in your daily routine. Over the course of a career there are years of potential improvement. Make good use of it.

References

American Psychological Association. "Stress in America Findings." (November 9, 2010): 5, 6. Accessed July 27, 2012. http://www.apa.org/news/press/releases/stress/national-report.pdf.

Cain, Susan. "The Rise of the New Groupthink." *NY Times.* Last modified January 3, 2012. http://www.nytimes.com/2012/01/15/opinion/sunday/the-rise-of-the-new-groupthink.html?pagewanted=all.

Caroll, Joseph. "Workers' Average Commute Round-Trip Is 46 Minutes in a Typical Day." *Gallup.* Last Modified August 24, 2007, http://www.gallup.com/poll/28504/workers-average-commute-round trip-minutes-typical-day.aspx.

Ericsson, K. Anders. "Expert Performance and Deliberate Practice: An Updated Excerpt from Ericsson." Last modified 2000. Accessed July 27, 2012. http://www.psy.fsu.edu/faculty/ericsson/ericsson.exp.perf.html.

Gonzales, Jan. "The Downside of a Smartphone." *Popular Electronics Reviews.* Last modified February 7, 2012. Accessed June 18, 2012. http://www.popularelectronicsreviews.com/the-downside-of-a-smart phone.

Paninos, Jason, and Scott Hollenbeck. "Sole Proprietorship Returns, 2009." Internal Revenue Service. *Statistics of Income Bulletin* (Summer 2011). Accessed July 27, 2012. http://www.irs.gov/pub/irs-soi/11spsumbulspreturns.pdf.

Planning Library
Programs for Patrons

BETH NIEMAN

Story times, crafts, and summer reading programs are some well-loved activities children look forward to at their libraries. Sadly, sometimes the library staff dreads them! Hosting children's programs on a small budget or with a limited staff can present a big challenge for librarians. There are so many factors outside the librarian's control: we usually don't know ahead of time exactly who is coming to our programs, how old they will be, or whether they will be reasonably well-behaved. Crying babies may interrupt a program carefully prepared for school-age children. Inattentive parents may allow youngsters to misbehave in the library and cell phones sometimes ring in the middle of a read-aloud story.

All of these unknowns contribute to librarians' stress. While there are many factors you can't control, the good news is that, with a little planning and preparation, you can minimize the chaos and consistently present programs enjoyable for everyone — even the librarian!

Get Ahead

It's never too soon to start thinking about your next program. If you're in charge of your library's summer program, get in the habit of gathering ideas all year long (more about how to organize your ideas later).

Of course, you start with an idea for your program. Perhaps you are one of the many librarians who uses the free Collaborative Summer Library Program materials offered through your state library. You may choose to draw many of your ideas from your professional resources shelf, or even from the Internet. Maybe you're ready to start an entirely new program, perhaps for toddlers and parents in your community, or a regular story hour for preschool children.

Although you know what stories you would like to share, what song or finger play you want to teach, and what craft you'll make afterwards, you also need to plan ahead for unexpected circumstances. That means not only having a plan for your how you expect the program to go, but also some last-minute backup ideas.

- If you plan a read-aloud program, be sure to choose several books that go with your theme. It's better to have too many than too few; you don't have to read them all. With a variety of selections at hand, you can choose the ones best-suited to your audience once they arrive.

- When presenting the same program to several groups, you may find that different groups relate better to different books. If a story doesn't seem to go over well with the first group you have, substitute one of the others you selected for the next program.

- Not all books make great read-alouds. Books with a lot of dialogue can be confusing for listeners to follow, unless you're very good at creating different voices for the characters. If you're new at presenting story time programs, practice reading aloud to get familiar with the stories you'll be sharing.

- Use both fiction and non-fiction books to keep story time interesting.

- If a craft is part of your program, plan an optional "bonus activity" for the kids who work quickly and need something more to do while others finish up. Picture books, easy floor puzzles, sturdy cars, and blocks are great for young children. Older children might enjoy coloring, more challenging puzzles, or a board game. The idea is to keep restless children busy, not bored.

- Have extra craft supplies on hand so you can accommodate the group if you have more kids than expected show up. You can use up the leftovers another day.

- If possible, allow yourself a day or two each week when you do not have any programs scheduled. If you are responsible for a summer program, it's good to discontinue all library programs the month before your summer program begins. This allows you several weeks to put the finishing touches on your crafts, make sure you've received all the books and supplies you'll need, and line up any guest speakers.

You're Not Alone—At Least, You Shouldn't Be!

Librarians can become so passionate about their work with young readers that they feel they must "do it all," from leading infant lap sit programs and summer reading to running a teen group and offering parent events.

You're a librarian, not a superhero. It's important to have at least two or more staff members (or a staff member and a volunteer) for each program to help things run smoothly. While the librarian is occupied presenting the program, helpers can perform several important tasks:

- Your helper can get a head count. This is useful not only for your library's monthly statistical report, but also to make sure you have enough supplies on hand for everyone.

- If necessary, helpers can quickly set up additional craft stations while the librarian is reading to the children.

- If you have planned music or a digital slide show, a helper can run the equipment while you focus on your presentation.
- A helper can discreetly remind kids who are disruptive to remain quiet, or find out if they need something.

Another important reason to have at least two people running a program is in case of a minor emergency, such as a child needing a bathroom break; a helper can show the child where the bathroom is while the librarian continues with the program for the other kids.

Are We Having Fun Yet?

One of the biggest challenges (and sources of librarian stress) is balancing fun with appropriate library behavior. It's best to address behavior problems and expectations early on in your program rather than try to regain order after things are already out of control. A simple announcement about basic library rules before your program begins is a good reminder for your library visitors. If you're lucky enough to have a library with a program room separate from the rest of the library, your job is somewhat easier because noisy activities can be removed from quiet areas in the library.

Parents and other caregivers can be your biggest allies (or your biggest hindrance) in helping maintain order. Remember, among all their choices for things to do, parents have chosen to bring their kids to the library because they believe library programs have something of value to offer.

- Let parents know you appreciate that they bring their kids to the library. Say "Thanks for coming today!" or "Hope to see you again soon!"
- Greet parents and kids with a friendly smile, and try to learn their names.
- Be courteous to library visitors by starting your programs on time; reward those who are punctual instead of making them wait for latecomers.

When you announce a library program for a certain age group, you can be sure some younger brothers and sisters will come along, too. Plant the idea in parents' minds that they can leave the program room if babies get fussy. A non-confrontational way to do this is by making a general announcement such as this: "If any of the little ones get restless during our story, please feel free to step outside the room with them until they are relaxed again."

Even if you make your expectations plain ahead of time, some parents are not sensitive to when their children are becoming disruptive. You shouldn't have to fight to be heard and the children and parents who are paying attention and are interested in what you have to say should have their needs respected, too. If someone is disruptive, it's okay to pause, put your book on your lap and say, "I'll just wait a moment for everyone to get settled. Is everybody ready?" This isn't singling out anybody, but conveys the message that the kids need to quiet down in order to proceed. Just remember to say it with a smile!

- Be sure to address proper behavior in the library at the beginning of the program, when you have everyone's attention.
- Small children are usually very eager to learn and follow the rules. To help them be quiet, you can ask them to pretend they have a mouthful of marshmallows or bubbles as they walk through the library to the story room.
- Watch your audience for signs that your program is going on too long or is no longer holding their interest. If there's a lot of noise and misbehavior, it may be time for you to introduce something else — a song, some physical activity, a guessing game, some riddles, or even head to the craft table early. Sometimes you have to be flexible!

What about horseplay or other serious discipline problems? It's important to speak up to children — and especially to their parents — when they are acting inappropriately (your guide will be your library's patron conduct policy). Not only do misbehaving children need to be redirected, but other children and parents nearby are watching to see what you will do and will take their cues from the way you respond to poor behavior.

Safety is important, too. Many parents and grandparents have fond memories of spending time in the library as children, and sometimes think public libraries are a safe place to drop off children. Depending upon your library's policies, it's a good idea to let parents know that you recommend they stay with their children, because the library is a public building and the library staff has no control over who might make contact with unsupervised kids.

Good Help Is Hard to Find

It's hard to offer programs if your library is understaffed. If this is a problem at your library, recruiting some able volunteers may be the answer for you. But where and how do you find them?

During library programs, you might spot a few parents who seem really on top of things. They always arrive on time, their kids are well-behaved, and they seem to take charge of the activities going on at their table, helping all the children — not just their own. Let these wonderful people know how much you appreciated the way they stayed to help clean up, or engage them in conversation about what they enjoy about the library programs. When one of your library staff calls in sick and leaves you short-handed, you can ask these parents to help set up or assist kids with their crafts.

Here are some more places to look for competent and willing volunteers:

- National Honor Society: Kids who are doing well enough at school to be tapped as members of the NHS are often highly motivated. Local chapters sometimes require their members to put in a number of community service hours to maintain their membership.
- Teens who "age out" of summer reading for younger kids, but still love the library: Some teens prefer to take on the role of assistant rather than participate in programs.

- Homeschoolers: If you notice school-age children making regular library visits with their parents at hours when children are normally in school, they may be home-schooled. Families who homeschool often seek out ways to become involved with their communities as part of their education and can make wonderful volunteers.
- Scouting Organizations: Both Boy Scouts and Girl Scouts place a high value on community volunteering for their members. Call your local scouting agency to see if they can recommend older kids looking for opportunities to help out.

Never fail to thank volunteers—they deserve it! A round of applause at the end of a program or, even better, a hand-written note from you, lets volunteers know their contribution is valuable. With positive feedback, volunteers are more willing to share their time, or even recruit some additional helpers. If it's in your budget, some library "swag" is usually welcome, such as a program t-shirt for summer reading volunteers.

Small Budget, Big Fun

It's no secret that library programs cost money, whether it's spent on books, art supplies or special performers. It can be a big worry, wondering if your program budget will cover the cost of the kids who attend. However, librarians have a secret weapon: people like us! Many folks believe in what we do and what libraries stand for. They are willing to donate time, and sometimes even money, to help us do it. To coax the most from your program dollars, reach into your community to find willing presenters for little or no cost.

A presentation by someone with special expertise on just about any topic makes for a fun and interesting program. Local government and non-profit agencies are often willing to send over a free speaker to address a group of children and parents at the library (they need to show they have made outreach efforts, just as librarians do). Possibilities abound, but here are a few ideas:

- Zoos and aquariums
- Sanitation or water department for a recycling program
- State and national parks for nature programs
- Scouting organizations for programs about wilderness survival, camping, etc.
- Local artists or crafters to demonstrate their skills and teach a simple project
- Therapy dog and handler to do a program about pets and service animals
- Ask a local person with an interest in theater to head up a summer acting program for teens; this provides an activity for the teens as well as a free "theater day" experience for the younger kids who come to watch the show.
- If you are in a rural area, there may be state funding for outreach programs from nearby cities; your state library is a good place to get more information.
- Make the most of your speakers' visits: ask ahead of time if you can assist in preparing a craft or activity to go along with the topic.

Make-and-take crafts seem to go along with many library programs, but as with speakers, funding can pose a problem. One option is to buy craft kits to hand out for kids to assemble, but these can be really costly and sometimes are not well-made, which makes them a poor investment. Kits have to be ordered ahead of time, too; if there are delays, you may not have enough to go around.

Librarians can save on program costs and still provide exciting arts and crafts projects by using materials on hand. Cardboard tubes can be recycled into animals, puppets, rockets, and so much more. If you expect large crowds in the summer, this free craft supply can be a lifesaver. Another plentiful "freebie" art supply is the egg carton. Egg cartons can become aliens, insects, flowers and other simple objects. Discarded CDs and DVDs from your library collection can also be recycled for crafts.

- Ask your library staff, members of the library, Friends, and the building custodians to save recyclables. Set up a convenient box where items can be dropped off anytime.
- Librarians often choose a story time theme and then pick out stories and crafts to pair with it, but you can also develop a program idea around a craft supply you have in abundance. Use recyclable items and save the money in your craft budget to buy embellishments such as sequins, beads, feathers, and the like.
- If you like to use the Internet for crafty inspiration, it's fast and easy to do an image search. You can quickly view the results for photos of crafts which look age-appropriate for the group you're working with and it's much faster than opening numerous text links.

Get Organized

One problem with all the great ideas from the Internet is figuring out a convenient way to organize them. Ideas are no good if you can't find them when you need them!

Some librarians find that Pinterest, a social networking website, can help them easily gather and share the ideas they find on the Internet. Members sign up for a free account, and then create "boards" where they can "pin" images from websites. This is an excellent, no-cost way to organize craft ideas, books, snacks, games and more, especially for a large, ongoing project like your summer reading program. You can create one "board" and "pin" all the ideas you like so you don't have to print out pages and keep them in folders. Or you could create a board just for crafts, one for books, etc. You can freely share with and borrow ideas from other pinners, too!

If you have an art supply closet or cupboard, consider making a list of the things kept on each shelf and tape it right to the cupboard door so you (or a volunteer who doesn't know where you keep everything) can quickly glance at the list and locate whatever is needed. Organize small items such as beads, corks, stickers, jingle bells, pom poms and the like in stackable, see-through plastic containers (these can be labeled with a list of their contents as well).

Once you have your supplies organized and your craft ideas picked out, it's time to put your plan into action.

- Whoever is teaching a particular craft should try it out ahead of time. This serves two purposes: you end up with a nice sample craft to show the children, and you will quickly find out whether the craft is well-designed and will turn out as expected.
- Modify the craft as needed to match the age of kids you're expecting. The younger the child, the more preparation you need to do ahead of time. For example, children younger than five have trouble using scissors because their motor skills are not yet developed. It is enough of a challenge to present them with pre-cut elements to color and assemble.
- Save painting projects for special occasions when you have plenty of time. Plan enough time for projects to dry. Volunteers can apply a base coat of paint to crafts ahead of time to prepare the surface for decorating.
- Because children have no control over when they will be brought to the library, make sure library craft projects can be completed in one session. Projects that require more than one session to complete may mean that some kids don't have the chance to finish theirs.
- If you want to do a more elaborate project, consider what things you could prepare ahead to make the best use of program time.
- Place craft items in small bowls or divided trays so you can quickly "set the table" with craft supplies. Empty frosting containers work well for holding colored pencils, washable markers, crayons or scissors.

Evaluate Your Experience

Not every program goes as well as you hope it will, in spite of your best efforts. It's important to make a note of what things didn't work well, as well as what did work well. Keep track of the things everyone enjoyed so you can do them again! Ask yourself and your helpers questions like these:

- Was this program topic well-suited for the age group advertised?
- Was the craft too difficult, and thus frustrating, for the kids? How could the staff have prepared the craft better ahead of time?
- Did we try to do too many things or cover too broad a topic?
- What went right?

Expect the unexpected. Planning ahead for a program you're presenting is one thing, but what if a Boy Scout troop arrives unscheduled for a tour, or a school group calls at the last minute to let you know 25 kindergarten children are on the way? There's no need to panic. The easiest thing to do is to prepare a couple of story kits you always keep ready to use at a moment's notice. A kit can be a bag or a box; inside are a story book you know well and some props to go with it, coloring pages or other handouts, and a few quick ideas for a song, finger play or game you can share. You come out looking like a winner because you're prepared!

Enjoy yourself and the kids will have fun, too! While it's true that library programs can be stressful, hosting events at your library can also be a very enjoyable way to interact with young library patrons and their families, especially when you are relaxed and having fun yourself. When families return with their children to the library again and again, you'll know you have captured their attention and helped them realize that libraries are great places for kids to be!

The Benefit and Implementation of an Employee Yoga Program

Kymberly Anne Goodson

Originating from ancient Indian disciplines, yoga is a 5,000 year old mind-body practice combining physical postures with breathing and meditation. Once obscure yet growing, a 2007 national survey found yoga among the top 10 alternative medical practices with roughly 6 percent of U.S. adults using it for health purposes in the past year (National 2012). Another study showed 4 million American yoga practitioners in 2001 growing to nearly 14 million by 2011 with half practicing at least once a week (May 2012).

In 2007, the University of California, San Diego (UCSD) Library began offering yoga classes for its employees. Aware private companies were introducing health club memberships or classes to employees to improve wellness and consequently attendance, the Training Coordinator proposed the idea for yoga classes to the library administration. Recognizing the library's limited budget, she explored options like yoga, aerobics, and kickboxing through the nearby campus athletic center. Yoga worked best because it could be accommodated in an existing library space, required little equipment, and wouldn't disrupt patrons.

Health Benefits

Offering myriad health benefits, yoga can be a cost-effective way for employers to lower their healthcare costs, offer employee preventative care, and reduce absenteeism. As such, yoga is often among multiple activities included in a broader employee wellness program. Related to the workplace, yoga can improve focus and concentration, increase morale and productivity, and help alleviate eyestrain, carpal tunnel syndrome, back pain, and other ailments related to computer work and prolonged sitting. It can help employees cope with emotions, deal with tension between co-workers, and relax during business travel. Some of yoga's many health benefits include:

- Reducing stress and anxiety
- Increasing physical flexibility, strength, and balance
- Improving muscle and joint conditioning

- Promoting relaxation and combating depression, fatigue, and insomnia
- Lowering blood pressure and heart rate
- Easing arthritis, back, muscle, and other pain
- Increasing energy and mental clarity
- Managing chronic allergies and diseases like diabetes, asthma, or heart disease

Overall Employee Wellness

Public libraries sometimes host community yoga classes or demonstrations. Less common are libraries of any type offering yoga classes for their employees. Alternately, examples abound of yoga's inclusion in corporate employee wellness programs. Despite limited budgets, expense cutting, and layoffs, workplace yoga has significantly grown in the past decade. According to yogaforbusiness.com's CEO, 5 percent of U.S. companies provide yoga classes for their employees, hoping to reduce employee stress and lower healthcare costs (Doherty 2002). Yoga can contribute to efforts to promote employee wellness, disease prevention, and physical activity and encourage employees to take personal responsibility for their health and healthcare decision-making. A deputy director from the National Institutes of Health, who also teaches yoga classes for NIH employees, encourages providing as many stress management techniques to employees as possible (Shepherd 2009).

Examples of employers of all sizes offering employee yoga are found nationwide. Smaller companies include Plexis Healthcare Systems, Hospice of Arizona, Industrial Light & Magic, Airport Appliances, Applied Signal Technology, Citizens Gas & Coke Utility, and Roche Diagnostics. Larger corporations offering employee yoga include:

- Apple Computers
- ChevronTexaco
- Dow AgroSciences
- EATEL Corporation
- HBO
- Kaiser Permanente
- Kraft Foods
- Nike
- PepsiCo
- Prevention Publishing
- Sony Corporation
- Toyota of America

When employed at Princeton University, one UCSD employee previously participated in lunchtime yoga in a library conference room. However, the program wasn't funded by the library and participants were charged to attend. Like at UCSD, sessions were taught by someone affiliated with campus recreation services. Ohio State University's employee wellness programs stem from its mission to improve OSU employees' physical quality of life. Health screenings and exercise classes complement teaching of yoga exercises. Stretches and postures, also taught to do at one's desk, help to release stress and improve circulation and posture (Narita 2005).

The technology firms Google, Asana, and Twitter offer yoga to their workers in support of employee well-being. The ubiquity of technology, smartphones, and social media can lead to burnout and the need to unwind and refresh. New Mexico's Sandia National Laboratories offers onsite yoga to increase relaxation, renew energy, reduce stress, and clear the mind for its 8,300 employees. Siebel Systems Inc. offers yoga to employees 4 times weekly. One participant says it helps him "gain mental clarity and reduce the stress caused by staring at a computer all day in a hyper-competitive field" (Doherty 2002, 3). Recognizing its inability to offer high salaries, the environmental charity, Eden Trust provides onsite employee yoga through a total reward approach.

An Airport Appliances administrator admits that offering twice-weekly yoga to employees is selfish. "The healthier our employees in mind and body, the better off we are for the portion of their life they give to the workplace" (Doherty 2002, 3). LaFrance Associates spend $1,000 monthly offering weekly yoga to its 10 employees to support work-life balance and reduce employee tension (Doherty 2002). Homebuilder Shea Homes is considering lowering health insurance rates for participants in its employee yoga program, as it did for employees who quit smoking (Natale 2007). The wellness program at Central States Health & Life Company of Omaha, which includes yoga, has resulted in "stronger morale, higher levels of productivity, and reductions in healthcare expenditures" (Schott 1992, 98). Market research firm SalesQuest's mission includes promoting employee health and productivity while striving for fewer employee absences. Rather than onsite yoga, it funds unlimited employee attendance at a nearby yoga studio. Its director appreciates that companies understand how yoga can increase their bottom line while keeping employees fit physically and mentally. Explaining its offering of yoga for stress reduction and relaxation, an occupational health nurse at Citizens Gas & Coke Utility recognizes regular exercisers are healthier and have less sick time (Weaver 2001).

Benefits Beyond Health

Yoga offers workplace benefits beyond employee health as well. Explaining the team building and other reasons for implementing its employee yoga program, Maureen Harden, the UCSD Library's AUL/Administrative Services, wrote to the author, "Staff from all levels of the organization participated and built interesting bonds." She notes that yoga was successful in getting people to talk to each other and fostering new social interaction. Other benefits include:

- Building teams and relationships
- Allowing staff to meet each other and interact outside traditional work relationships

- Increasing employee creativity and productivity
- Refreshing workers midday
- Providing a sense of community
- Promoting a positive self-image and a person's sense of well-being
- Improving morale

Workplace Yoga

Yoga suits the work environment well for several reasons. Participants can wear street clothes if they prefer not to change into workout gear. Gym memberships can be costly and some dislike the atmosphere of a gym. Other reasons supporting workplace yoga include:

- Accommodating a variety of age, flexibility, and fitness levels
- Being convenient and easier than visiting the gym
- Participants not smelling badly or needing to shower afterwards
- Being relatively inexpensive
- Requiring little administrative overhead or equipment for company or participant purchase besides an instructor
- Working in a space most organizations likely already have without modification

UCSD Library Yoga Program

Recognizing yoga's myriad benefits, the UCSD Library established an employee yoga program in 2007 after its Training Coordinator investigated options and introduced a proposal to the library administration. Though unfamiliar with use of yoga in other libraries, the library's Maureen Harden embraced the idea and was instrumental in identifying needed funding. In a recent e-mail, Harden listed reducing stress and improving staff well-being among primary motivations for supporting staff yoga, though she recalls being met with skepticism when sharing UCSD's plans with fellow LLAMA administrators and others at ALA.

Logistics

The UCSD Library program was arranged through UCSD's Campus Recreation. Its FitLife program supports convenient, affordable fitness and wellness activities for UCSD personnel. FitLife Mobile offers customized classes led by qualified instructors and is taught on campus, but outside of Campus Recreation facilities. Examples of FitLife classes include core conditioning, Pilates, yoga, meditation, and relaxation massages.

Library classes are taught by a FitLife Mobile instructor who is also an academic counselor for Computer Science & Engineering. She completed Campus Recreation's Yoga Teacher Training in 2006 and occasionally teaches other university fitness classes.

The library pays $40 per yoga class through a separate budget established for health & wellness events. Expenses to this account include yoga, CPR certification, Rape Aggression Defense training, and other occasional events. Though separate from money funding of more traditional training activities, the budget is managed by the library's Training Coordinator because of associated learning components.

Sessions are offered in a multipurpose room in the public area of the building housing the most library staff. Classes are held Tuesday and Thursday year-round from noon to 1:00 P.M. Some participants change clothes for the class, while others don't. Participants use and store their own yoga mats. At the instructor's suggestion, library training funds were used to purchase specialized equipment like foam blocks. Extra yoga mats were purchased for employees who forgot theirs or want to try yoga before buying one. These blocks and mats are stored in the multipurpose room.

Yoga classes are restricted to library employees with no sign-up needed to participate. Campus Recreation requires participants to sign in at each class, which serves as a waiver releasing the instructor, library, and university from liability in case of participant injury. No reports of injury to library yoga participants have ever been reported. Storage of attendance records from these classes, split between Campus Recreation and Library Human Resources, are incomplete. If attendance statistics are important for justifying on-going program support, other libraries are advised to maintain such records within the library.

Since its inception, several dozen library employees have taken part in the yoga program with over a dozen attending regularly at least once weekly. Some attend every class; others go when they can. Every department is represented in the classes. In its first year, the library offered 96 yoga classes, followed by 99 in 2008/09. Typical attendance was 10–15 per session both years. The number of classes has remained roughly the same over the years. Despite regular staff turnover, participation rates from 2007 through 2012 have remained consistent.

Participant Feedback

Six UCSD employees were interviewed about their yoga program participation. Interviewees praised the library's program for being convenient and free, saving them time and money. Several thought it preferable to visiting the gym before or after work and so convenient it's hard to make excuses not to attend. Others appreciate that yoga provides welcome personal time separate from that devoted to family, work, or other commitments. Two interviewees commented they find it incredible to forget about stresses and focus on one's immediate state rather than work while at yoga.

Interviewees also appreciate the program's support from library administration, quite different from the individual choosing to visit the gym at lunch. One offered, "The idea that my employer pays for and supports yoga is a huge benefit." Another agreed, "I feel like it's OK to take that break in the day, since it's offered by the library."

Library participants appreciate the break from sitting at a desk and in front of a computer. One interviewee described feeling more chaotic and disorganized when she hasn't been to yoga. All mentioned feeling better after attending yoga, even when reluctant to take the time to do so. One noted that attending yoga even once weekly reminds her to breathe correctly, stretch, and move her body over the rest of the week. Other health benefits of yoga participation mentioned include:

- Reducing stress, tension, and fatigue
- Feeling more mentally alert, focused, creative, and productive afterward
- Feeling renewed and refreshed
- Providing relief from feeling overwhelmed
- Feeling more positive about the working environment
- Gaining perspective
- Staying calm and balanced
- Interacting with co-workers from other areas of the library
- Centering oneself
- Staying healthy and in shape

Several interviewees who began participating shortly after their hire liked meeting colleagues across the library and sharing camaraderie by attending yoga. One library staff member commented how yoga participation has broadened her social circle in the library and translated to deeper and broader working relationships. She explained feeling more comfortable approaching and working with those she knows from yoga and making the time productive by chatting about work before or after class.

Barriers

Despite its convenient location and time, interviewees still mentioned difficulty getting away from work regularly, particularly between frequent meetings. Some noted feeling awkward wearing workout clothes around colleagues or feeling guilty for taking additional time away from work to eat after yoga.

Having attended yoga only once, one interviewee explained she doesn't participate because she found it more stressful than stress relieving. While she enjoys yoga, she finds it awkward and difficult to pull away from work in the middle of the day. Special Collections interviewees mentioned the difficulty of accommodating both yoga and lunch midday. While other staff can attend yoga, eating at their desk before or afterward, food restrictions in Special Collections eliminate that possibility for those staff.

Program Success

The UCSD Library yoga program has been a strong success, enjoying wide support from library administration and regular participation by a core group. One program devotee returned as a volunteer following retirement and selected his workdays specifically to permit continued yoga participation. Even staff who don't attend the yoga classes appreciate that the library provides and supports the activity. Staff interviewing candidates for open positions proudly mention the yoga program and candidates are excited to hear about the unique offering. One interviewee who joined yoga after her hire said hearing about it in her interview impressed her and she appreciated that yoga classes were supported by the library.

Recent years, marked by new strategic initiatives, significant annual budget cuts, and a complete organizational restructuring in the library, have been particularly stressful as employees have continued to provide quality service with reduced staffing and resources. Yoga's calming effect proved welcome and beneficial in the stressful times for library employees since the program started in 2007. Noting her added stress from the library's ongoing reorganization, one interviewee looks forward to yoga and uses it to maintain a positive outlook.

Maureen Harden described being proud of library administration for supporting the program and strongly recommends it to other libraries. Participants frequently told her, even after her retirement, they enjoyed and appreciated the yoga program. She often received positive comments about it and said staff were concerned yoga might be cut during the budget constraints of recent years. The library hasn't performed a staff survey about the yoga program, but all interviewees said they would be disappointed if it were ever eliminated.

Starting a Program

Libraries considering establishing an employee yoga program should keep several considerations in mind, beginning with offering classes for free or at a low cost to participants. Yoga need not cost the library a great deal. Shea Homes pays an average of $85 per class, charging employees $5 per class. Citizens Gas & Coke Utility charges employees $2 per class, with the company paying the remainder. Others, like UCSD and Sandia National Lab, don't charge participants. At $40 per one-hour session, the UCSD Library pays roughly $4,000 per year for nearly 100 annual yoga sessions—a quarterly program cost of less than a single trip for one to ALA. In addition to keeping participant costs low, other tips include:

- If you plan to charge employees, offer free trial sessions and ensure a positive experience so attendees are comfortable and interested in returning.
- Create a supportive and encouraging, rather than threatening or competitive, class environment.
- Ensure support within library administration so staff are comfortable taking time to attend.
- Alert employees that all age and fitness levels can be accommodated.
- Despite its Eastern spiritual beginnings, exclude any spiritual component from workplace yoga.

- Though some organizations offer one-time or periodic workshops as part of a larger wellness program, offer classes at least once weekly for maximum benefit.
- Identify the best class time (before/after work, during lunchtime).

Surveying employees in advance isn't essential, but may lend support or build enthusiasm for a yoga program. Employee input can provide insight on preferred program logistics, such as class timing and frequency. The healthcare corporation, Kaiser Permanente, surveyed employees for ideas on its employee wellness program. Suggestions included herbal medicine, meditation, stress reduction, relaxation therapy, low-fat cooking, physical flexibility, self-defense, weight management, women's health, aerobics, and yoga.

The UCSD Library's employee yoga program remains a clear success after 5 years. Employee yoga classes in a wide range of workplace settings offer numerous benefits to participants and the organization. Such a program can be replicated to suit a spectrum of library environments and budgets, for a relatively low cost and with little overhead, through a variety of implementation options.

References

Doherty, Brendan. "Company-Sponsored Yoga Helps Anxious Workers Breathe Easier." *San Francisco Business Times*, June 28, 2002.

"Kaiser Wellness Program Shaped by Employees." *Employee Benefit Plan Review* (May 1998): 49.

May, Patrick. "Tech Warriors Unplug for Yoga Respite." *San Jose Mercury News*, January 17, 2012.

Narita, Emi. "Ohio State U.: Yoga Relieves Ohio State U. Employees' Stress." *The America's Intelligence Wire*, August 2, 2005.

Natale, Tony. "Work-site Yoga Classes Reduce Stress: Employees Find Lunchtime Sessions Helpful, Convenient." *Tribune* (Mesa, AZ), December 15, 2007.

National Center for Complementary & Alternative Medicine, National Institutes of Health, "Yoga." Accessed June 4, 2012. http://nccam.nih.gov/health/yoga.

"SalesQuest Adds Fresh Veggies and Yoga to New Employees Benefits Package." *Business Wire*, August 15, 2007.

Schott, Fred. "Wellness with a Track Record." *Personnel Journal*. 71. (1992): 98.

Shepherd, Leah Carlson. "Yoga Can Help Employees Stretch Away Stress, Anxiety, Burnout." *Employee Benefit News*, April 1, 2009, 36.

Tramer, Harriet. "Meeting for Meditation; Workplace Yoga Programs Can Help Boost Employees' Wellbeing." *Crain's Cleveland Business* (January 23, 2006): 16.

Weaver, Gregory. "More Indianapolis-Area Companies Help Employees Realize the Benefits of Yoga." *The Indianapolis Star*, February 19, 2001.

Librarians Helping Each Other: A Staff StressBusters Program

AISLINN CATHERINE SOTELO *and*
SHIRLEY A. HIGGINS

The University of California, San Diego Libraries maintains a dedication to helping employees manage their stress. Whether in the form of official library programs, or staff-administered programs and activities, the Libraries understand the benefits of helping employees manage their stress levels. One cannot open a magazine, or visit a news website without seeing countless articles and studies focusing on the negative effects stress can have on your psyche and the physical repercussions for your body. With increased budget cuts, library staffs are frequently required to assume more responsibilities with fewer resources and as a result often find their stress levels rising. Working in an environment with administration support for stress relieving activities benefits both the employee and the employer. Organizations often are a reflection of their leadership, and if leaders place a value on the human aspect in the workplace, employees recognize and appreciate they are an important and valued member of the team working towards common goals.

As a method for helping employees learn to manage stress, the UC San Diego Libraries offer yoga classes twice a week, a wellness program, and a library staff administered StressBusters program. The StressBusters program is a self-sustaining program that hosts stress relieving events for staff. In this essay, we will describe the impetus for creating such a program, describe the program in detail, evaluate the effectiveness of the program based on participant survey results, and provide instructions on how to implement your own StressBusters program in your library.

Why Create the StressBusters Program?

In 1994 UC San Diego Libraries embarked on a redesign process that would affect all levels of the organization. The Library Administrative Team appointed a group named Committee on Restructuring for Distinguished Information and Library Services (Cordials) to manage the process. Cordials, which included the University Librarian as well as the Deputy UL, was composed of staff from various areas and departments and represented all levels and classifications of Library employees. This group had responsibility for determining how the organizational structure would change in the library and how. Cordials' members received intensive training in organizational dynamics and team building. Over the course of several months we determined it was necessary to change the focus of the organization as well as how we conducted business.

The user became our focus and shared decision making was the way we would govern. The Libraries would change how we made decisions about resources and priorities, how we communicated, and how we measured, recognized, and rewarded performance. Such fundamental change affected all employees at all levels. A series of mandatory all staff training sessions were provided to communicate expectations and to build skills needed for shared decision making. Cordials also recognized such extensive changes could cause stress for many staff and ways to relieve stress was discussed. Recreational classes, massage, team-building activities and similar ideas were suggested and discussed in the group, but in the midst of California state budget woes of the early 1990s, we had no way to fund these activities.

What Is the StressBusters Program?

Recognizing many staff had skills, interests and hobbies they might share with others, Shirley Higgins came up with the concept of a self-empowered staff group who would coordinate stress relieving activities and events, and the StressBusters program was born. As a newly empowered employee, Shirley took charge of the idea and sent a call to all library employees interested in developing StressBusters to attend a brainstorming meeting. Over twenty-five library employees, including librarians and staff at all levels, attended the first brainstorming session and others who could not attend in person sent suggestions over e-mail. We framed the guidelines together:

- no monetary support from the Library
- events would take place during the lunch hour (employees who normally had a half hour lunch period were encouraged to seek support from their supervisors to attend a one hour event)
- most events would be single, rather than continuing events
- StressBusters would be held approximately once a month
- StressBusters would be open to all employees
- all employees were welcome to initiate and host events

We came up with a variety of ideas but the real challenge was to get volunteers to host events such as teaching classes. Shirley hosted several events the first year and helped others to advertise and plan their events. We branched out and incorporated some after-hours events including two camping trips per year in the local mountains. Eventually StressBusters became somewhat self-sustaining and many staff planned and hosted events on their own.

The hope was StressBusters would evolve into a self-governed and self-perpetuating leaderless program, so over time, Shirley stepped back from organizing and only hosted a few events per year. Over the years, in the absence of strong leadership, StressBusters lost some focus and many events were billed as StressBusters were not about relieving stress for employees. Also, the diversity of events decreased as the number of hosts shrank and crafts became the chief function of the events, which had limited appeal. StressBusters dwindled to an occasional event attended by twenty or fewer employees in an organization of approximately two-hundred.

Listed below are the various types of events that took place in the early years of StressBusters.

Past Events
Astrology charts
Camping
Country Western dancing
Money management (4 repeats—VERY popular)
Nature photo walk
Paper Theater
Viewing videos
Walking group
Walking tour of the Stuart Collection (2 days)

Parties
Cookie decorating and Christmas movie
Getting the jump on Christmas Cards luncheon
Holiday potluck party and publication of the recipes
Potluck & recipe swap
Potlucks (numerous, with themes)

Crafts
Beaded bookmarks, snowflakes, needle-weaving
Craft show and sale
Decorating Christmas ornaments: balls, bells, felt, stockings
Desktop fountains
Gift-wrapping techniques
Decorating hats for the Library Staff Picnic
Jewelry: bracelets, earrings (3 separate events), flag pins, necklaces
Learn to crochet
Learn to knit ("graduates" created a weekly knitting group)
Magnets and tacks for bulletin boards
No-knit scarves

Origami flowers

Paper ornaments (stars, recycled card balls)

Patterned-darned bookmarks

Pompom creatures

Snow globes

T-shirt/sweatshirt appliqué and painting

Tassels

Topiary

Valentine cards

Wash cloth bunnies and rolled newspaper baskets

Wreaths (Christmas, Corn Husk, Fall, Spring)

The UC San Diego Libraries are again challenged to change dramatically and will be reorganized in 2012. Confronted with radical change, stress levels are elevated, and the need for stress relief is tangible. It is time to restore and reenergize StressBusters! New partners were recruited to help add energy and fresh ideas. To reach a new audience, Aislinn Sotelo and Shirley have started a regular StressBusters feature in the monthly library newsletter. The StressBusters column format includes:

- fun things to do
- tips and tricks and interviews with library staff on how they relieve stress
- a recipe and cooking tutorial every month
- a craft for the month

One of the "fun things to do" each month will be one of the new StressBusters events planned for the year so people get a preview of activities to come, and those who cannot attend can do the activities on their own. To ensure a variety of events, we actively recruited colleagues with various talents to assemble a diverse activity program that includes: a potluck; creating a terrarium; an Iron Chef Library competition; a lecture on bread baking; a lecture/demo on pickling; learning to play a musical instrument in an hour; putting together a choir to perform at the annual staff holiday party; and forming a walking group.

Is the Program Effective?

Since the university is currently going through a new Library-wide reorganization and we want to promote our existing StressBusters program, we determined now was the time to assess and reflect on our current program. To determine the effectiveness of our current StressBusters program, we came up with a series of questions to be presented to staff who have participated in, hosted, or have chosen to not participate in StressBusters activities.

Our method for information gathering was to send an e-mail to all Libraries staff asking for voluntary survey participants. Our volunteers could then answer the questions by sending an e-mail reply, a telephone interview, or an in person interview. The following questions were posed:

1. Have you ever attended a StressBusters event?
2. How often do you attend StressBusters events?
3. If you have never attended a StressBusters event, or have stopped, why? (i.e., do the activities not appeal to you? Dates and time don't work for you?)
4. What are your favorite types of events (ex. crafts, potlucks, newsletter, physical fitness?)
5. Would you be interested in more physical activities like soccer, prepping for volleyball, the Chancellor's 5K, bring back walking on the trails (faster and slower).
6. Have you ever led a StressBusters event? If so, how did you find the experience? (rewarding to share your hobby, stressful? Is it worth it?)
7. Have you ever continued with a hobby you've learned during StressBusters?
8. Do you feel your relationship with your colleagues has improved?
9. Do you have any suggestions for improving the StressBusters program?
10. Do you have suggestions for additional StressBusters activities?

Yes!

The majority of survey responses were overwhelmingly positive. We had thirty-eight respondents to our survey. Of those thirty-eight, six have never attended a StressBusters event. Of the thirty-two who have attended StressBusters events, the frequency of participation ranged from attending only one StressBusters event to participating in ninety percent of the events offered. The majority of participants attend two to three times a year.

Those who had never attended or who stopped attending stated that timing was an issue and/or the cost was prohibitive, or, they were not interested in the activities offered, namely crafts.

Timing

Timing was one of the biggest constraints for attending StressBusters events. Timing concerns ranged from fitting in a StressBusters activity and eating lunch into one hour, or their schedule only permits a half hour lunchtime total, finding the time in the workday to spend on a StressBusters activity, and scheduling conflicts with reference desk responsibilities.

Cost

The cost of StressBusters activities was stated as being prohibitive. StressBusters activities are usually kept at a cost of $5 to $10 to cover the cost of supplies, if there is a cost at all. Despite these efforts, cost continues to be a concern, and offering more free activities is something that should be considered.

Types of Activities & New Hobbies

Of the respondents who stated the types of activities offered did not appeal to them, many mentioned crafts were not appealing. Some even mentioned doing crafts stressed them out! Others noted they stopped attending StressBusters because they found other extracurricular activities to do during their lunch time, like swimming at our campus pool.

Interestingly, the majority of respondents stated their favorite activities were crafts, but crafts were also the biggest deterrent for others attending! The StressBusters program is fluid and in order to meet the goals of the program, we want to make sure we are appealing to the broadest audience. In our survey we posed questions to help us evaluate our current offerings and give us ideas for future ones.

We found crafts and potlucks were the overwhelming favorites. Additionally, there were strong proponents of more physical activities, and equally strong opponents of physical activity. An overwhelming majority of respondents mentioned their favorite activities to include holiday themed crafts, potlucks, and jewelry making.

Furthermore we found that most participants of StressBusters events who responded to our survey have not continued any of the activities they have been introduced to through StressBusters as hobbies. Those who have, stated they picked up knitting again, have made more desktop fountains, and many respondents started making jewelry after one of the jewelry making classes.

Physical Activity

Just as there was a split between those whose favorite StressBusters activities were crafts, and those who avoided crafts, there were some respondents who were enthusiastic about including more physical activities, and those who were completely uninterested. Of those who were enthusiastic about more physical StressBusters activities mentioned they would like to participate in sports such as soccer and volleyball on the weekends, nature walks identifying native plants on campus, and trail walks around campus.

StressBusters Leaders

Of the thirty-eight respondents, four had led StressBusters activities. Only one of those four stated they found prepping to lead a class stressful. The other three found leading and prepping for classes to be rewarding and stress relieving. Additionally, they enjoyed teaching something they loved to others.

Suggested Activities

Some of the most interesting things we learned from the survey were in response to the question about suggestions for additional StressBusters activities. Respondents listed:

- jumping rope
- card and scrapbook making
- recipe swaps (i.e., cookie exchanges)
- once a month potlucks on campus or at a park for a game day/picnic (water balloons, soccer, family day)
- happy hours

- book clubs
- tours of the campus sculpture collection
- more physical activities
- pickling and bread making classes
- gardening
- introductions on how to play poker, backgammon, bridge (and other games)
- improvisation
- craft sales
- stretching
- meditation
- bookbinding and book arts
- introduction on how to use Twitter
- organizing a home photo collection
- quilling
- drop in themed lunches (vegetarian, gluten free)
- gift wrapping sessions before the holidays
- board games

Stress Relief

Perhaps the most important part of the survey summarized whether we were fulfilling the mission of the program. Does StressBusters accomplish its goal and help relieve stress? The majority of the respondents answered positively about the StressBusters program making an impact on their stress management. Also, we learned participants felt their relationships with their colleagues have improved as a direct result of participating in StressBusters activities together.

Almost every single survey respondent who had participated in StressBusters and/or read the StressBusters section of the staff newsletter stated it has helped them relieve stress. A lot of respondents used the phrase "morale boosting," when describing their experience with StressBusters. People noted they especially appreciated Stress-Busters during the reorganization currently going on in our Library. Having a Stress-Busters event or taking the time to read the StressBusters column in the staff newsletter helped a lot of staff break up the long workday. Some respondents shared they often feel overwhelmed by their workload and it helps to take a break and do something fun like a craft, or socialize at a potluck. One respondent said she really enjoyed reading the interview section of the StressBusters newsletter where we interview someone from Libraries' Administration about how they deal with their stress. They said it was nice to know others are feeling stress and learning what steps they are taking to relieve or manage it. The few who stated StressBusters or the newsletter was not stress relieving for them either did not provide a reason why, or they stated taking the time for Stress-Busters was stressful. Overall, the response to the program was positive.

Relationships

Only a few survey respondents said they did not feel their relationships with colleagues had improved, and not one said any relationships had worsened! Many people stated they appreciated being able to meet colleagues from other departments they would not otherwise have met through participating in StressBusters. One participant noted they actually felt more comfortable approaching and working with people they had met and spoken to informally during StressBusters activities. Someone also shared a past Stress-Busters walking group has become a close group of friends outside of work. One participant noted they appreciated that there is no hierarchy during StressBusters. No one is anyone else's boss and everyone is on equal footing. Another participant stated that conversations inevitably turn to work during the sessions, and it's a good laid back environment to actually get some work accomplished while de-stressing.

Improvement

Additionally, we wanted feedback on ways to improve the StressBusters program in general, and survey participants had some great suggestions.

Respondents' suggestions for improving the program included hosting follow up sessions so people could finish any craft projects they may have started, but need help finishing. Some said they would like to have StressBusters events hosted more regularly, such as once a month. One suggested some StressBusters take place after work instead of during lunchtime. Also participants mentioned the level of difficulty of activities could vary to keep it interesting for all. Another person suggested there be more of an effort to distinguish StressBusters events from Library Training sponsored events, just to help differentiate the two programs. Others mentioned changing the location from our main library building to another location some of the time, to make sure events start on time to prevent rushing, and to advertise more.

How to Host a StressBusters Event

If you are planning to implement a StressBusters Program in your library, you can learn from the experience of the UC San Diego Libraries and the survey responses. To help with the logistics of planning, the following guide has been provided to help you plan successful events:

1. Find a host
   - Put out a call for volunteers
   - Invite interested staff to attend a planning meeting
   - Recruit select individuals
   - Recruit a team
   - Pick a date/time
   - Lunch hour
   - After hours
   - During work hours
2. Test run the event for timing/Prototype a craft
   - Determine materials needed and cost for instructor and students
   - Can students supply their own materials?

- Determine whether to charge a materials fee and if the fee should be collected in advance or at the event
- Determine whether you need to limit attendance
- Do you need helpers?
- Decide if RSVP required
- Do you need special equipment for music, videos, or other media?

3. Advertise the event at least 2 weeks prior to the date
   - Date
   - Time
   - Cost
   - RSVP

Send a reminder e-mail the day before the event to all or just people who have returned their RSVPs. Be sure to photograph the event and ask permission to share photos. Finally, send e-mails to all library staff after the event to share the fun and stimulate interest in future events.

The UC San Diego Libraries' Staff StressBusters Program has been successful at helping employees relieve stress by organizing events and activities among colleagues. Staff has been able to sustain the program for the last eighteen years without any financial support from the Libraries (though they have been very supportive in time and space, planning, organizing and teaching amongst ourselves.) The program has been fluid throughout the years, which undoubtedly has contributed to its success. It is important to remain flexible and gauge the needs of your staff.

De-Stressing: Conscious Choices at Work and Home

Maryann Mori

In my most stressful experience as a librarian, I saw the wrinkles appear on my tired face seemingly overnight, and my hair literally fell out by handfuls. I was a library director. The stress I experienced as a director was not from being in a bad situation. On the contrary, my position was a good one; I had capable employees, good support from my community, and my library was located in a "good" area that faced little or no serious problems with vandalism or behavior. Yet the position was still highly stressful simply because of the constant demands, and those demands took a noticeable toll on my physical well-being. I have heard from other library colleagues who have said their stress-related problems included physical symptoms such as stomach and digestive ailments, insomnia, and severe headaches. Other colleagues have mentioned various emotional problems that have developed from job-related stress: an inability to remain focused on a task, extreme dependence on a substance (such as food or cigarettes), depression, even strains in family relationships.

Yet, most any employee within a library can become overwhelmed by stress due to poor working conditions or bad employee relations. When job descriptions are not clear, when staffing cuts make more work for fewer employees, when employees and positions have not been adequately paired, or when budget deficiencies mean doing more with less, those situations can create added stress to any library employee. And stress can be miserable. During my high-stress job at the library, I discovered and practiced some simple steps that eventually brought calm and relief back into my life.

I believe a primary contributor to stress among library employees is due to trying to live up to everyone's expectations. For employees such as a director, the board may be "the boss" in theory, but in practice the director must answer to everyone, including the city council, city department heads, all library staff, the public, and the library's Friends & Foundation organizations. Other library staff may face similar situations as they contemplate the number of people they must please, including a direct supervisor, co-workers, department heads, a branch manager, director, story time parents and assorted patrons. That's a lot of people to try to please, and suffice it to say no one can be all things to all people. When I came to realize I had to be true to my personal convictions, and do what I firmly believed was the best action for the library as a whole, I was relieved from some of the stressful burden that comes from trying to be a people-pleaser. Realizing no matter how hard I tried, I would never be able to please everyone, I vowed simply to be friendly, hard-working, conscientious and professional. If anyone would not be happy with those traits, then I told myself there was not much in life that *would* please them. Shakespeare wrote, "...to thine own self be true," and his statement is a good one for those individuals who find themselves in a position where they must answer to many people.

A Three-Step Plan

Another lesson I learned was that I could alleviate some stress by simplifying, delegating and eliminating some of my duties. I started with simplifying. I streamlined some of my tasks, as well as some of the tasks of the employees at my library, and I made a few basic changes that brought better efficiency and ease of work for staff. Developing a better work environment created happier employees, and happier employees made me less stressed. A previously cumbersome check-in area became a more efficient check-in station by relocating a desk and establishing some designated sorting shelves. Creating a few Excel spreadsheets proved far more practical for various statistical record-keeping than previous ways requiring use of an adding machine. Opting not to attend every optional meeting, but only some of those meetings, opened a few spots on my previously packed calendar. I also made the time to establish a decent filing system (both for hardcopy and online documents) which, although it took some time to initiate, simplified my organizational needs and made locating documents faster and easier.

Next I moved to delegating. My predecessor had maintained a hefty file of library invoices and a spreadsheet of expenditures. I talked with my city finance officer and learned she was already maintaining those same records with some efficient software. She offered to establish a log-in identification for me, so I could access the software and view any invoice or expenditure I might need to examine. And she provided me with line-item breakdowns or budget figures any time I made the request. Realizing I could simply delegate this particular task to her, I stopped maintaining the kind of records my predecessor had kept. It was a huge burden off me! In another situation, I asked an employee to begin running the monthly statistical reports and just give me the totals for the various categories. Asking one of my capable employees to do this task allowed me to focus on using the data for my own reporting purposes.

I then began to eliminate some activities from my "to do" list. I was determined to focus on doing a few things well rather than trying to do many things in an only passable manner. To begin cutting back on over-commitments, I decided which skills seemed to be my forte,' or which ones were my passion within librarianship. I focused on those, even though it meant a few of my other interests had to wait. I also calculated which of the services my library provided were the best ones or the most appreciated by the community. I suspected spreading the library (and its staff) across a huge spectrum of offerings could be a contributor to a stressful work environment. To begin analyzing which skills/

services/talents my library and I did best, I started making a list. I talked with staff and colleagues. I asked them what they believed were my strengths, as well as what they saw as the strengths of the library. I asked people to help rate this list for me. I considered next which of those skills most benefited my library as programs or services. Again, I rated them or asked staff and patrons to rate them. I chose the top two or three from the list. I focused on those skills and programs in order to develop them to the best of my and my library's abilities. I allowed other offerings and activities to wait until such time as I could begin to refocus on them or until I could adequately train another employee to assist with them.

I am convinced another big contributing factor to high-level stress is long hours at the office. As a library director, I could easily have worked sixty hours a week. Fifty plus hours became routine for me. It was only after my board president saw my timesheets and demanded (kindly) that I limit my hours did I try very hard not to work more than 45 hours a week. By eliminating just a few hours a week, I helped alleviate some stress simply because I was able to be with my family more often. I had to remind myself I did not need to be a martyr; the library survived before I arrived there, and I knew it would be able to survive without me. My unnecessary, extra hours were not doing as much good for the library as they were doing harm to my physical well-being. I realize some library employees are in a position with a specified, limited number of hours, and those employees may find it difficult to complete all of the assigned tasks during their scheduled work time. I recommend to employees in that type of situation to talk with a supervisor about the possibility of getting the hours increased or about eliminating or delegating some of the responsibilities. Prioritizing and working smart as well as hard can only go so far in making the impossible possible; employees should express concerns to a supervisor and attempt to find suitable solutions that will not only benefit the employee's personal well-being but ensure quality services and programs are part of the library.

Applying the Plan Elsewhere

In addition to simplifying, delegating and eliminating some of my work-related tasks, I applied those techniques to my personal life. I started limiting my outside activities. I really enjoy presenting at library conferences, serving on library-related organizations or committees, teaching courses at the local college, and writing professional articles. Likewise I enjoy commitments to non-library organizations, which have always seemed like a good way to "get away from it all" and leave library stress behind. But when some of those activities — whether professional or personal — turned from a blessing to a burden, I realized I had overcommitted myself and simply added to my stress. What may have started as a means to alleviate stress, actually added to further demands, deadlines, and frazzled nerves. I dropped out of a few social organizations and did not renew my "officer terms" with some professional groups. While eliminating some of those activities proved to be a difficult action, in the long run, I was glad I did it and found not having those additional commitments really did relieve some of the stress I had previously felt.

Furthermore, I took the goal of simplifying, delegating and eliminating duties and applied it to my home life. Anyone living with other family members knows the demands from those additional family members can often increase stress. During other high-stress times of my life, I trained my children to do their own laundry, solicited teen family members to help prepare meals on certain nights of the week, and informed my family clean towels would be stored in a large basket (without being folded) instead of being carefully folded and stacked in a closet. Reducing and delegating household chores was a tremendous help in alleviating some stress-inducing ailments. More recently, I have hired someone to regularly do the yard work and have even hired someone to do house-cleaning on a few occasions. I have learned the value of my time is worth more than the cost of hiring someone to do those types of household jobs.

Listeners and Mentors

Everyone needs a sounding board, and I did not discover this fact soon enough. A sounding board might be a best friend, a significant other, a colleague or a trustee. I believe a neutral third party is the best option for a sounding board. When I was undergoing a time of significant stress, my spouse especially understood my need to talk about the situations and allowed me thirty minutes each evening to discuss my day, including my struggles. I never expected any kind of comment or advice from him; I simply needed him to listen. Finding someone who will just listen is a positive step in relieving stress, but I firmly believe it is necessary to limit the amount of time spent talking about the stress factors; there is a difference between letting it all out and rehashing it over and over again.

In addition to a sounding board, a good mentor can be invaluable in relieving stress. A mentor — someone else in a similar library position — has probably experienced the same kinds of situations and can not only provide advice on how to handle those situations, but can give comfort by being someone who has "been there, done that." Just knowing I was not alone in my situation was a huge stress relief! I chose another library director in a town where I had formerly lived to be my mentor. He was far enough removed from the situation (geographically) to be neutral, yet close enough to it (professionally) to be sympathetic and helpful. The wonderful thing about having such a mentor is the relationship often becomes reciprocal as both individuals realize they have a trusted friend and comrade in the library field.

Sometimes a group of colleagues can be a good way to give comfort and assistance in a stressful situation. In my career, I was once part of a small group of librarians (all of whom held similar positions) who met quarterly for lunch. We had no real agenda for our meetings, but we all knew the value of those meetings and took comfort from each other's presence. Sometimes we would present a certain situation and ask for advice, but often we would purposely refrain from library talk and just relax amidst one another's company. The time out of the office was appreciated by all of us. I now encourage colleagues to form a "librarians' club" of their own and make it a routine event.

Get Away from It All!

During some of my extremely stressful library experiences, I often recalled the old commercial where the woman was obviously going through a lot of stress, and in desperation she asked for Calgon, a bath soap to "take [her] away." Everyone needs to be taken away from time to time. Whether it is with a bubble bath or a vacation, some time away from the library will do both the employee and the library some good. After all, a stressful employee tends to reflect stress within the workplace, which can negatively affect the entire workplace environment. While an actual vacation may not be possible, a few simple indulgences of pampering can do wonders to alleviate stress and restore sanity.

Here are some simple get-away-from-it-all activities I found helpful in reducing stress and I have suggested to other library colleagues:

- Designate a certain time of the day or week to "unplug." Turn off the computer, shut off the phone, and disconnect any other gadgets or gizmos that could lead to work-related activities.
- Take a lunch break — a significant break to leave the office and/or the library. Eating outdoors can be a simple and inexpensive way to get out of the library for a few minutes each day.
- Take a mini-vacation to a nearby town — if not for the weekend, then at least for the day, or visit some of the local museums, parks or tourist attractions that are typically overlooked by residents.
- Visit a salon or spa for a new hairstyle, a massage or the works!
- Arrange for one day per week to be a "night out" or at least a "night off" — an evening where a special meal is the focus. Break out the good china, visit a new restaurant, or try a new food. Even a frozen meal prepared in the microwave can become special when served on nice dishes with a glass of wine or cup of flavored tea. Splurge a little!

Throughout my time in a high-stress library position, my one-day-a-week treat was Friday evenings. On Friday night my husband would prepare an extra-special multi-course meal. I'd get out the good china, the nice placemats, the linen napkins and the fancy tableware. It was a special event I looked forward to every week. I made it a priority, as did my spouse, because we both knew the invaluable health benefits it provided in reducing stress levels. While not everyone is blessed with a resident cook, the important thing is to have something special to look forward to at the end of the work week.

Hobbies and Health

Some overstressed library staff have found hobbies to be instrumental in alleviating their stress-related symptoms. Scrapbooking, restoration activities (furniture, cars, etc.), photography, painting, needle work and music (learning or playing a musical instrument) have all been favorite hobbies among some of my colleagues. I play a couple of musical instruments, and I am determined to make one hour a day (minimum) the time I would devote to my hobby. While there were times when the extra hour proved difficult to fit into my already burdened schedule, the hour proved to be quite therapeutic by allowing me to focus on my own skills and interests. It was always an hour well spent.

Another sure-fire way to get rid of some stress is to burn it up — literally. I learned to burn up stress by burning some calories. I have personally found that exercise invigorates me in a way no other stress reliever can do. A hard, fast walk can be a great way to vent frustrations! I know of someone who believes in the therapeutic art of boxing and joined a kick-boxing class as her means of relieving stress. For me, cycling became a preferred way to relieve stress. With the wind blowing on me, and my legs pumping away, I can literally feel the stress being lifted away with each turn of the bike wheel. When I discovered a bike trail leading from my home to my library, I rode my bike to work on occasion — nearly 15 miles away. And I actually looked forward to it! Not only did the exercise burn off the steam of stress, but I avoided heavy, frustrating traffic contributing to my stress levels before and after work.

In addition to exercising, I also made it a point to eat and sleep well. Being under the burden of a stressful job situation proved bad enough, but not taking care of my personal health only exacerbated the situation. I now avoid high-calorie junk food and empty calories (except for an occasional splurge). Instead, I eat a diet rich in vitamins, nutrients, fruits and vegetables. I try to get to bed at a decent hour and do all I can to get restful slumber. While it is easy to dismiss these actions because I think I do not have time for them, the fact is these are simple, inexpensive ways to make drastic improvements in alleviating stress.

An old saying is "Silence is golden," and I found the sentiment to be true when I was trying to find ways to relieve stress. Although broadcast news could get my mind off my work, and music could be energizing or relaxing on days when I drove to work, I often found the best sound from my car radio was *nothing*. Sometimes I amazed myself at how different I felt after driving to or from work in complete silence. It became a time for personal reflection and meditation — a tremendous benefit to reducing stress. I now regularly practice moments of silence in my car, home or office and have found the absence of additional noise helps calm my spirit.

In a few instances, colleagues have attempted to follow my advice but still found themselves in unbearably stressful situations. For those individuals, the best way to relieve the stress was to leave the job. It did not mean leaving librarianship, however; a new position within the same library or a change to a different library system became a good career move for some of those friends. Their courage to move on showed me that change can often become a way to branch out to new and better career offerings. Finding a library job conducive to one's talents and temperaments is often the ultimate way to minimize stress.

Journaling Your Professional Life: Appreciate the Journey

CRISTINA HERNANDEZ TROTTER

During my graduate studies I attended an ALA-sponsored leadership conference. After two days of soaking in the advice of experienced librarians, all the attendees received a handsome bound notebook. Our mentors encouraged us to document our professional journey. As a long-time diarist, I appreciated the idea of journaling about my career dreams and goals, and yet, the pages of that blank journal intimidated me. I held on to that journal, but I would not write in it for years. I still wrote in my cheap little notebooks, but my musings were deeply focused on my personal life. Almost ten years of professional experience, transitions and growth were just minor footnotes in my journal.

Maybe it was the pressure of a new middle management position or maybe it was the strain of trying to support a family in a time of recession, but I recently realized I could use a more productive way to focus my thoughts and concerns about work. So I returned to the journal given to me years ago and started writing.

In the meantime I have come to appreciate why the words journey and journal share the same French root word — *jour,* a day. Our professional journey is made by one day's work following another, day after day. Journaling about this daily progress keeps us on track while slowing us down enough to appreciate the journey.

The Benefits of Journaling

Journaling has long been recognized as a powerful tool for coping with stress and improving performance. Ira Progoff started offering his Intensive Journal Workshops in the 1960s. His 1971 collaboration with the New York State Job Training Program demonstrated journaling exercises contributed greatly to the participants' ability to find and maintain employment, secure better housing, and become more financially independent (Sealy 1977).

Since then studies have shown journaling benefits not only our mental health, but also our physical health. The studies of James Pennebaker are often cited as demonstrating the positive psychosomatic effect of expressive writing which are less doctor visits, less sick days off work, and heightened immune function (2011, 420–422). In addition, his research provides evidence that the repression of emotional thoughts increases stress levels and negatively affects health (Petrie 1998). Pennebaker has also investigated how journaling affects our ability to adjust during stressful life changes. For instance, his 1994 study demonstrated that recently laid-off professionals who used journaling techniques found new employment more quickly (2011, 421).

Few studies have focused specifically on journaling as a means for coping with occupational stress. A meta-analysis compared the effectiveness of various types of occupational stress management programs. Journaling was included as "alternative treatment," but the authors could not draw any conclusions on its comparative effectiveness due to insufficient data. However, the researchers did conclude that cognitive-behavioral therapy was the most beneficial intervention program for reducing occupational stress (Richardson 2008).

Unfortunately, formal psychotherapy is too expensive and time-intensive for most employers or employees to consider. This is where journaling comes in. As Kathleen Adams reminds us in her book *Journal to the Self*, we all have the option of leaning on our "79 cent therapist" (6). The price of notebooks might be slightly higher now, but Adam's point remains strong — all we need is a notebook, a pen and some time to write. We can become our own helpful therapist.

Why Journal About Work?

A journal provides a private place where we can lay out our thoughts without judgment or censorship. The freedom of expression afforded by the private journal allows subconscious ideas and concerns to bubble to the surface and take form. Author Joan Weimer celebrated journals as "a place to pursue a feeling or a dream instead of forgetting or evading it" (Bender 2001, 61). It is a place where we can surprise ourselves. By putting feelings into words (or drawings) we are able release, identify, and work through our emotions. As we ruminate on the past and imagine the future, we find ourselves questioning our behaviors, recognizing strengths and weaknesses, and formulating new perspectives. When we begin journaling about our work and career, all of these benefits extend to our professional life.

"Paper is more patient than people," wrote Ann Frank in her famous diary (1991, 154). This statement rings particularly true at the workplace. Professionalism often prevents us from expressing our honest reactions to situations at work. By writing freely about our frustrations and concerns in a journal, we begin to seek solutions rather than just venting to co-workers. The work journal becomes a record of our professional development, where we lay out our goals and fine-tune strategies. We hone our communication skills through the simple regular practice of writing. As we read back through our entries we can identify cycles of productivity. More importantly, journals help us to integrate our mental life with our professional life.

Honoring Our Inner Work Life

"As people arrive at their workplaces they don't check their hearts and minds at the door," wrote psychologists Amabile and Kramer, explaining why they had asked 238 knowledge workers to complete daily dairy entries for four months (2007, 74). Amabile and Kramer were investigating the connection between the work performance and "inner work life," which they define as all the emotions, perceptions, and motivations constantly passing through the mind during the workday. According to their 2011 article, "The Power of Small Wins," an analysis of nearly 12,000 diary entries found the strongest factor affecting our inner work life is our ability to make progress in meaningful work (73).

An unexpected result of the study was the helpfulness of journaling. Many of the participants expressed their appreciation for participating in the study. Even when the daily journaling felt forced and time-consuming, participants reported several benefits from taking the time to review their feelings about the workday. They were able to identify those reassuring signs of progress, strategize in the face of setbacks, and better understand their relationships with others. The authors announced on their *Harvard Business Review* blog that they had been so impressed with the benefits of journaling that they decided to start keeping their own work journals (HBR Blog, 2011).

Bound or Unbound? Print or Electronic?

What form your work journal takes is a matter of taste. Some prefer bound notebooks, others spiral. Some like the neatness that lined pages encourage, while others like the freedom to draw, doodle, and let words explode on unlined pages. Others prefer to go the electronic route. They might type faster than they write, they do not like the messiness of their own handwriting, or they like the mobility of an electronic journal. Handwritten journals have some advantages worth considering. They provide us with an opportunity to step away from keyboards and monitors which dominate our work life. They help to slow us down enough to focus on reflection. They make editing more difficult which reduces self-censorship. Furthermore, handwritten journals allow us to draw and create mind-maps.

On the other hand, electronic journals offer the powerful advantages of keyword searching and password protection. The mobility of electronic journals is very appealing. Many applications and websites allow journal entries to be accessible and synced across multiple devices. You can categorize your type of entries for easier discoverability in the future by using tagging features. Also, you can easily copy and paste into an electronic journal.

Journaling Techniques

I generally subscribe to the "just start writing" philosophy of journaling. In her book *Leaving a Trace*, Alexandria Johnson includes a quote worth remembering from Katherine

Mansfield's personal journal, "It's very strange, but the mere act of writing anything is a help. It seems to speed one on one's way" (2001, 21). And yet, sometimes we get stuck. We do not know how to even begin. This is where journaling techniques and prompts are helpful. There are many helpful books about journaling that offer various suggestions on how to get the ink flowing (or the keys clicking). I have selected a few common techniques I find most applicable to the workplace:

The Unsent Letter

One safe way to release pent-up frustrations is through writing *but not sending* a letter. We have to hold a lot back at work. Professionalism and good old-fashioned common sense help us to hold our tongue during disagreements. Often we walk away feeling like we never got our point across. Suppressing these frustrations simply adds to our stress levels. The unsent letter not only provides an emotional release, but also helps you to clarify your position when you feel misunderstood. Addressing a specific person forces you to stop and consider what you really want that person to know. Whether you are writing to your co-workers or patrons, you finally get an opportunity to really tell someone (yourself) how you feel.

Because the unsent letter is personally addressed to someone, it is important you do not accidentally leave it for someone to find. Also, this is not a journal entry you should compose in your e-mail client. One final drawback of the unsent letter format is that you might feel so much better after writing the letter you might be led to believe it is a good idea to send it. The most important thing to remember about the unsent letter is this: DO NOT SEND IT!

The Dialogue

Dr. Ira Progoff dedicates six chapters to the Dialogue technique in his book *At a Journal Workshop*. Kathleen Adams calls it "the Swiss army knife of the journal toolbox," and covers it in the longest chapter of her book *Journal to the Self* (1990, 102). So with the hope I am not over simplifying this technique, I will say it is basically a scripted dialogue between you and someone (or something) where you write both parts. It looks something like this on the page:

Me: I am really tired of you asking me to do your research for you.

Patron: But you make it so much easier.

Me: It is not my job to do your research for you.

Patron (*Legitimately surprised*): It's not? Really? (*In a whining tone*) But I don't know how, and I already got my hands full having to write this paper.

Me: Yeah, when I think about it, finding the articles and books for you sure sounds a lot easier and faster.... Oh, I am so conflicted!

(*Patron stares blankly and says nothing.*)

At this point, Adams would encourage me to respect the silence and take a moment to ask, "What does my heart say?" Instead, I ask my better professional judgment to guide me, and I decide to finish with this:

> ME: How about this? I'll talk you through the steps as I help you find articles in one database. And then you can search other good databases on your own later. Are you even listening to me?
>
> PATRON (*Lowers phone briefly*): Yes, sorry. You realize they do not teach us this in class. I do not even know how to get started. If I close my eyes and pretend like it doesn't exist, this assignment will just go away, right?
>
> Me: Sorry, but no. Here let me help you get started ... (*still slightly exasperated*) but you have to put the phone away!
>
> PATRON (*Puts phone down*): Yes, ma'am.

Success! I feel better already. This is the idea of the dialogue technique, to work through troubling situations with people. While there might be a certain amount of venting or complaining, this technique forces you to try to understand the other person's perspective.

In addition to dialogues with people, Adams lists other types of dialogues we can have, including dialogues with events and circumstances, our bodies and our emotions, and our work (1990, 102–122).

Sixteen Topics

"Topics du Jour is a journal technique that allows you to start moving mountains, one boulder at a time," according to Kathleen Adams (1990, 167). In its original version, Topics du Jour is a journaling technique where you create a numbered list of 31 aspects of your life you want to track and develop. You then begin journaling about the topic corresponding to today's date. In a month's time you will revisit the topic. This format assures you are monitoring your progress and development in those important areas of your life. However, Adams suggests when using this technique for business purposes, it is more beneficial to create a list of just 16 topics that you review on a bi-weekly basis. She also recommends writing a two-week plan on days 15 and 30, with an overall review on those months with 31 days.

Here is what my 16 topics would look like:

1. Customer Service
2. Collection Analysis and Development
3. Online Resources
4. Communication with my boss
5. Communication with my staff
6. Genealogical collection
7. General helpfulness
8. Statistics and reporting

9. Organization of stacks and work areas
10. Time management
11. Management of staff's responsibilities
12. Promotion of resources
13. Professional development of staff
14. Professional development of self
15. Two week plan
    ...Repeat...
16. Overall review

According to Adams, you can spend as little as fifteen minutes a day focusing on your Topic du Jour to reap the benefits (1990, 167–171).

Make a Plan

If you are feeling overwhelmed by unfinished work projects and unmet goals, you might be suffering from the Zeigarnik effect: nagging thoughts about some outstanding business that intrusively and involuntarily pops into our minds. When you feel like you are on the losing end of a long to-do list, it is difficult to stop rushing ahead and take time to write. But this might be just what you need.

In their book *Willpower*, Baumeister and Tierney discuss how one of the best methods to tame the Zeigarnik effect is to simply make a plan. The authors' review several studies that demonstrate writing a specific plan to address some unfinished business can help clear your mind. Even though you have not made any "palpable progress" on the project, your unconscious mind will stop nagging you and allow you to concentrate on the task at hand (2011, 83). The best part is you not only have a clearer mind, but you now have a plan.

Gratitude List

"One of the most important writing techniques for boosting happiness revolves around the psychology of gratitude," concludes Richard Wiseman in his book *59 Seconds* (2009, 21). Numerous studies have demonstrated that "counting our blessings" is beneficial to both our mental and physical well-being. One study asked participants to simply create a weekly list of five things for which they were grateful. These participants reported a significant increase in happiness and health, as compared to other participants whose list-making focused on either hassles or neutral events (22). It is easy to overlook the little details that make our work more pleasurable. It is so easy to focus on the negative. Take the time each week to make a short list of the good things in your daily work life. You might surprise yourself and discover it is not so bad.

Reflective Practice

If you want to use your journaling efforts to truly maximize your professional life, then I recommend you take the time to learn the art and skill of reflective journaling. Reflective journaling is a technique that asks you to review your performance in a specific situation, critically analyze the outcomes, and consider possible changes for the future. It requires you to question your own behavior and motivations. Such self-questioning encourages us to break free of rote behavior that stems from either personal habit or professional inculcation. It helps us to consider how our professional performance affects others, identify areas where we can improve, and maximize learning (Forrest 2008). The ultimate goal is to become a more reflective practitioner.

Reflective practice is an important skill prescribed in the professional literature of various fields including education and librarianship. The ability to reflect on our own professional practice is so important that some consider it a core competency. The UK's Chartered Institute of Library and Information Professionals (CILIP) requires candidates seeking chartership to provide evidence of their ability to reflect critically on their own performance. CILIP offers numerous courses in reflective writing to help members provide such evidence in their portfolios.

One recommended structure for reflective writing follows a six-stage questioning process suggested by Gibbs in *Learning By Doing*, which has known as Gibbs' Reflective Cycle (1988):

1. Description: What Happened?
2. Feelings: What were you thinking and feeling?
3. Evaluation: What was good and what was bad about the experience?
4. Analysis: What sense can you make out of the situation?
5. Conclusion: What else could you have done?
6. Action Plan: If it arose again, what would you do differently?

Conclusion

Successful journaling can benefit your mental and physical health while reducing stress. It helps to maximize performance and enjoyment both in your personal and professional life. Here are some tips to consider as you begin journaling:

- Make time to write in your journal. It benefits you even though you are busy
- Select a journal format that works best for you
- Quiet the inner censor. Express your thoughts and concerns freely
- When you need help working through a specific situation or concern, try using a journaling technique such as the unsent letter or the Dialogue
- When you write, dig deep. Question yourself and your preconceptions

- Practice gratitude and recognize even the smallest progress in your workday
- Keep it Private! Do not leave your journal out (or on the screen) for someone to read

In his classic self-help book, *7 Habits of Highly Effective People*, Steven Covey promotes journaling as part of the seventh habit, "sharpening the saw." He says, "Keeping a journal of our thoughts, experiences, insights and learning promotes mental clarity, exactness, and context" (296). This context is often forgotten as we rush through the workday. By journaling we begin to tune into what is going on both around us and within us. We allow ourselves to see where we have been, where we are, and where we want to go in our careers. Our journals remind us our professional life is a journey, and it is a journey we make one day at a time.

References

Adams, Kathleen. *Journal to the Self: 22 Paths to Personal Growth.* New York: Grand Central Publishing, 1990.

Amabile, T. M., and S. J. Kramer. "Four reasons to keep a work diary," HBR Blog Network. Last modified April 27, 2011. http://blogs.hbr.org/cs/2011/04/four_reasons_to_keep_a_work_di.html.

_____. "Inner Work Life: Understanding the Subtext of Business Performance." *Harvard Business Review* (May 2007): 72–83.

_____. "The Power of Small Wins." *Harvard Business Review* (May 2011): 71–80.

Baumeister, Roy F., and John Tierney. *Willpower.* New York: Penguin, 2011.

Bender, Sheila. *Keeping a Journal You Love.* Cincinnati: Walking Stick Press, 2001.

Covey, Stephen R. *The 7 Habits of Highly Effective People.* New York: Fireside, 1989.

Frank, Anne. *The Diary of a Young Girl: The Definitive Edition.* Ed. Otto Frank and Mirjam Pressler. Trans. Susan Massotty. New York: Doubleday, 1991.

Forrest, Margaret. On Becoming a Reflective Practitioner. *Health Information and Libraries Journal.* (2008) 25: 229–232.

Gibbs, G. *Learning by Doing: A Guide to Teaching and Learning Methods.* London: Further Education Unit, 1988.

Johnson, Alexandra. *Leaving a Trace: On Keeping a Journal.* Boston: Little, Brown, 2001.

Pennebaker, J.W., and C.K. Chung. "Expressive writing and its link to mental and physical health." In *Oxford Handbook of Health Psychology*, ed. H.S. Friedman, 417–437. New York: Oxford University Press, 2011.

Petrie, K.P., R. J. Booth, and J.W. Pennebaker. "The Immunological Effects of Thought Suppression. *Journal of Personality and Social Psychology* 75 (1998): 1264–1272.

Progoff, Ira. *At a Journal Workshop: Writing to Access the Power of the Unconscious and Evoke Creative Ability.* Los Angeles: J.P. Tarcher, 1992.

Richardson, K.M., and H.R. Rothstein. "Effects of Occupational Stress Management Intervention Programs: A Meta-analysis." *Journal of Occupational Health Psychology* 13, no 1 (2008): 69–93.

Sealy, S.A., and T.F. Duffy. "The New York State Department of Labor Job-Training Program: Applying the Progoff Intensive Journal Method." (1977), Dialogue House Associates. Accessed on July 18, 2012. http://www.intensivejournal.org/specialized/article_training.php.

Wiseman, Richard. *59 Seconds: Think a Little, Change a Lot.* New York: Knopf, 2009.

Avoiding and Recovering from Burnout

Samantha Schmehl Hines

Are you having a hard time being polite to patrons and fellow library employees? Do you feel a headache coming on Sunday evening as you consider the work week ahead? Are you not loving the work of librarianship the way you used to? You may be approaching burnout in your career. I faced burnout shortly after I was awarded tenure at my position as the Social Science Librarian at the University of Montana. I found myself drifting through the day. No projects could really engage me any more in the way they used to. I dreaded talking with coworkers about what I was working on. Web browsing, nibbling on hidden stashes of chocolate, and watching the clock became irresistible pastimes. It was especially embarrassing considering I had just published a book on how to be a productive library employee! Eventually I realized I was suffering from burnout and made some changes to improve the situation. To deal with burnout, it is important to first realize what it is; then, examine some approaches to avoid burnout for ourselves and for our organizations; and finally, look at ways to deal with burnout once you or your colleagues have succumbed.

What Is Burnout?

Burnout is defined in the Oxford English Dictionary as "physical or emotional exhaustion, especially caused by stress at work; depression, disillusionment." In today's fast paced society, it is easy enough to imagine our jobs causing this sort of exhaustion, especially in library-related workplaces. The constantly changing technological resources, the ever-present funding pressures, the trend to do more work with less people, money and time, can all add up to a stressful and disillusioning work environment. Library work lends itself to stress by interruption from patrons and coworkers, and can be occasionally monotonous. How many times can you answer the question "Where's the bathroom?" or unjam a printer before feeling a little distressed?

How can librarians differentiate burnout from simple tiredness or other frustrations? Burnout is a process that can be seen, and is not the result of just one incident. Burnout goes beyond simple annoyance or even depression. Dr. Herbert Freudenberger, who developed the concept in the 1970s, identified an outline of several phases leading up to burnout. A partial list relevant to our profession includes:

- A compulsion to prove oneself: working beyond the point where others would give up, in order to demonstrate one's worth or value
- Neglecting personal needs: particularly not eating or sleeping adequately
- Withdrawal: becoming uncommunicative with co-workers or family and friends
- Depersonalization: seeing those you work for and with as less than human, as interactions rather than people
- Depression: the situation seems especially hopeless and unsolvable

A full list of phases along with in-depth discussion of burnout is available in Dr. Freudenberger's 1980 book, *Burnout: The High Cost of High Achievement*. In my own experience, I found myself withdrawing from co-workers and working harder than I probably needed to in order to prove I was worthy of tenure. I worked nights and weekends on my book or on committees for professional associations. Although I achieved my goals of tenure and publishing my book, I succumbed to burnout.

Burnout is a serious issue that goes beyond simple stress. It can lead to physical illness, addictions, or even suicide in some cases. Thankfully, reports of job-related suicide among librarians are somewhat rare, but many people have experienced the Sunday evening headache or stomachache when contemplating the work week ahead. I mentioned my own problems with excessive web browsing and consuming too many sweets. These are fairly mild problems but still impacted my health, restricted connecting with my coworkers, and prevented me from getting my work done. Beyond the personal effects, an employee suffering from burnout is not a fully productive employee, and a library employing burnt-out workers will not be able to function well. Dealing with burnout allows the individual and the library to best accomplish their joint mission.

Burnout is not necessarily about being overworked, although that certainly contributes. It is more often about losing motivation and feeling unappreciated. Burnout can be best described as a sort of disequilibrium, or an imbalance. The most well-known test for burnout, the Maslach Burnout Inventory, measures workers on three aspects of their work life: exhaustion, cynicism, and professional efficacy, to highlight the ways in which an individual may be out of alignment (Maslach, Jackson and Leiter 1997). A quick web search for the test will bring up several examples, some of which you can take and score yourself. The official test can be purchased at MindGarden.com; but an online, less-thorough, version is available from Mindtools.com.

The Best Cure for Burnout

The developer of the Maslach Burnout Inventory described the opposite of burnout as engagement: feeling energetic, involved and efficient (Maslach and Leiter 1997, 24).

The best cure for burnout and way to return to engagement is to try to regain a sense of balance and of what is important. However, it is easiest all around for you and your workplace to avoid burnout in the first place. The most effective approach to reducing or avoiding burnout is for employees and employers to work together if possible. Following are some guidelines I have developed based on Judith Seiss's 1992 book that employees and employers could jointly apply to avoid burnout-prone situations.

1. Know your best daily schedule and work environment, stick to it, and take frequent breaks.

Every person has a natural rhythm to their day and how they work best. Some library staff prefer to get into work early before everyone else arrives to work on tasks uninterrupted. Others find later evening hours good for that kind of focused work. Yet, other librarians prefer a bustling workplace while others cannot concentrate without quiet. It is vital to recognize what is best for your work environment and attempt to honor that as much as possible. It is also vital to take lunch and other short breaks throughout your day, away from your workspace. You may feel like you get more accomplished if you power through, but you will likely end up burnt out. Breaks refresh you and help you work harder and smarter. This is also true with vacations. If you think you are so busy you cannot take a vacation now and then, you are headed toward burnout. Every workplace can and should survive the occasional employee absence. If not, then this is a serious situation that must be addressed with your library's administration as soon as possible.

Employers should be as flexible as possible toward the ways in which their employees work. By granting every employee his or her own workspace that can be customized helps. For example, employees who have the ability to control lighting, seating, or are allowed to listen to music can make a workspace much more inviting and comfortable. Flex hours or allowing work outside the library can help too. Some employers fear the loss of control this can imply, but the benefits to the employee and workplace can outweigh these concerns.

2. Develop good time management skills.

Developing good time management skills can help ward off problems by allowing you to feel more in control of your schedule and your work. If your schedule feels impossible to deal with or track, taking necessary breaks will feel impossible and your work life will clearly suffer. Use one of a librarian's best coping skills and read up on the issue. A couple of good books on time management are: one I wrote in 2010 called, *Productivity for Librarians,* and Judith Seiss's 1992 book, *Time Management, Planning and Productivity for Librarians.* Skills presented in these books can help you get a handle on responsibilities you should be doing and when. These works can help you lay out a manageable schedule, set goals, create effective to-do lists, and plan for completing tasks and projects.

3. Set realistic goals for your work.

In order to avoid burnout, it helps for workers and institutions to set realistic goals. What would be most important to you and/or your library: writing a book for your tenure dossier or teaching more classes? Both may be asking too much. Goals for workers should be set jointly by employees and supervisors which focus on the most important needs of an institution, so it is easy for both to tell what is important work needing to get done. Together decide what may be negotiable. Part of setting these goals is taking a realistic look at time commitments. Employers and employees both need to recognize there are only a set number of hours in the day, and be cognizant of how much time is needed to complete tasks.

In addition, having activities outside of the workplace helps lessen burnout. Workers and employers should recognize the best employees have interests outside of work, whether they are family, hobbies, sports, or charity work. These outside interests can help save employees from becoming too involved in their work and starting on the path toward burnout.

4. Set specific and concrete limits on your tasks and time.

Oftentimes librarians feel as if we are in competition with one another to prove how busy we are. "I worked eight hours from home this weekend," I might say to a colleague. "That's nothing, I worked twelve hours," says my colleague. This type of conversation is a sure sign of librarians headed toward burnout. There should be a firm and respected "quitting time" for employees. Supervisors should not have to take work home, nor expect our subordinates to take work home, on a regular basis. Librarians need to have lives outside of work. Along these same lines, employees need to be able to say "no" to tasks and assignments that are extraneous to our goals and/or the institution's goals. It is wonderful to be valued by colleagues, but it can be overwhelming to receive many invitations to speak, present, write, or serve on committees. Setting firm and concrete boundaries on how you will spend your time can help.

To set limits effectively, first of all, know your institution's and your priorities. Secondly, try to maximize opportunities to meet these goals, and pass on other opportunities. Librarians cannot "do it all" as we might like. If we have to choose between staffing the reference desk and preparing for teaching a class, knowing your priorities can help you make the choice. Once you are knowledgeable about these goals you are enabled to justify requests for more funding and support to your administration. Thirdly, be realistic and concrete in your limit-setting. "No more working at home" may be too vague and unlikely a goal. "No working at home before the kids go to bed" or "No working at home after 9 pm" is more tangible and more likely to be carried out. The later goal allows some wiggle room for those times when working at home is the best answer for your personal work situation. Develop the ability to say no to opportunities that will not help you meet the objectives you have set for work.

When You or Your Employees Are Burnt Out

For librarians that suffer from burnout, the most immediate solution is to take a break, for as long as possible, as soon as possible. To begin to deal with burnout, separate the worker from the work situation when possible. Take a vacation or ask your supervisor for help with your existing workload, or help your employee revisit their workload. Then analyze, jointly with your supervisor or employee, how the work situation can be improved for all involved. What are the priorities that your institution has, and what limits need to be set by the employee? How can the work environment be modified for comfort and a better routine? What are your personal or outside priorities as an employee and how can you protect them? Both the employee and employer must communicate with one another to answer these questions. Outside help can often assist in this communication. Employee assistance programs, where available, can be a great boon. If that is not an option, bringing in an uninvolved supervisor from another branch or department to act as facilitator can help start the process.

How to Deal with Burnout on Your Own

What if you are on your own dealing with burnout? In my own situation I had a fairly unobservant work environment and had become isolated from my coworkers. Since I was attuned to the issue from writing my book on productivity, I noticed my lack of motivation early on, and was able to take some steps to address the problem. First, I took some time off of work. I had some vacation days to use up and tried to have a relaxing few days away. I made myself as unreachable as possible by going camping with my family and attempted to not think about work at all. Next, after I had returned from my vacation I revisited my goals for my career and thought about why I felt disconnected and unhappy despite all I had accomplished. I found that I was in need of a major change and decided to look for a new position. However, I knew that I would need to secure recommendations and continue working on projects to build my resume. Fortunately, this proved to be motivating enough to get me back to work and I found a new position within two years. The new position has been revitalizing and work now seems fun again, even though I am doing more than ever.

Additionally, I have made some lifestyle changes by building relationships and activities outside of work, and have attempted to become less of a "type A" personality driven by achievement. I talked with a mental health professional through my Employee Assistance Program to get some practical advice on how to make these changes last. I ensure that I take breaks regularly and, while I still tend to have a stash of chocolate in my office, I try not to sit and eat it while I browse the Internet. Most of all, I keep a close eye on how I feel, how I work, and attempt to avoid falling into patterns that could lead me back to burnout.

The best way to recover from burnout is to not succumb to it in the first place. Keep an eye on best work practices for you and your employees. Form good practical goals in concert with your institution and set limits on what you and your employees do. Work based on these goals will help avoid a dangerous situation. To steer clear of burnout:

- Know your best daily schedule
- Take regular breaks

- Manage your time well
- Set specific and concrete limits
- Have realistic goals and expectations

When it becomes too late, adopting moderate changes in work and lifestyle can assist us in overcoming burnout, although sometimes a sweeping change like a new job will be the only cure. Librarians will likely continue to feel busy and overworked, since that seems to be the nature of the modern workplace especially in libraries. Additionally, remaining mindful of potential imbalances we can make the most of what we do and minimize the risk of burning out.

References

Freudenberger, Herbert. *Burnout: The High Cost of High Achievement.* New York: Anchor Press, 1980.

Hines, Samantha. *Productivity for Librarians: How to Get More Done in Less Time.* Oxford: Chandos, 2010.

Maslach, Christina, Susan E. Jackson, and Michael P. Leiter. *Maslach Burnout Inventory, Third Edition,* edited by Carlos P. Zalaquett, Richard John Wood. Lanham, MD: Scarecrow Education, 1997.

Maslach, Christina, and Leiter, Michael P. *The Truth About Burnout.* New York: Jossey-Bass, 1997.

Seiss, Judith. *Time Management, Planning and Prioritization for Librarians.* Lanham, MD: Scarecrow Press, 1992.

V: Juggling Responsibilities

The Real Cost of Doing More with Less

PAMELA O'SULLIVAN

It's eight in the morning, and you have just arrived at work. Three people have called in sick, there is a professor with an urgent research request, two students who need help, and you're due at a meeting. As you check the reference schedule, you dial the professor's office. Speaking with him, you glance at the research question one of the students has circled on her assignment. Professor taken care of, you send student one to a database with a few quick instructions and pick up the materials you need for your meeting. As you gather your materials, you call a colleague's office to ask him to cover the reference shift, and pass the second student on to him. By 8:15, you often feel as if you've been working for a full day.

These days, multitasking is considered a necessary part of many workplaces, yet studies indicate it may have a deleterious effect on both productivity and quality of work (Jarmon, 2008; Adler 2012). Although some people seem to thrive on the constant adrenaline rush, for most of us, it can be exhausting. Is there an alternative? Many of us would shake our heads no, as staff and budget cuts have left us with workloads that must now be spread over a smaller number of staff. With administrators expecting services to be kept to the same standards—or higher!—library staff find themselves overworked, stressed out, and unable to effectively plan for new services.

That's where the analogy to the Pied Piper comes in. We all are familiar with the story; the piper got rid of the rats for the townspeople of Hamelin, and they decided to ignore the agreement they'd made with him. In return, he took something far more valuable—their children. What I'm suggesting is, rather than get to the point where you have to call in someone to take care of your impossibly large workloads, or find your health, job and/or family compromised, you need to deal with the problem immediately.

Sounds impossible, I know, as many of us already feel overwhelmed and overworked. However, by stepping back a little bit, you'll be able to envision strategies that can transform the way you work. All of these are simple, take no money or resources, but some do require commitment by the whole staff to be truly effective. There are parts you can do on your own that will help you in your day-to-day routines.

Strategies to Reduce Your Stress at Work

1. Stop Multitasking

Although it may seem counterintuitive, stop multitasking. While multitasking may give you the feeling that you are getting more done, and often gives others the impression you are a highly productive worker, studies show the opposite is actually true. Multitaskers can lose as much as 30 minutes of every hour, which has a serious drain on true productivity. Conversely, if the multitasker is able to keep up their productivity level, it is often by subjecting themselves to a much higher stress level (Crenshaw 2008).

How does one stop multitasking in a setting (the workplace) in which it has become the norm, and for many, it is the way they went through college and graduate school as well as any other positions they've held. One way to gauge the extent to which you engage in multitasking is to record for a couple of hours just how you spend your time. Include everything—staff and student queries, the task or tasks you are trying to complete. You may find, as the woman in Crenshaw's "The myth or multitasking," that you aren't doing things simultaneously, but rather shifting attention constantly from one item to another. The result is that no one task holds your attention completely. So while it looks on the surface that you have accomplished a great deal, the reality is that at least one of the items left finished at the end of your block of time could have been completed if you had avoided checking e-mail, answering the phone, and handling each question then and there as though it was vital to the continuance of the world as we know it.

2. Organize Your Day

Take a look at your workday, and try to organize it in a way that makes sense to you. I know we sometimes have limited control over our schedules, but if you have even a basic plan in place you regain some measure of control and thereby reduce your stress level a bit. Prioritizing your tasks and projects, and pruning unnecessary distractions, can go a long way toward helping you rein in your workload and reduce the amount of stress you are under. For example: during an 8 to 5 workday, you may have only one or two hours in your control. Set a time limit for answering e-mail and voice mail, look over the tasks you have to complete and assign a time to each. Finish as much as you can on one task before opening another, or, if you're going along well on one, put off a different task on your list until your next block of free time.

3. Align Tasks During Less Busy Times and Delegate

What about those of us who have no free time—the librarian or library media specialist who is a one-person staff? That's admittedly more difficult, as you don't always have the freedom to put up the "closed" sign for an hour or even 30 minutes. Try aligning your tasks with less busy times, if you can, and take advantage as much as possible of time-saving aspects of technology, discussed below. At the same time, try to avoid unnecessary overwork. Delegate where you can, even if you feel you're the only one who can do it right. You may be pleasantly surprised at what other staff come up with.

Don't create work, setting up projects that don't really need to be done in order to tweak a few things. If it's working, and working well, put your ideas on the back burner until such time as you are less busy. Once you've done your website and it's working, for example, don't tweak it every couple of days—leave it alone long enough to get some feedback.

4. Turn Off the Distractions

Do you really need to check your e-mail every time a new message comes in? Or be up-to-the minute on tweets? Is there truly someone who needs to hear your contribution to an on-line discussion within thirty seconds of you seeing it? Of course not! However, immediate responses to e-mail and tweets can make us feel productive, and they are often something we can do in just a few minutes. Step back for a moment and look at what is happening—for every few minutes you spend on an e-mail, you also need a period of time to mentally re-align with the task at hand.

What about the distractions you can't turn off—co-workers, supervisors, students and faculty? It's tempting to say you have to be available to them all the time, but is that true? If you have an office you can close the door and put up a "busy" sign—then stick to it. Let your supervisor know what you're doing, let your co-workers know, and do it regularly until it becomes a habit and a boundary those around you respect. If you don't have an office with a door, find a sign to put up, put some headphones on, and keep working on it until those around you realize that you're serious. (Another possibility is to find an empty meeting room and take a laptop or tablet if you have one, along with whatever portable project you're working on. Should customers, co-workers, or students complain that you are less accessible than formerly, then you could point out you are actually more accessible to them in the times you set aside to meet with other people, for you are less distracted by the projects that are being interrupted and can focus entirely on the moment.

5. Make Technology Your Ally

Use your voice-mail, auto response on e-mail, any applications that can save you time in gathering the information you need on a regular basis. Most software applications gathering information can give you the information relatively quickly. Make sure you and your staff know how to use the applications so that the data going in is as accurate as possible, and the data you get out of it will be reliable. For example, if you are using an on-line reference form, make sure all the staff enters information in the same format using all initials in capitals or lower case, but not both.

Set up your e-mail so items that you receive regularly, such as listserv messages, go straight into folders rather than cluttering your in-box. This will reduce the time needed to go through your e-mail, as you can leave all the listservs until you have some free time, without leaving your inbox overly full. Additionally, if you have access to a tablet or iPad for meetings, consider taking your notes in electronic format, which will save you the time of transcribing later.

6. Practice the Art of Saying No

Librarians tend to think we must take on each task thrown our way in order to be considered productive and hard-working. Consider the person asking you to join yet another committee or take on another library program has no idea of all you are doing. Let them know, and negotiate if possible, to reduce your responsibility in some other area. I know that, too, will seem impossible in these times of reduced staffing, but it is important you let others know when you feel you are at your capacity — and not when you're already so thinly spread that one task more or less won't make a difference.

Try enlisting the assistance of other staff. Many people will balk at becoming a member of a committee that could sit for the entire academic year, but a team that has a specific beginning and end date and a specific expected outcome will often be of more interest to other staff. Team-based projects can be a way to accomplish more without leaving everyone feeling overworked, so long as you use teams to carry out specific projects over a pre-determined amount of time.

A necessary step in making team-based projects workable is tearing down silos in your institution. If you can call on those who have the best skill set for a particular project, the work will go more quickly and be distributed more equitably. Look at your staff as a large team rather than a series of departments and it will be easier to work together.

7. Network Effectively

Time spent catching up with colleagues is not necessarily time wasted. However, make sure to mention to colleagues the projects you're working on and anything that has you feeling stressed or isn't coming together the way you'd like. Actively seek suggestions and seek out new contacts who can help you with your projects. This should be more than a collection of folks you can call on when you need to vent — though it's important to have those as well! You need professional contacts who can provide different perspectives and advice.

Other Steps to Alleviate Stress

There are other steps you can take to try to mitigate the effects of stress in your workday. Again, not all of these will appeal to, or be practical for, all readers.

Create a stress-free zone: ideally two, one for home and one at work. Your stress free zone can be a corner of an office, a quiet, less-used part of your library, or a bench outdoors. The important thing is to designate a place and not allow stress to follow you there. If you have children at home, creating a stress-free zone may be difficult. Some, like me, use the car as a stress-free zone. During my commute, I listen to the music I want (or none at all), but I try not to use the morning time to mentally prepare for my day or the evening commute to rehash anything that went wrong during the day.

Take time for yourself. This is an oft-repeated maxim, but it bears one more repetition. I speak with many librarians who feel guilty taking time for them, or who feel that it's impossible to do so with a heavy workload that leaves them constantly playing catch-up. The reality is, like multitasking, not taking time for you leads to lower productivity and higher levels of stress. This is also another area where teamwork and networking can be helpful. There are probably people on your staff who could take over major tasks that can't be automated or put aside for a few days. Call on them, and expect to return the favor sometime.

Take time that is not devoted to household maintenance, personal business or health care. *Take a day or two every semester that is just for you*, and do whatever re-energizes you. I like to go to a park with a cooler of iced tea and a good book, and sit by a stream reading. A friend likes to ride long distances on her bike, and another likes to browse at a local outlet mall without a list of "must" purchases. If you can't take a day, take a half day or a couple of hours. A friend who is a birdwatcher will leave a few minutes early, drive home by a different route, and spend an hour in a local bird sanctuary. Another will treat herself to tea at a local tearoom.

The main point of all of this is to find ways to reduce stress in situations where you can't realistically reduce your job duties permanently. By working smarter, taking steps that can reduce stress and increase productivity, and remembering to take time for yourself, you can do it all without having to pay the piper.

References

Adler, Rachel F., and Raquel Benbunan-Fich. "Juggling on a High Wire: Multitasking Effects on Performance." *International Journal of Human-Computer Studies* 70, no. 2 (2012): 156–168.

Crenshaw. Dave. *The Myth of Multitasking: How Doing It All Gets Nothing Done.* San Francisco: Jossey-Bass, 2008.

Jarmon, Amy L. "Multitasking Helpful or Harmful." *Student Lawyer* 36, no. 8 (2008): 30–35.

Meeting the Demands of Teaching

Marcia E. Rapchak

Many reference librarians see their jobs evolving in a variety of ways, and they may be surprised how much instruction beyond the reference desk they are being asked to do. Job titles shift to show this change as "reference and instruction librarian" becomes a popular replacement for "reference librarian," particularly in academic libraries. Teaching more than just the occasional instruction session can cause a significant amount of stress, but there are strategies for dealing with this new responsibility.

Some library instructors may feel a bit of the "imposter syndrome" felt by teachers who are questioning their worthiness, and this can cause stress. Not having the formal training can lead to this feeling, but realize you are the expert in your field and you have something valuable to teach. However, having important information to impart, and the ability to create a few PowerPoints or to demonstrate how to search a database, does not create an effective teacher. For me, the most effective stress reliever when it comes to teaching is being an engaging instructor who helps her students learn valuable information and helps them understand the importance of this valuable information. I still have improving to do, but by seeing professional development as an essential aspect of my job, I continue to see more student engagement and to feel less stress while teaching.

Professional development for any instruction librarian, regardless of experience level, can energize an instructor and improve the classroom experience. I find this is a great defense against teacher burnout. For college or university librarians, opportunities for pedagogical professional development should be plentiful; many colleges and universities have a dedicated center for faculty development and support in teaching. These centers often have development materials, individual consultations, and workshops librarians can attend. Workshops allow librarians to interact with other instructors at the institution, which has the added benefit of creating networking opportunities. If your college or university does not have a teaching center, see if any of the programs with many teaching assistants have new instructor trainings you could attend. Though there may be some discipline-specific information shared at these programs, they include sound pedagogical practices applicable to multiple disciplines.

Professional development opportunities extend well beyond workshops at one's own college or university, though; conferences related to teaching can provide a way for librarians at any institution with instruction duties to improve their teaching abilities and reduce stress. There are both information literacy conferences and conferences on higher education issues that cover pedagogical strategies. Some of these are:

- Library Orientation Exchange (LOEX)
- Librarians' Information Literacy Annual Conference (LILAC)
- EDUCAUSE
- Association for the Study of Higher Education (ASHE)
- Conference on Higher Education Pedagogy from the Center for Instructional Development and Educational Research (CIDER)
- The Teaching Professor Conference

To prepare yourself for effective teaching, familiarize yourself with professional standards. ACRL's Information Literacy Competency Standards for Higher Education are the accepted information literacy standards of the profession, and many university or colleges use these as the basis for their own institutional information literacy standards. Of course, if your institution has its own documents on information literacy, then make sure you are familiar with those. If your library doesn't, then consider authoring them to keep your program focused on particular learning outcomes.

Join listservs that relate to information literacy and library instruction. These allow posters to exchange tips and ideas, and offer a venue for asking any questions occurring during the year. Two listservs are very popular:

- ILI-L — ALA/ACRL Information Literacy Instruction Group
- INFOLIT — Information literacy for school, academic, and public libraries through AASL

These allow information to be sent to your e-mail and for you to engage in discussions with other instruction librarians.

Read the literature important to pedagogy and educational theory, along with the important works for information literacy instruction. The resources that explore theory and link this to application are the most useful to me. Authors like Paolo Friere and John Dewey (that's right, John, not Melvil) are very influential in the world of education, and becoming at least familiar with them is essential. Bloom's Taxonomy offers a way for instructors to understand how to form effective learning outcomes emphasizing a variety of skills, including higher order thinking skills. These resources provide important theoretical backgrounds to help in your understanding of pedagogy. Several books exist about information literacy instruction. My favorites include:

- *Information Literacy Instruction: Theory and Practice* by Esther Grassian and Joan Kaplowitz
- *Reflective Teaching, Effective Learning: Instructional Literacy for Library Educators* by Char Booth
- *Teaching Information Literacy: 50 Standards-Based Exercises for College Students* by Joanna Burkhardt, Mary MacDonald, and Andrée J. Rathemacher

Follow blogs through RSS feeds (this way the information comes to you rather than you tracking down the information) on pedagogical issues and information literacy. There are a number of blogs out there providing innovative teaching strategies, theoretical backgrounds, new instructional technology, and more. Don't feel you have to read every blog out there on library instruction which will only cause more stress but do subscribe to your favorites. Some RSS feeds I subscribe to include:

- Information Literacy Weblog
- Info-mational
- In the Library with the Lead Pipe
- Journal of Information Literacy

These include personal blogs, organizational blogs, and journals, all of which inspire me with new ideas and important updates relating to information literacy.

Visit repositories that collect learning objects and sharable educational materials. These include:

MERLOT — Multimedia Educational Resource for Learning and Online Teaching

Connexions

NCLOR — North Carolina Learning Object Repository

Gateway Educational Materials

There are various states with their own learning object repositories, and a quick Google search will lead you to others. These, along with open courseware, make finding activities, lesson plans, tutorials, and readings very easy. Of course, you can search for these things through a search engine, but the repositories often provide metadata and reviews that can help you evaluate the educational materials listed.

While finding resources about information literacy from a variety of places is important to building up your teaching repertoire and reducing stress, don't forget to talk to the other librarians engaged in instruction at your institution. You will not have to look far for innovative ideas in instruction: your co-workers, if they are engaged in instruction, have an original take on teaching the concepts you cover in your sessions. Ask to observe some successful teachers at your institution so you can implement some of their strategies.

Managing a classroom can create stress for those who are not used to teaching (and even for some who are!). One way to help the class session go smoothly is to make sure you are prepared; talk to the professor if the library instruction session will be held for a class. Look at the syllabus and related assignment materials, and see if the instructor has an extra textbook or reader you could examine. Speaking the language of the class and making your session truly relevant will keep students engaged and impress the professor.

For instructors teaching a for-credit class, prepare, but don't over-prepare. Write out your learning objectives for the day and determine what activities will allow you to reach those learning outcomes. Don't script your every word, and leave some room for flexibility in the class session. The beauty of teaching a class multiple times is you can cover and correct information missed in the previous sessions.

If you worry your instruction abilities need improvement, let someone non-threatening (a peer) observe your teaching. Talk to the observer about what feedback you want, and then offer them your ideas for the session and any relevant class materials you have. After the observation, sit with them to discuss what they saw in the class. If the class experience they describe is not the session experience you wish to create, work with the observer to create small, attainable teaching goals. For example, if you tend to mumble at the end of sentences, make a goal of clearly annunciating every word during an instruction session. The observer can attend your class again and let you know how well you met these goals. Improving your teaching abilities may include some initial stress as you work through problems and acknowledge deficiencies in your teaching, but ultimately by improving your teaching abilities, you will reduce the anxiety you feel when teaching.

Another way to improve your teaching and reduce stress is to figure out what the students would like to be taught. Ask them for feedback before and after sessions such as in this form.

Sample Student Feedback Form

Please answer the following questions as honestly as possible:

What did you find most helpful in this session?

_____

What do you wish we had talked about more?

_____

What did you learn in the activity on identifying scholarly articles?

_____

Any other comments?

I have gone into course-related instruction sessions where the students did not have a project, and I asked them using Poll Everywhere what they wanted to learn from a selection of choices. I was prepared to cover any and all of it, but they were topics I was very comfortable with teaching and did not take too much time to prepare. When you ask for feedback from students after instruction, make sure to ask them about your teaching abilities and to ask them what they learned in the class. You can ask them what they liked or didn't like in the class, but try to keep the focus on the learning and the presentation of the material; this way the feedback focuses on what you and the students did, not you personally. Ask them questions like, "What was the most important thing you learned from this session?" or "What are you still confused about after this session?" Focus on the feedback providing constructive criticism or praise, and ignore the feedback that is general or cruel. Let students know how other students' feedback has been implemented, and this will show you are a conscientious teacher, and it will help build a positive class environment (even in a one-shot) that reduces stress.

A positive class environment is my goal for every session and course I teach, and this diminishes stress not only for me, but also for my students. Know you can't make everyone happy, but aim to engage the entire class. If you find yourself focusing on students who are not as engaged, make eye contact with attentive students every few minutes and give them positive feedback by smiling and/or using open body language. Focusing too much on the students who are not engaged will alienate those students who are interested in what you have to say. If you expect and assume the best out of your students, not just when it comes to learning, but in behavior, most of your students will reach to achieve. Assume your students will respect you and respect the classroom. Make these expectations clear and model them yourself. If a student seems to be bored or inattentive, do not assume they are bad people or they are trying to make your life miserable — this will only increase your stress. Instead, assume the student may be confused or have some other issues going on in their lives. If a student is disruptive, talk to them in private to understand what may be the trouble. Generally, this will lead to a better understanding and greater satisfaction on both sides.

Juggling teaching duties with other library duties can be difficult, especially for those librarians who teach for-credit classes. Make boundaries clear with your students— let them know when they can contact you and when they can expect an answer. If you are teaching face to face, set aside an hour each day for answering student e-mails and concerns, and then do not answer anything that is not an emergency for the rest of the day. Online courses require more contact from instructors, but setting aside time throughout the day when teaching online to work with the course allows you to keep instruction and your other responsibilities separate. For example, decide you will check on the students and the course at consistent hours every day and then no more.

Leave work at work if possible. Taking work home can sometimes be necessary, especially if one is teaching, but doing so only adds to the stress of instruction for librarians. I find even if this means I have to stay late or come early, leaving the work only for the workplace is better on my psyche. Recognize and meet due dates, but give yourself some breathing room. When I teach a for-credit class, I have a tendency to try to grade everything all at once, especially if I am teaching online. Give yourself some time for grading (if you are lucky enough to be a grader), and give yourself several sessions of lesson planning throughout the week rather than marathon grading/planning.

Save your course materials and keep them well organized. Being able to revisit materials used in similar sessions can help with time management. This doesn't mean you should repeat the same lessons over and over year after year, but revising course materials often can work well for reducing the time constraints of teaching many classes in a short period of time. If you know another librarian has recently taught a similar class you are going to teach, ask them to share their materials and make changes as necessary.

Set time before and after class sessions for yourself. This, of course, is not always possible, but when you can, set off a half hour to an hour before class to think about what you are going to cover and your approach. I will tell people I am busy during this time and will not schedule meetings or desk time, even though I do not have any appointments. After classes, I like to have time to read over any formative assessment material and think about what went well and what I could improve next time. I'm usually tired after teaching, so I like to take this time for some quiet (and maybe a snack!) to regain energy.

Keep a teaching journal to help you reflect on your teaching experiences. This will enable you to vent if needed and to think about ways to improve your own instruction skills. I have a journal with three columns: the first column allows me to provide a summary of what occurred during the session; in the second column, I write about what went well in the class; in the third column, I write about any issues or problems and how I plan to overcome these in the next session. Make sure to include in your reflection concrete, achievable goals so you can document your own improvements as an instructor.

Teaching can be psychologically difficult, especially for those who did not anticipate the amount of teaching duties that would come their way when entering the library profession. Teaching includes public speaking, and, for many academic librarians, public speaking in front of both peers (a faculty member) as well as students, creates stress in many people. An instructor's knowledge (or lack of knowledge) is exposed, and the chance for vulnerability and embarrassment is high. As a friend and mentor once said to a class of future librarians, "Just accept that you will have a little bit of dread before you teach." Recognizing anxiety is a normal part of the teaching experience, not an indication you cannot teach, can actually help to reduce the stress that accompanies teaching.

Teaching is ultimately a learning experience. Learning includes experimenting, failing, and revising, so being flexible and open to change will not only allow you to deal with the stress of teaching, but it will make you a better teacher. Understand teaching has its struggles, but if you take it seriously, manage your time, and make room for reflection and improvement, and then it will not be something you dread but something to which you look forward.

Employee Empowerment
as a Strategy for Supervisors

James B. Casey

Stress in the work place generally carries negative connotations, but not all stress is destructive and self-defeating. Sometimes stress can be positive and productive. Part of the reality of any professional employment involves working overtime to meet deadlines managing large volumes of work and tackling intellectually difficult problems. For many hard working librarians, the entire absence of stress would be almost intolerable. However, the anxieties caused by fear of failure, micromanagement by supervisors and conflicting claims for credit can often generate an unnecessary, toxic stress in the workplace that undermines creativity and diminishes productivity. While employees are subject to an array of their own personal stress issues, supervisors are in a strong position to use empowerment techniques to carve out a workplace where toxic stress and negativity can be minimized while encouraging risk taking and creativity.

The best characterization of an attitude that supervisors can adopt to reduce negative stress in the workplace was efficiently encompassed in the witty description of one of his ministers sometimes attributed to British King Charles II. This invaluable administrator was said to be "Never in the way, never out of the way." The unobtrusive, but alert and readily available supervisor can lift many sources of negative stress through empowerment.

Employees Need Space

A supervisor who needs to feel manifestly and constantly in-charge can sometimes be very much "in the way" of employees trying to do their jobs. Staff members need leadership and guidance in the form of training, structuring of meetings and occasional prompting to move projects forward. Nonetheless continuous and meticulous oversight of large and small tasks by the supervisor can cause nerves to fray and preclude productivity. Employees need the space to do their jobs and to know there is a supervisor who is "never out of the way" to whom they can go with questions, requests for assistance and sometimes for reassurance.

In order to be effective as an empowering leader, a supervisor simply must accept that "being right" is far less important than "doing right." The omnipresent manager who needs to feel in control is unlikely to accept criticism or contradiction well or acknowledge there are a variety of ways to address problems and accomplish objectives. The misguided notion that admitting error and entertaining criticism are signs of weakness confuses strength with obstinacy and inflexibility. The objective of "doing right" can be undermined if a supervisor is so intent upon "being right" that productive collaboration is precluded. One of my prior supervisors adopted the practice of excusing librarians who voiced opposing viewpoints from staff meetings and lavishing praise on those who agreed with her. Whether congratulated or ejected, my stomach was in knots.

How Not to Lead

Previously, I had some supervisors who very clearly insisted on being treated as "the boss" in every conceivable interaction, large and small, and who viewed disagreement to be tantamount to disloyalty. In one instance, a controlling supervisor expressed concern that a draft of strengths and weaknesses of the library's collection did not conform to his own previous list. The newly submitted list was prepared by a committee he had appointed earlier. Instead of examining the veracity of the suggestions presented, he viewed them as a challenge to his authority. Fearful remarks were voiced at staff meetings by this supervisor." It makes me look bad. Are they trying to take over?" There were naturally some trusted insiders who were sufficiently subservient while others who had the temerity to disagree on occasion were thus considered to be enemies. The segregation of employees by an insecure supervisor into lists of friends and enemies adds an entire element of stress unrelated to organizational objectives. In a later incident, I found my own areas of disagreement with one supervisor who blurted out: "I wish that I could put my brain in yours!" The need for the supervisor to "be right" and to feel "in-control" caused considerable stress among staff members, but involved even more self-inflicted stress on the supervisor. In an environment where insecurity and fear emanate from the top, ambitious and talented employees often leave and the library remains crippled by turnover and inertia.

The controlling supervisor who must approve and check every minute piece of work coming out of a unit or department not only implies basic mistrust in subordinate staff to do their jobs, but creates backlogs and an invariable drop in overall productivity. One supervisor with whom I worked was personally very able, but insisted on checking every one of the thousands of books ordered by the professional librarians on her staff before they could be shelved. The release of new books to the public was delayed and a message of mistrust and subordination was conveyed to the staff librarians. The person who eventually succeeded this controlling manager lifted the checking of every order and empowered her librarians with full responsibility for their selection areas. One of the librarians commented to me with a smile that the change of boss was like having an entirely new job.

Good Supervisors Do

An empowering supervisor once assigned me an area of responsibility, arranged for thorough training and presented me with a clear set of expectations. Then, he provided me with the authority and support needed to do the job. On the occasions when I did make errors, he was there to help. Additionally my supervisor was available for the exchange of ideas, sharing of information and aided in the procurement funds for proposed projects. My work was evaluated in the privacy of an office while affirmation was lavished publicly. Although the work load was extremely heavy, the stress of getting work done in a timely manner was affirmative rather than corrosive and disconcerting. I could look forward to going to work, handling huge assignments and feeling gratified when I received a "well done" during or at the end of a project. For some reason, this supervisor was not universally popular, but accepted the fact and refused to react with fear and hostility towards subordinates. The refusal of the supervisor to allow personal agendas and fears to become a diversion empowered employees to focus on the work at hand and to devote energies to accomplishing the library's goals.

A good leader delivers focused and constructive criticism as well as praise. The best approach is to deliver constructive criticism privately with the employee and preferably in writing, with emphasis on the behaviors and performance issues that need to be addressed. The supervisor should strive to expunge all emotion and anger from the framing of critical comments, but expect an employee may react with anger and/or sometimes with attacking remarks when discussing a performance appraisal. It is for this reason an emphasis should be placed on the confidentiality of the assessment process and be communicated in personnel policy documents and procedures (Trotta 2006, 121–124). We all make mistakes and have deficiencies in our performance, but official recognition of those issues should never be the subject of open forum discussion. Supervisors who fail to confront employees personally and privately for deficient performance, and especially those who discuss such issues publicly, undermine the confidence of all employees in the integrity of the assessment process and create a huge source of toxic stress in the workplace.

More Ways to Be an Energizing Leader

Good performance needs to be recognized publicly. In this case, a supervisor needs to be every bit as assiduous and precise as she/he would be in criticizing unacceptable performance. An empowering supervisor should be hesitant to accept personal credit for accomplishments of the staff, but needs to be extremely careful to make sure that those employees who labored long and hard to achieve success are given due credit. For instance, crediting "John" when things go well should be a public celebration in which the empowering supervisor recognizes "John" for a job well done. If "John" has leadership potential, he will also acknowledge others on his team and his supervisor for their hard work and support. Precious few of us who work in the profession of librarianship do so for money alone. All of us want to feel the fruits of our labor are significant and make a difference. The supervisor who fairly and consistently identifies and recognizes employees for jobs well done is encouraging all staff members to redouble their efforts.

When things go wrong, a good supervisor will invariably accept a sizeable share of the responsibility for the failure. Sometimes the use of the word "we" in a description of a misdirected project can undercut the stress and fear of subordinates. Instead of saying, "John failed to consider staff scheduling" the empowering leader will say in public, "We failed to consider staff scheduling." The assessment process can sort out areas of account-ability in private, but the conscientious and responsible supervisor will always accept a share of the failure.

Communication Is Important

Tangled lines of authority can produce considerable negative stress. For senior super-visors who manage other supervisors, it is important to avoid intruding upon and con-travening the relationship of the staff members with their direct supervisor. It is possible for a well-intentioned library director to undercut the credibility of a subordinate super-visor. Senior managers who proclaim an "open door policy" in an attempt to stimulate productive communications may inadvertently open the door to malcontented employees who want to carry complaints, advice, and gossip to the top. If an employee feels com-fortable in circumventing a direct supervisor and going to the top manager, the lines of authority could be tangled to the detriment of the entire organization. An empowering senior supervisor will adhere to the lines of authority and thereby affirm the credibility of all subordinate supervisors. Library employees have enough stress in their jobs without the added quandary of trying to determine who is actually in charge.

One of the realities supervisors of larger departments and libraries should understand and accept is a significant number of subordinate staff members will be far more knowl-edgeable in many aspects of their work than you might be as their supervisor. For example, there are many library directors I know who might be comfortable giving a story time for young children or working at a reference services desk, but who know next to nothing about cataloging, building maintenance or information technology. Nevertheless, empow-ering supervisors can focus on substantive outcomes and results in evaluating the per-formance of staff members with unfamiliar skill areas. An able library director who knew next to nothing about municipal finance made it a point to ask questions of his library business manager and the city business officer until he came to a clearer understanding of that aspect of his responsibilities. A good leader will strive to understand and appreciate the important aspects of library operations with which she/he is unfamiliar. Furthermore, she/he will be able to convey that to governing bodies such as boards so the staff members who labor in these areas will know their contribution is appreciated and valued.

Some supervisors can create an entire universe of unnecessary stress by focusing incessantly upon very small or even petty issues in disciplinary proceedings. For example, I am aware of supervisors who base an inordinate amount of weight on infractions such as tardiness, spelling errors, or even failing to smile sufficiently. There are undoubtedly positions where spelling accuracy and punctuality are extremely important, but in many professional library and senior management level positions, these infractions should carry far less weight than larger issues of competency and unit performance. An empowering supervisor will understand and give greater value to the larger issues and outcomes of a manager's area of responsibility. A good supervisor will distinguish those situations where characteristics such as creativity and productivity may be of greater consequence than meticulous punctuality. One misguided director I knew seemed to be incapable of formulating substantive criticism and affirmation for the performance evaluations of a highly productive and creative department head, but belabored issues such as arriving late by as little as two or three minutes. After one or two years, the department head left for a working environment where competency was valued.

How Supervisors Can Reduce Stress in the Workplace

Sometimes negative stress can be "busted" or diminished in disarmingly simple ways during the course of a work day. Supervisors who make it a point of exchanging brief pleasantries with staff members, bringing in treats for the team and remembering first names can sometimes relieve tension. This can be especially helpful in cases where there may be a negative "buzz" in the air. One empowering supervisor who had been subjected to a great deal of hostile comments from staff who had been angry about recent performance evaluations, made a point of addressing these staff in a collegial manner in public. For example, he praised them for some of the good work they had done in general meetings. This positive attitude in the face of hostility, undercut the negativity and cynicism of toxic stress. A supervisor sometimes needs to exemplify a positive attitude and focus on the accomplishment of institutional objectives and unit projects.

Not every staff member is a "high achiever" and few will be the recipients of commendations for significant accomplishments. However, annual awards for length of service, perfect attendance and other achievements allows for an opportunity to congratulate staff members and undercut tensions. Even acknowledging all staff members on their birthdays and providing tangible recognitions such as gift cards can create a sense of good will. Modest budgetary support for staff appreciation should be provided and staff designated to insure the details of this effort are carried out on a consistent basis. When employee recognitions are not distributed fairly and consistently with a concrete outcome, they will soon lose credibility. Some examples of low cost or no cost recognitions for raising morale might include letters of commendation, designation of special parking places for "employees of the month" and sharing patron letters of praise about employees with board members.

Staff meetings where small or large groups can be gathered together offer golden opportunities for empowering managers to publicly acknowledge staff members who have performed well and to allow relevant input and questions. Also, it might be perfect in combination with distribution of awards and recognitions. Meetings are sometimes difficult to schedule in busy libraries and can be expensive if you consider the salary and benefits costs of everyone in the room for one hour or more. However, the payoff can be priceless in employee motivation and what they give to the library. The supervisor will need to have an agenda, focus on issues affecting the whole library (not personal matters) and sufficient substantive content to make the experience productive. Such meetings can provide the empowering supervisor with an occasion to lay out the progress made by the library, its impact on the community and the contributions made by staff members who may not realize how their labors impact the larger reality.

Supervision in a modern library setting is not for the insecure and "faint of heart." It is definitely not recommended for persons seeking a high comfort level and escape from stress. Empowering supervisors will:

- Give employees space and authority to do their job
- Provide training and be available to assist
- Trust employees
- Praise in public and criticize in private
- Offer constructive criticism/and confidential evaluations
- Provide treats or awards
- Accept responsibility for projects gone wrong
- Give credit where credit is due
- Encourages risk taking and creativity

In this fast paced world of librarianship, supervisors need to assume leadership by empowering subordinates, subduing negative stress and fear by focusing energy and time on addressing institutional goals and completing objectives.

References

Disher, Wayne. *Crash Course in Public Library Administration*. Santa Barbara: Libraries Unlimited, 2010.

Hakala-Ausperk, Catherine. *Be a Great Boss: One Year to Success*. Chicago: American Library Association, 2011.

Montgomery, Jack G., and Eleanor I. Cook. *Conflict Management for Libraries: Strategies for a Positive, Productive Workplace*. Chicago: American Library Association, 2005.

Stanley, Mary J. *Managing Library Employees: A How-to-do-it Manual*. New York: Neal Schuman, 2008.

Stueart, Robert D., and Maureen Sullivan. *Developing Library Leaders: A How-to-do-it Manual for Coaching, Team Building, and Mentoring Library Staff*. New York: Neal Schuman, 2010.

Trotta, Marcia. *Supervising Staff: A How-to-do-it Manual for Libraries*. New York: Neal Schulman, 2006.

VI: Easing Stress on a Budget

Affordable Library Makeovers

SHARON M. BRITTON

When I interviewed for my position as Library Director at a regional campus in Ohio, the first thing I noticed was how outdated the library looked. I had heard and read excellent things about the services offered by the library, the wonderful, helpful staff that always had time to stop what they were doing to help students, the infinite array of research resources available to students, faculty, staff and community users through OhioLINK. I was well aware of this incredible service, which supplemented the libraries very adequate, but small collections. What I hadn't heard about, and hadn't seen until I arrived on campus, were the much too crowded together workstations, the multicolored chairs which I came to call the "psychedelic" chairs flanking long, heavy tables, the outdated furniture of other kinds, and how closed off the various areas of the library felt in an attempt to form separate spaces out of what was essentially one large L-shaped library. It was a library that cried out for updating and opening up.

None of this deterred me from taking the job because the services and staff were what really mattered and still do. But I secretly thought, "We have to do something to make this a more comfortable and inviting place for all, including the library staff themselves." When one works in a kind of antiquated dreariness all day, it can be very stressful. I came to learn that was indeed the case with my new colleagues. Also, as is the case in many small libraries without a lot of funding, there was only so much money to go around here. The current budget had to be used to provide the best educational resources and desired spaces possible to our students. Shortly after my arrival, I had to write my first budget for the upcoming academic year. It was then I realized with certainty, that it was going to take some brainstorming, grant writing, begging and cajoling to make even small changes to the appearance of the library that would relieve the stress of the library inhabitants and help make the library more welcoming.

In addition to the obvious reasons for wanting the library to be warm and inviting, there was the issue of staff morale, and the added stress placed on them by working in a cheerless environment. Their feelings were obvious in many of our conversations in my first year. I came to share their frustration with having to make do, receiving hand me down furniture or equipment left after some other unit on campus had received a makeover. We knew the library was not slated to be next in line for improvements in the near future. Nor were we optimistic about the library receiving infusions of money to make the needed changes. The staff was doing such a good job of helping our students with their research needs, thoughts of the environment in which they were doing it, wasn't seen as a problem to anyone. It wasn't terrible, but we knew it could be better. Again undeterred, my thoughts of changing things no longer secret, the staff and I began to brainstorm about ways in which we could make the library more physically open, and to identify cosmetic changes that would lift their spirits and ease the stress of "making do" every day.

They all liked the idea of identifying things we could do with what resources we had, and that is how we proceeded. Most of the staff talked about our new plan to students and faculty when appropriate. Our Assistant/Instruction Librarian touted it in her faculty committee meetings and in the classes she taught. And I became the campus nudge for the library in my administrative and faculty roles or in conversations with the Deans. Whereas before, the library had been very much "under the radar," we began to do what we could as administrators, faculty members and staff, to bring it up to the surface and beyond. I wanted the library to be on administrators' minds in any positive way possible. I wanted librarians and staff to be included on committees as appropriate, and prevent people from asking the question, "Why would someone from the library want or need to be on this committee?" As Director of the Library, I became a member of the Administrative Directors group, which had not been the case with past directors. Slowly, we were showing up on more radar screens.

What We Did on Our Own

GRANT WRITING FOR SIGNAGE

The first thing we did was to think about new signage throughout the library. I wrote and received an internal campus grant to purchase new signs. The ones that had been hanging had been made by the previous Director in a labor of love. However, they were old, faded, and much too small, 18" × 5" with a beige background and small black stick on letters. I was told the background had once been white, but had faded with time. They could not be read until one was standing directly under them. The new signs were bright blue with large white lettering, and were now 47" × 11". Each sign announced the Classroom, Library Staff work area, Quiet Study Area, Information Desk, Writing Lab, and Conference Room. These new signs were incredibly exciting to us, and they changed the appearance of the library immediately. Of course, the new signs were more than cosmetic. They also assisted the patrons in navigating the library on their own. The signage turned out to be a great solution not costing us anything.

GRANT WRITING FOR NEW FURNITURE

I also wrote and received a grant from a local organization for the purchase of laptop tables, which had been requested frequently by students. We also bought nesting MI6 chairs from KI, to accompany them. We selected bright blue swirling fabric that matched the color of our new signage, and other chairs in the library. This further helped to enliven the space. Incremental changes were occurring and people were complimenting the staff, making us all feel better about our evolving library.

It Can't Hurt to Ask: Renovation and Reallotting

During the summer of 2007, a planned renovation of what had been called the East Lounge was about to take place. The lounge was a huge cafeteria-like room, which was used for meetings. It was to become the college bookstore. Its furnishings consisted of several round tables with bright blue, heavy plastic chairs with metal legs. They were quite attractive, and they matched what was becoming the "décor" of the library. All of the furniture was slated to be removed and sold. Our Assistant Librarian suggested we ask the Director of Budget and Operations if we could have some of the round tables to replace our bulky wooden ones, and most of the blue chairs to replace the psychedelic ones. He consented, and the exchange took place. These new tables and chairs provided alternative seating to the huge tables, most of which were underutilized because 2 students would sit at far ends of them if they didn't know each other. Now two people sitting at a table was fine, or they could be used for students needing to have group discussions about assignments. We were working together to improve our work space, which contributed to a feeling of camaraderie, raising morale even further.

The "Walk Around": Move It All About

At a library staff meeting, the Assistant librarian came up with the idea of doing a "walk around." We all walked around the entire library together, each person pointing something out, no matter how small, that could easily be moved, painted, discarded or re-purposed to continue our improvement project. I took notes and compiled a list of the ideas. This was like a brainstorming session on the move. This exercise in itself lifted spirits immensely. We could feel our stress levels decreasing again, by virtue of the fact we were doing something, not just wishing. Everyone liked the idea that they were being consulted. It made them feel more in control, and confident they were changing what they could to brighten things up and to improve study spaces for our students. Small steps are always better than none. Among the things identified were: removing another huge table at the entrance of library, removing the top shelves on the former indexes tables, removing overgrown, scraggly plants from the entrance way, removing an under-utilized desk in front of the Circulation Desk; replacing a crowded coffee service table with another two tiered table from elsewhere in the library. Before we started to make these small, but mood lifting, stress reducing changes, two of the staff had dubbed themselves, "The Beatification Committee." One was a trained artist and the other just had artistic taste. They used to joke that they were a committee with no money and no power. While they still had no money, they now knew some changes could and would be made.

Some of what we did after the walk around really opened up the library. As all long time librarians will remember, before the days of the Internet and online databases, most libraries had a series of long, heavy wooden tables. At these tables patrons could write down citations from the print indexes such as Reader's Guide, which were housed on shelves on the upper portion of these desks. For those new librarians who may not remember these, they were very high and in our case, anything but conducive to allowing light to fill the area. Our library had two of these in the center of the library right behind the crowded computer workstations. As one can imagine, this divided the area and gave the space a dark, closed in feel. Since most of the citations and articles listed in these indexes were now available online, they were virtually never used. So despite the antique traditional appeal these tables might once have had, they had outlived their purpose and were removed from the library. We kept some of the indexes covering the years prior to our online access, and moved them to low shelving units toward the back of the library. The front area of the library beyond the Circulation Desk was now clear of furniture except for our workstations. The staff could now see students using the workstations, and were better able to surmise when they needed help. Again, this was a two birds with one stone solution—a brighter, more open area, and enhanced ability to anticipate our students' need for assistance.

All of us were feeling very energized, and everyone knows increased energy and enthusiasm about a project, are two great stress relievers. Staff members were enthusiastically making new suggestions weekly. After the removal of the index tables, we honed in on another section of the library, the Archives. Our library houses the campus Archives and any documents sent to us from our main campus. These archives are all paper files and are housed in six scratched gray, metal file cabinets. These had been placed in a solid row between the front lobby area, and a small lounge area. The original thought had been the cabinets would make this area resemble a separate room. But in our stress busting, morale raising mode, these were seen as another hindrance to the open feel for which we were now striving. They had to go. We have a small Quiet Study area in the rear of the library with a wall that was a perfect location for these. We moved them into that room, and it now seems like they were always there. The archived materials were as easily accessible as they had been, but the cabinets were no longer a blight on the newly evolving appearance of the library. We now had a clear view from the entrance, to the rear wall of the front half of the library.

What We Did with the Help of the Administration

One of the library's staff members and I served on a committee called the Retention Initiative Implementation Team, or RIIT. The committee had been appointed by the Dean of the College, and was comprised of people representing a wide spectrum of the college academic and support units. We were charged with looking at all aspects of student retention on campus. The Chair of the committee was a dynamic, organized Associate Dean, who encouraged us to brainstorm. And brainstorm we did. After weeks of discussions, arguments and agreements, we developed a huge spreadsheet of ideas, and divided them into short and long term initiatives. We had decided to define "retention" very broadly because we all agreed the physical plant of the college was an important element contributing to students' feelings about their college. The committee decided upon some areas that needed upgrading, and happily the library was on the list. As a result, we became the beneficiaries of some wonderful projects intended to enhance the services in the library, and as a side benefit to us, these projects improved staff morale and lowered stress levels.

- The first project identified was the painting of all the walls. In the end, this became one of the biggest stress relievers of all. The library's walls had all been painted institutional beige. If they had ever been bright and cheerful, they had been dulled by years of dust, sun and age. In the summer of 2009, the physical plant people painted the entire library a cleaner light yellow hue. To compliment this new look, we selected a bright blue paint for two accent walls that matched most of the chairs in the library.

- The next thing that was done was the removal of all curtains from the windows throughout the library. They too were very old, and blocked the sunlight that should have been allowed to shine through the floor to ceiling windows. To all of us, it was like a literal breath of fresh air, albeit sunshine this time. It was incredible what affect these two things had on the appearance of the library. The staff enjoyed these changes every time they walked around and observed the light hitting the beautiful newly painted walls. Occasionally, I saw them literally smile at the difference in the rooms.

- The next target was an alcove with "comfortable" seating. This area became irreverently known as "the dead deans" area for the 5 foot portraits of former Deans, although one of whom was still very much alive. These paintings were rather creepy looking down on students studying or sleeping. We were very happy to have them removed. To this day we don't know where they went, but may they rest in peace.

What We Did with the Help of Other Faculty or Units

- One of our art professors generously framed and donated 16 modernistic prints of art work done by his students in past classes. These were abstracts of varying themes, each one done in bright reds, blues, greens or purples. They beautifully accented the newly painted walls and added additional color. The next assistance came from our Chair of the Visual Computer Technology (VCT) department, who allowed us to display a rotating collection of the VCT students' photography. One of our student assistants, a VCT student herself, mounted pictures and changed them every few weeks. This display is prominently hung on one wall as users round the corner to the book stacks, Writing Center and group study room. Both of the latter rooms were built with the RIIT money and became two incredible boons to the library in themselves. This rotating exhibit serves two purposes, to further beautify the library, and to display student art.

- Our main campus library donated several sections of shelving they had removed for discard—yes another discard, but one that matched our other stacks and was very much needed. With this donation, we were able to shift the crowded monograph collection, and to eventually move our circulating journal collection into the circulating stacks. This freed up space behind the circulation desk for our last, project, one made possible by a bequest from an area library devotee, upon her death.

What We Did with the Best of All, a Bequest from a Community Person

In the summer of 2009, we were surprised to learn of a bequest of funding to update the library for our students. This was given to us by an area woman who had passed away. With this bequest, received annually for a number of years, we are able to phase in projects every two years. With the first of the money, we discarded the crowded tables that had housed computer workstations replete with hanging wires, no space between workstations for students to put their belongings, or to afford them any privacy in their research. We replaced these computer tables with what I call the "wavy workstation" tables, beautiful workstations modeled after one at my previous library. In the first weeks after their installation, we collected students' comments. A typical comment was much like this one: "The new stations are great. I love the layout. It offers privacy, but a group of two can still work together efficiently." We also bought additional MI6 stackable chairs on casters for ease of movement to anyplace in the library, or for group study.

Our final project is in development and will be a modern, more functional Circulation Desk with work areas for staff and an office for the Assistant Librarian who had given up hers to me when I arrived. A staff work area will be moved from the technical services area in the back room to the front desk area to better assist users.

While some of what I have described in this essay did cost money, none of it came from the library. The administration paid for the removal of curtains, the donation of the round tables and blue chairs, and provided the labor for the painting. RIIT funding provided the paint for the group study room and Writing Lab. A grant provided funding for the signage, laptop tables and chairs. Finally, the wonderful donor gave us much needed funding to make the biggest improvements. She will never know what her gift did to brighten our environment and provide relief from the stress caused by formerly dingy, dark surroundings.

There will always be irate patrons, changes in policies or demands from Administration, or the public, that may temporarily return feelings of stress to us. However, what we accomplished through the changes implemented in this essay has made our work environment more comfortable, more open and inviting, and has relieved our stress as much as a day at the spa may do for some.

Most of what we achieved can be accomplished by any library staff. Do your own "walk around" and see what changes can be made. I can guarantee it will be worth it.

In summary:

1. Brainstorm with your staff to develop immediate and inexpensive ways to make small changes to your environment. As noted, it is truly amazing how seemingly small improvements can turn drab into fabulous, and lift staff spirits.

2. Take hand-me-downs and discarded items of furniture, equipment, or art work, but *only* if it's in good condition, looks new or can be made to look new, and truly enhances your space. Otherwise, you are just taking another person's junk and making your space junky as well.

3. Re-purpose your existing furniture or other items, as we did with our coffee cart. If they had a function in a certain area once, and no longer make the space comfortable or appealing, try it elsewhere. It might just look completely different for a different purpose, and make that space more functional as well.

4. Be on the lookout for donations from other area libraries, your own faculty or local companies. Make sure you have a way of transporting your new treasures, so that it doesn't cost you much to retrieve them.

5. Talk to your administrators or supervisors to ascertain if there is any way they can paint, clean or remove something from your area without charge to you. Provide valid compelling reasons and emphasize that you are trying to make improvements frugally.

6. Identify and write grants to compliment your library budget, especially if it's small. Writing grants can be fun. They take a little work, but if written well, one day, you may be rewarded with a small influx of money for your library, almost like a gift. As noted in this essay, we purchased signs, tables and chairs with grant money.

7. Don't be afraid to ask for what you need. The worst that can happen is that the answer will be no. If we hadn't asked for the chairs from the renovated lounge, our students might still be sitting on "psychedelic" chairs.

8. Have fun making the changes. It's the best stress reducer of all.

Funding Your Media Program in Lean Times

BARBARA FIEHN

We all know our new reality is making do with less. Budget reductions have affected libraries of all kinds. Generally with reduced budgets have come staff reductions, shorter hours of operation, and cutbacks in programming, materials, and promotions. This new reality has created stress as everyone tries to squeeze more money out of existing funds and seeks alternate funding sources. We are seeking new strategies to bolster our program goals without spending funds. Stress develops through trying to do at least the same things with less money. It is time to reduce this stress by looking at our work through lenses more compatible with a new financial reality that has the approval of your supervisor, board or principal.

Analyze Reality

The place to begin is with an analysis of where you are and project where you can go. This is a good time to take a second look at the vision, mission, goals, and objectives for your library. Are they still valid as guiding documents for your library? As you are working on this, begin thinking about the core values. What is most important to your library, to your patrons? Reduced budgets and staffing means you must change something. Continuing on your old path will create increased stress and ultimately failure of library functions. Some ideas for stress-reducing changes are

- Identify old patterns that need updating. Look to save time: time is money and lack of time causes stress. Eliminate tasks not necessary to basic functioning.
- Revise collection development plans with more emphasis on patrons who come through the door. This helps reduce stressful purchasing decisions. Replace popular books that are lost, because they circulate. Do not worry about replacing other materials or completing series.
- Drop print periodicals orders for titles covered in your databases to reduce expenditures.

- Send overdue notices via e-mail or print only every third or sixth month to save paper, ink, distribution costs, and staff time. If someone asks for an overdue book, follow up with the person who has it checked out. Overdue notices are stressful for everyone.
- Give volunteers more responsibilities to reduce stress on staff who cannot deal with everything that needs to be done.

Budgeting

A written budget, based on your revised mission and goals provides direction for programming and purchasing. Use statistics from your annual reports as you plan. A written budget:

- gives you more credibility and directs your path, reducing decision-making stress
- requires you to organize your priorities and arguments
- makes you look efficient and professional
- gives your administrator something to think about after you have left the office
- provides rationale for new purchases

Shifting Funds (K-12 Schools)

As you build your budget, look carefully at what you are paying for; can you shift the funding to some other budget? Can you justify this shift? Budgeting is stressful even in good financial times. In tight budget times, librarians' stress levels rise as they try to find funds for needed materials, equipment, and programming. Shifting or offloading budget items can help free up funds for other areas of the budget.

Argue for budgeting online databases as district-wide expenses. These databases benefit all faculty and staff and most students. The district technology budget is a logical place to shift money. Likewise, the library management system's annual support is district-based rather than a building expense. Maintenance of a district-wide automation system is a benefit to the whole district. Funding should be from a district library or technology budget. Another place to shift funds is for equipment that is, in most cases, a capital outlay expense and funded by building and technology budgets. This helps in maintaining equity between buildings in districts where there are perceptions of "have and have not" buildings.

Carefully look for occasions where you can get materials for the library on someone else's budget or for free. Specialized curriculum support materials housed in the school library traditionally are purchased through the library budget. In buildings where departments have budgets, these purchases can be offloaded to the individual areas or a shared budget. Perhaps your budget pays for supplemental reading program materials, specialized periodicals, or math manipulatives. Every dollar you save turns into money to build your collection and helps to reduce stress about providing requested materials.

For years, I never purchased pencils, pens, crayons, and markers. The custodians picked up these items as they cleaned and gave them to me. At the end of the school year, I collected these items from students as they cleaned out their lockers and desks. I also picked up pens, notepads, and sticky notes from conferences I attended. These pick-ups reduced the money I spent on supplies, allowing me to spend more on essentials or even some nonessentials I could not otherwise afford.

Purchasing at a Discount: Books, Databases and Online Resources

Everyone loves a bargain. Anytime you can take advantage of group purchasing or book fair perks through vendors such as Scholastic, outlet mega-sales, or Amazon.com discounts. From the community solicit titles that can be donated by parents, local businesses, and civic groups. These acquisition sources will help you ease the stress of how you will manage with a reduced budget.

Let's talk about wise strategies for purchasing online resources. Your first task is identifying the best online material for your needs. There are many choices, and you must make decisions because you cannot have them all. Everything is negotiable. Let the company representative know what you can afford and see if they will work with you. Understand that pricing of some products is less flexible because of set costs to the company. There are usually a variety of pricing options. Go into negotiations with data on your previous usage, including average daily attendance by the schools in your district. Be a strong negotiator.

A purchasing cooperative will usually obtain lower-cost bids than individual schools or school districts. The larger the buying power, the greater the savings. There are a wide variety of purchasing collectives available such as your regional library systems, regional library cooperatives, and even statewide cooperatives. Most require membership and offer very competitive pricing on supplies, databases, and other items. Let the co-op know the products you would like to see. One nice thing about group buying is that the cooperative will help deal with order problems and re-negotiate the contracts. This reduces your own stress of dealing with pricing negotiations.

Each dollar of the budget saved, off loaded, or partnered, is money saved to meet the goals of the library. Stressing over budget problems will not go away, but can be reduced by creative thinking and reprioritizing. Too many librarians passively accept their budgets as delivered from the money holders. Being active in securing the best possible budget may actually reduce your overall budgeting stress.

Fundraising

Fundraising has never been intended to replace the regular budget, but it is necessary to support special collections and programs that strengthen your library. By developing creative fundraising ideas, you not only engage the community, but also build relationships, which often translate into various kinds of support for the library. In times of budget shortages, some school libraries use fundraising as their only source of money for new purchases. By spending a little time planning and brainstorming for fundraisers, you can minimize the stresses of a reduced budget.

Public libraries have long relied on their Friends of the Library group to support the library through various fundraisers. School libraries have relied on the local parents' organization for additional funding. It may be time to expand this group to include advisory committees, library pages, teen groups, school service clubs, and other volunteer groups. Creative ways to raise smaller amounts of funds are becoming popular in many libraries. These activities usually involve sales and are called mini-fundraisers. These may include book sales and vending machines monies which sell everything from basic school supplies to headphones and flash drives. Additionally, fundraisers may encompass before and after school sales of coffee and snacks. Some library groups are involved in raffles, gaming day, and movie afternoons selling pizza, pop, and popcorn. Other special calendar day sales consist of selling baked goods such as slices of pies for Pi day.

Book Fairs

Traditionally, a standard of elementary and middle schools, book fairs can raise a considerable amount of money. When the funds are used to purchase materials from the book fair vendor, the funds tend to be extended through additional discounts. Book fairs are time intensive and can be managed by volunteers. Scholastic has been the predominant book fair vendor in schools. However, local bookstores as well as chains, such as Barnes & Noble, should be considered. In planning a book fair, ask for inclusion of materials relevant to teachers and parents in addition to student materials. Also, consider book fairs with online vendors. Several companies specialize in online book fairs, which greatly reduce the time investment for library staff. Mackin Educational Resources offers a unique online fundraiser that collects funds for your library.

Solicited Donations

Libraries have a limited history of soliciting donations from patrons. The traditional profile has been materials gifted from community members, birthday or memorial books. Now is the time for libraries to reach out to the community and let businesses, civic groups, and individuals who know there is a need for quality materials for the collection. Before soliciting gifts, check your selection policy and administration. Your policy should state that all gifts are subject to the same criteria as purchased materials. Place this information in your solicitation materials along with the statement that unsuitable materials may be donated elsewhere. Acknowledgement of library gifts is vital to good will and good manners. Have a template on your computer you can use to thank donors. Carefully word this document and do not place a value on gifts. Be sure to include a statement that the donor must verify any valuation or tax deductibility. Mail the acknowledgement as soon as possible after the receipt of the gift.

Keep a wish list of materials you desire on hand and updated. You can include other items, not just books: list needed supplies and other items such as CDs, audiobooks, hand sanitizer, and tissues.

Contact businesses and fraternal organizations in your community, such as Kiwanis or Rotary clubs. They are often willing to make the same types of donations as parents and community members, and many have among their goals an interest in supporting education and literacy. An insurance company may have up-to-date road atlases to donate. A grocery store may donate snack food for reading promotion parties. Other businesses will have office supplies or promotional gifts. You have to let them know what you can use. You—and they—may be surprised at how much small but essential donations can help stretch your budget and reduce your stress.

Check with corporate supports by starting close to home then branch out. Most of the big box stores have community service grants for organizations managed through their local nonprofit offices. Have your needs list ready when you approach them. Target your list to items they carry. Be prepared to fill out a form or grant paperwork. If you are located in a small, rural community, go to the nearest regional shopping town or city. Be creative: a local furniture or carpet store may be able to provide a colorful carpet for the children's storytime area. A lighting store may provide a reading lamp for a dark corner. A florist or garden supply store may provide plants or supplies to bring a little green decor into your library.

Branch out to larger corporations. Search the Internet for companies interested in literacy and contact them about your needs. Contact Scholastic Book Fairs for their list of Literacy Enhancement Supporters.

Cultivate Allies and Grant Writing

- PTA/PTO
- Administration
- Teaching Staff
- Parents and Students
- Vendors

Let your allies know you are sincere in your desire to build a strong library media program. Make them aware of outdated or inadequate collections. Tell these potential supporters stories about what you are doing, what you are trying to do, and what you can do with additional support. Let them know about state and national standards, and summarize research reports about the importance of libraries. Use the ALA and AASL advocacy toolkits.

Big dollars and little dollars are out there waiting for you through grant writing. Check the Internet, professional organizations and journals. Let others know you are looking for grants and are willing to collaborate with other libraries and organizations. Vendors will often hear about grants, so do not hesitate to ask them. Federal grants may be too complex for you initially, but do not discount them. Take a course in grant writing. If one is not available locally, try to find one on the Internet or get a book or two and educate yourself.

Other Low-Cost Ideas to Reduce Budget Stress

Professional journals often look for reviewers for upcoming books and other library materials. Contact popular library journals and include a sample review, following the specific review style. Once you establish a relationship with the review editor, she or he will send you material to review. The number of items sent to you will vary. Generally, you will get a shipment about three times a year, and you can sometimes add the reviewed materials to your library's collection. This is a way to keep up with currently published materials, and you can often add popular titles to your library at no charge.

Many materials vendors have periodic sales. Find out when they are and target purchasing to those dates, when possible. Know what your collection needs; do not purchase titles just because they are on sale. Tie purchases to specific goals and objectives and curriculum needs. Reviewing circulation data can help you make wise purchasing decisions.

We all recognize the value of materials available on the Internet. The problem is identifying the great and good from the poor and worse. How do you get these materials into the hands of your patrons?

The first step is to organize usable, free material on your library's website. Identify what materials you will provide, develop an organizational structure, and then begin adding links to helpful resources. Check nationally acclaimed library websites for great ideas and useful tools. For example, Joyce Valenza has an outstanding reference blog for her high school students called the *Springfield Township High Virtual Library*, which may give you ideas for your site. Include online versions of age-appropriate materials:

- Search engines and directories: Search out those most beneficial to your patrons. Google is fine but there are so many different tools to use. I recommend doing a search for "search engines list" to find lists of good search engines and directories for a variety of users. One I go to for specialized search engines is "List of Search Engines by Type of Search."
- Basic reference tools (almanacs, dictionaries, encyclopedias, etc.): The abundance of these tools makes the job of selecting the right ones for your library difficult. You may want to check Library Spot as a starting point or for links appropriate for children. Another useful resource is Great Websites for Kids: Reference at ALA.org.
- Magazines: When you have to cut your magazine budget, add your favorite magazines' links to your website. While content and quality vary, the free online site is better than having nothing. Do not overlook professional journals. Many have very useful websites, some with free access to older articles.

- Newspapers and news sites: Search by newspaper name or by best newspapers— pick regional, national, or worldwide favorites. Keep a balance of liberal to conservative, local to global news. When looking for news sites for children try searching "newspaper websites for kids." There is an amazing selection of free news access.

- Graphic novels: There is a wide variety of graphic novels and comics available online. Reduced budgets make it difficult to stock as many print copies, as you would like. Use the free Internet sites to appease your avid readers. Ask aficionados for their suggestions. Words of warning, not all online graphic novels are child or young adult appropriate. Digital Tools for Teachers lists a number of sites appropriate for children. For primary students and international students try Toons Reader.

- Book and eBook sites: Linking to book and eBook sites presents some problems. The good news is, there are thousands of public domain works available. A caution: Many online books are self-published, with little or no editorial supervision. The following directory sites are a good place to begin:
  — The Online Books Page
  — Free Audio Books Online For Children
  — Free Children's Books Online Free Teen and Young Adult Books Online
  — Curriculum/Homework sites: While there are many curriculum and homework websites available, there is nothing like handpicking the best for your local community. A starting place is the following ALA websites: Best Websites for Teaching and Learning and Great Websites for Kids

Professional Development

When money for staff, operations, and purchasing is tight, professional development also suffers. Thanks to the Internet, a growing number of free or very low cost professional development options, such as webinars or online workshops, have developed. More become available each year. Check with your professional organizations and watch for announcements on library e-mail lists, or just search the Internet. The following are a few suggestions for professional development options online:

- *Booklist* Webinars
- *School Library Journal* Webcasts
- ASCD Webinars
- ASCD Courses (fee based)
- Educause Online events
- *Library Journal* Webcasts
- InfoPeople Webinars, Podcasts and Online Learning
- NCompass Live
- Webjuction (OCLC)

Working with an underfunded budget is always challenging because you are always juggling priorities and trying to make do with less. What is your library doing to meet your organization's goals? Set clear boundaries. Maximize the resources you have on hand to successfully beat the odds in challenging economic times. Careful planning and outreach, a little ingenuity, prioritization, and creativity go a long way toward building success in your library. There is no way to completely eliminate the stress of an underfunded library, but taking active steps to seek new ways of thinking about budgeting and providing resources to your patrons will help you manage the stress.

References

Kenney, Brian. "SLJ's 2011 Technology Survey: Things Are Changing Fast." *School Library Journal* 57, no. 5 (2011): 28–33.

Downsizing Stress:
Dealing with Budgetary and Staff Cuts

STACEY R. EWING AND JANELLE WEST

In recent years, academic and public libraries have suffered from massive budget cuts resulting in layoffs, hiring freezes, and reductions in acquisitions and services. Recent studies by the Primary Research Group reveal that in the academic library community alone, 35 percent of libraries have seen a reduction in budget over the past two years, with only 11 percent seeing a modest increase. Moreover, 32 percent of academic libraries anticipate budget reductions in the next three years (2012, 81–82). Not surprisingly, budgetary constraints are a primary stressor for many librarians and have become a source of widespread job dissatisfaction (Miller 2011, 52).

Given the unstable financial climate, budget instability will be a long-term challenge for most libraries. Nevertheless, it is vital for administrators, librarians, and staff to optimize their resources in order to work successfully within their budgetary constraints, while mitigating the inevitable stress that comes with fiscal uncertainty. The following case studies demonstrate how two academic libraries are dealing with budgetary challenges and offer examples of coping positively with the resulting stress on both institutional and individual levels.

Case Study 1: University of Florida (UF)

The George A. Smathers Libraries, comprised of the Health Science Center Libraries (HSCL) and the University Libraries (UFUL), serve over 50,000 students of the University of Florida and accommodate approximately three million in-person visitors per year. Although the HSCL is an important part of the University of Florida's library system, this essay targets budgetary issues relating solely to the University Libraries. In a recent peer review analysis comparing the UFUL to other institutions' resources and populations, the review found that UF libraries are under-funded and under-staffed. Despite protecting the materials budget through the most recent budget reductions, the cumulative loss of materials buying power since fiscal year 2007/2008 (through 2011/2012) has been approximately $2.7 million. This loss is projected to increase to approximately $3.4 million by the 2012/2013 fiscal year. Not only has the general library fund been weakened, but the entire budgetary source structure has not evolved with the times. The University of Florida University Libraries, on the whole, does not receive funding from student use fees. Additionally, the Libraries maintain the largest number of public workstations on campus, yet it only receives funds from the academic and research units of UF, with no supplementary funding from centralized IT (Russell et al., 2012). In effect, the UFUL has been given the responsibility of providing students with online access but has not been granted sufficient funds to do so. It is currently anticipated there may be another 5 percent cut in the 2013/ 2014 fiscal year, leaving the libraries struggling to predict which services and resources to further cut.

Case Study 2: University of North Texas (UNT)

The University of North Texas Libraries (UNTL) serve over 30,000 students. Unlike the majority of sister institutions, 96 percent of the Libraries' funding comes from student use fees. This funding model was adopted in 2004, at which time the student use fee was fixed at $16.50 per semester credit hour. Regrettably, the fee remains unchanged. Therefore, UNTL must rely on a steady increase in enrollment in order to keep up with the ever-increasing costs of materials, staffing, and maintenance. Unfortunately, during fiscal year 2011/2012, enrollment decreased by 1.5 percent. This decrease translated to a 3.5 percent, or $500,000, decrease in funding to UNTL, which, when coupled with projected cost increases in serials and technologies, translated to a $1.5M projected shortfall for fiscal year 2012/2013. Nevertheless, UNT aspires to become a top tier research institution, and this goal requires that the Libraries continue to build their services and resources, even as they face canceling $1M in materials and $500,000 in library services.

Limiting the Impact of Stress Through Innovation and Compromise

Libraries must limit the stressful impact of budget cuts through innovation, creativity, and flexibility. Admittedly, some of these solutions are based on unpleasant compromises, but in today's economic climate, libraries need to depend on invention and necessary concessions in order to maintain high levels of service.

Transition to Embedded Librarianship

For UF, this has meant providing library instruction with reduced staffing. When the first round of hiring freezes hit the university, the George A. Smathers Libraries endured a major departmental reorganization, and Library West (LW), the Humanities and Social Sciences branch, went from six instruction librarians to one. Due to the drastic decrease, it became necessary for LW to move to a mentor or "train the trainer" model of embedded librarianship. Each semester, all librarians are assigned between one and three teaching assistants (TAs) from UF First Year Writing classes. Librarians then correspond with the TAs via e-mail, sending lists of important resources and links to online library instruction resources to share with their classes. The TAs are provided with instant messaging service information, in addition to research assistance desk schedules of the various subject specialists, to pass along to their students. In addition, they are encouraged to schedule instructional classes, either at the library or in the classroom.

Supplementing Face to Face
Instruction Using Technology

In order to continue meeting the demand for library instruction with reduced staffing, it became necessary at UF to supplement face to face instruction with technology. To this end, an online/interactive library instruction tutorial was created for professors and TAs to assign as a graded class project. The tutorial was designed with interactive research modules, helping users develop basic information literacy skills by guiding them through the mechanics of researching at the libraries.

The librarians at UF discovered a valuable open source software tool from the University of Minnesota — the *Assignment Calculator*—and concluded it could benefit their students as well. The calculator software was modified to include resources specific to the UF Libraries. Students input the start and end dates of their research paper into the online portal embedded in the library webpage, then the calculator estimates the number of days needed to complete the project and generates a list of twelve steps guiding the user through the entire writing process. Each step provides a completion date, safeguarding users from falling behind in the writing process and ultimately guiding them to meet the assignment deadline. All twelve steps provide links to online library services, such as the Ask-A Librarian instant messaging service, in addition to internally and externally produced online guides such as the UF Libraries' *Avoiding Plagiarism Guide* and the Purdue Online Writing Center's *Tips for Writing Your Thesis Topic.*

In 2010, librarians secured a University of Florida University Libraries mini-grant to fund a project allowing student assistants to create library instruction videos for their fellow digital natives. The students were charged with developing content to produce twelve videos highlighting library services and resources. Although librarians supervised the video creation team, the students were largely self-directed and worked autonomously to design and produce the videos. The videos are located on the UF Libraries' YouTube channel and are archived in the UF Institutional Repository. Librarians incorporate these videos in their subject LibGuides by embedding HTML code from YouTube, while the First Year Writing Program Library Liaisons send links in periodical e-mails to their TA mentees, encouraging them to share the videos with their students.

Making a Positive Impact on Student Retention

Until recently, the UNTL student-fee–based budget was workable, but the sudden decline in student enrollment caused an equally sudden drop in funding. This is a stark reminder that student retention should be an essential goal of UNTL and other libraries whose budgets depend on student fees. In order to improve retention, UNTL must become an even more effective part of the overall quality of education at UNT. To start, departmental and library-wide assessments can be performed to discern ways of reaching out to the student body, ensuring students' intellectual needs are being met at the library. For instance, there must be a continued, active outreach effort, urging professors to integrate library tours and instruction sessions into their class calendars. It is fundamental that students be encouraged to familiarize themselves with the library and its staff in order to boost their potential for academic achievement. Certainly, librarians and staff on all levels of the library structure can contribute to success in this area by providing exemplary service and attention to the student patrons. In the end, students who are comfortable with the quality of their education will continue coming back for more.

CREATIVE APPROACHES TO STAFFING

Staffing during budget short falls are particularly challenging, so libraries should utilize creative solutions. For example, UNT and UF offer work study programs, through which student workers are funded partially by the state or federal government. As the libraries cut some of their library funded student assistant positions, they may choose to fill at least some of the gaps with work study students. In addition, both UF and UNT make use of the School of Library and Information Science (SLIS) interns or practicum students to temporarily alleviate staffing short falls on special projects. In another approach, one UNTL department found a creative way to fill a workforce need. The burgeoning special collections of this department required the attention of a fulltime librarian, but no funding was available for a new position. This department chose to satisfy the need by trading some graduate library assistant positions for a fulltime librarian position. While this tradeoff is not optimal, it proves departments can get what they need through bargain and compromise.

ADMINISTRATIVE TRANSPARENCY

Administrative transparency is vital while striving to provide necessary services on a depleted budget. In times of change, a workplace is particularly susceptible to widespread and negative rumors, breeding stress and anxiety in its workers (Bordia et al., 2006, 606). Although it may seem that closely guarding budget details will prevent rumors from swirling, withholding information often ignites the very speculation an organization wishes to suppress (Fortado 2011, 217). Therefore, library administrators should do all in their power to retain transparency as they weigh difficult budgetary considerations.

To accomplish this, the libraries at UF have again turned to technology. In 2008/2009, when the first round of tough budget cuts began, the UF Libraries began using blogs and a wiki. These tools help keep the 200+ employees of the library system stay informed of the subsequent reorganization and of the direct effects the budget has on library employees, facilities, services, and resources. Furthermore, the University of Florida holds town

137

hall meetings, which are open to all library employees, in addition to smaller, more frequent departmental meetings. All of these are efforts to communicate the facts and squelch rumors before they begin. Similarly, the dean of the UNT Libraries holds periodic "Dean's Coffee" meetings, through which he communicates news on the state of the budget and reports on the progress of various projects. During these meetings, he openly discusses the details of the budget, including the Libraries' strategies for dealing with the cutbacks, and he reserves ample time for questions. Efforts such as these go a long way toward limiting the negative impact budgetary issues can have on a library workforce. When employees are accurately informed, they are less vulnerable to the anxieties that go hand in hand with speculation.

REINFORCING SENSE OF COMMUNITY THROUGH COST EFFECTIVE MEASURES

Another way for library administrators to limit the stress spawned by cutbacks is to reinforce a sense of community within the library through simple, cost effective measures. One such measure was taken by the UF and UNT libraries is to celebrate the successes of library employees through public acknowledgement in meetings and newsletters. Additionally, both libraries present star performer awards, which include certificates of achievement and token gifts to deserving staff members. These types of affirmation boost morale and project the sense of a common mission, while inspiring employees to strive for excellence.

The UF and UNT libraries also foster a sense of community through library-wide or departmental get-togethers. Pot-luck style holiday or other themed parties may be held with minimal financial burden. For example, one UNTL department holds monthly pot-luck parties to celebrate birthdays or other milestones, and several other departments throw parties to mark special occasions. Similarly, multiple library branches at UF hold holiday themed pot-luck parties at least once a semester, making sure to include the student assistants. The deans of the UF Libraries hold small monthly breakfasts, with light refreshments and simple tokens of appreciation, for employees who have had birthdays. In the UF Libraries' IT department, members take turns bringing cake — bought or baked — to their monthly departmental meetings, giving the staff something to enjoy while working through the agenda.

These measures do not need to be reserved exclusively for the purpose of combating budgetary stress. Certainly, it is always important to provide a quality educational experience, make the most of your resources, prioritize good communication, and foster a sense of community. But when there is a budget crisis, these measures become even more essential.

Limiting the Stress: Individual Responsibility

As necessary as institutional and departmental efforts are, it is paramount that individuals take responsibility for managing their own anxiety levels. Ultimately you are in control of your response to stressful situations, and there are measures you can take to weather budget storms in a healthy way.

PROFESSIONAL DEVELOPMENT AND ROLE ASSESSMENT

While it may be tempting in times of budgetary stress to keep a low profile and cling to routine, this approach leads to stagnation at a point when it is essential to be proactive. Librarians can boost their job confidence and moderate their stress by remaining informed of developments in the field and by maintaining and acquiring new skills. Many libraries offer regular workshops, seminars, and webinars that help augment existing knowledge and skills. Grant writing workshops are especially valuable these days and are often offered free of charge.

A financial crisis at work also offers an opportunity to re-assess your role in the library. For example, a cataloger who finds his workload reduced because of cuts in acquisitions may want to volunteer to work on donated and "hidden" collections. On the other hand, a librarian who is suddenly challenged with a heavy workload due to staff cutbacks has the opportunity to refine his or her time management skills.

As you take on tasks, acquire new skills, and attend workshops and seminars, you should be mindful to keep your resume up to date. There are several online CV hosting sites that simplify resume updating, and some social and professional networking sites have professional features as well. LinkedIn, a popular, business-oriented social networking site, allows users to create a professional profile and list their present and past employment, as well as connect with friends and colleagues. BranchOut, an application for Facebook, is another example of a social media career tool. While you should always be careful about privacy concerns associated with any given third party application, Branch Out and LinkedIn offer an avenue of professional networking that could prove valuable to your career.

PROFESSIONAL ORGANIZATIONS: INTELLECTUAL RECHARGING

During challenging financial times, the importance of professional organizations cannot be overstated. On the national and state levels, library associations help library professionals keep in touch with what is going on in the field and with colleagues at other institutions. Through conference sessions and workshops, you can gain useful knowledge in areas such as new technologies and resources, juggling work and personal life, and dealing with budget cuts. Conferences provide the opportunity to recharge professionally, while networking and commiserating with others in the field. Sharing common experiences with your peers can help to alleviate stress; you will likely find that others have been struggling with challenges you thought were uniquely yours. Most importantly, the shared ideas and experiences gained at these conferences can be brought back home to benefit your institution.

With budget cuts happening in both public and academic library realms, professional library organizations can be a powerful voice of resistance. For example, when Florida suffered a 60 percent cut in the 2011 state budget, the Florida Library Association led in a massive library advocacy effort, which ultimately resulted in restoration of $21.2 million to libraries' budgets.

Personal Life: Tending to Your Physical and Emotional Health

Of course, none of the above measures will effectively reduce stress levels if you do not take charge of your physical and emotional health, and there are several measures you can take while at work. First, make it a priority to step away from the office periodically. Take time to occasionally eat lunch with a colleague, or use your lunch break to take a walk. Alternatively, take occasional short breaks to walk around the building or through the stacks, or simply stretch at your desk or in a stairwell. The light exercise will help get the blood flowing, and you can use the time constructively, keeping an eye out for maintenance or cleaning issues and for students who look like they may need help.

Your institution may even offer structured activities to keep your workday stress at a minimum. At UNT, massages are available at the campus health center within easy walking distance of the library. At UF, many of the librarians and library staff participate in Walking Gators, a group that meets during lunchtime for a one mile walk around campus. Other institutions likely offer similar activities that not only provide health benefits but are a great way to get out of the building and take your mind off of office stressors. As busy and distracted as you may be, work breaks are your right by law, and it is important to your own well-being to use them to your best advantage.

Additionally, it is important to maintain nutritional balance throughout the work day. Keep healthy snacks at your desk for the inevitable afternoon slump (or for days when you accidentally forgot your lunch at home). Snacks like granola bars, nuts, and dried fruit can be easily stored at your work space. Perhaps even more importantly, remember to drink lots of water throughout the day. Libraries are dry places, so when you feel like reaching for a Diet Coke or a third cup of coffee, grab some cold water instead.

The health advantages of a regular exercise regimen are well publicized, and librarians would greatly benefit from a regular workout schedule. Many institutions have exercise facilities on site, and low cost memberships are often available to faculty and staff. Both UNT and UF have faculty/staff gym memberships and offer programs such as meditation, yoga, and health assessment workshops. Also UNT has a Faculty/Staff Fitness Program, which allows longer break periods for staff members attending a fitness class during the work day. Look into what your institution offers, and take advantage of it!

Juggling Work, Family and Personal Life

Efforts to maintain a healthy perspective at work rely heavily on the balance between work and home life. This balance begins with leaving work stresses at work at the end of the day. This is not always easy. Many librarians are tempted to check their e-mail during off hours, and some may see repeated reminders of work on social media sites. Although these technologies seem to encourage 24/7 connectivity, it is perhaps better to reserve a time at the end of the work day to check e-mail one last time, then forget about it until morning. Librarians may also choose a pronounced separation between the work life and private life by not connecting with co-workers on social media sites. A healthy work/home separation is aptly illustrated by one UF librarian's mental approach: she allows herself to vent her work frustrations to her husband on the commute, but upon their arrival home, she shuts the door to the car and mentally locks her work stress inside it until the next day.

And when all of these measures still leave you feeling overwhelmed, many institutions offer counseling services that may help get you back on track. UNT's and UF's Employee Assistance Programs connect employees with free counseling services to address an array of issues, from financial problems to family turmoil to depression.

Conclusion

This essay touches on a few ways libraries and librarians can remain innovative and inspired despite a lean budgetary period. The University of Florida and the University of North Texas library systems continue working aggressively to reduce employees' stress through creative uses of technology, resourceful staffing techniques, communication, and community spirit. Also, it is the responsibility of each librarian to manage individual stress levels. With a little innovation and resourcefulness, libraries and librarians can navigate their way to a healthier, more balanced workplace, and in the end, a more efficient library system.

References

Borida, Prashant, Elizabeth Jones, Cindy Gallois, Victor Callan, and Nicholas DiFonzo. "Management Are Aliens!: Rumors and Stress During Organizational Change." *Group & Organization Management.* 31. no. 5 (2006): 601–621.

Fortado, Bruce. "A Field Exploration of Informal Workplace Communication." *Sociology Mind.* 1. no. 4 (2011): 212–220.

Miller, Rebecca. "Rocked by Recession, Buoyed by Service." *Library Journal.* 136. no. 10 (2011): 52–55.

Primary Research Group. *Survey of Academic Libraries: 2012–13.* New York: Primary Research Group, 2012.

Done in a Day: Effective Use of Volunteer Labor

JEFFREY DISCALA AND SHERI ANITA MASSEY

The goal of the school library program is to "ensure that students and staff are effective users of ideas and information" (ALA/AASL 2009; AECT & ALA/AASL 1998). The school librarian performs five roles to accomplish this mission: leader, teacher, instructional partner, information specialist, and program administrator. The tasks associated with each role are numerous, and often overwhelming: lesson planning, teaching, selecting, labeling, weeding, shelving, purchasing, evaluating, budgeting, monitoring, collaborating, advocating, creating, retrieving, disciplining, researching, advising, scheduling, developing, organizing, and so on. With a limited amount of time each day and a seemingly endless list of responsibilities, not only can the mission of the school library program can get lost, but the job-related guilt and stress can be soul-crushing. The goal of this essay is to position volunteering as a way to delegate tasks, alleviate guilt, reduce stress, and advocate for your program all at the same time.

Nonprofit organizations use volunteers to perform jobs that might otherwise be done by paid staff as a strategy to reduce costs during hard times (Fritz n.d.). Nicol and Johnson (2008) begin their chronicle of volunteers in libraries in the 1930s as the face of volunteering was changing from largely stay-at-home, middle-class housewives, to people of all ages and employment situations with a willingness to give freely of their time. McCauley (1976) wrote specifically about school libraries and the arrival of citizen volunteers in the late 1960s. Ironically, the rise in citizen volunteers was caused not by economic hardship as many might think, but by a time of prosperity for school libraries. Funds from the Elementary and Secondary Education Act (ESEA) increased library budgets and, consequently, the need for assistance in incorporating non-print materials and audio-visual equipment into the school library collection.

The use of library volunteers has advantages and disadvantages:

Disadvantages:

- Librarians sometimes see volunteers as a threat to paid staff
- The costs of training and maintaining a quality volunteer program can be a strain on resources; and
- Some volunteers can be unreliable (Tikam 2011)

Advantages:

- Well-trained volunteers perform a wide variety of services free of charge (Barack 2010; Farmer 2003; McHenry 1988)
- They bring new, innovative ideas to the program (Nicol and Johnson 2008; Tikam 2011)
- By freeing us from routine manual labor they allow librarians to refocus on their overarching mission, or "big idea" projects necessary for improving ourselves and our profession (Jacobson 2010; Nicol and Johnson 2008); and
- Most importantly, a volunteer can be an advocate with a deep, personal understanding of our ever-evolving libraries (Dickinson 2011; Jacobson 2010; Tikam 2011)

Today's volunteer may not have time to help regularly in the school library, but still has a strong urge to give back. For this group, volunteering on a one-off basis is best. One-off volunteering, also called occasional, on demand, done-in-a-day, project-based, or commitment-free volunteering, occurs when individuals commit to volunteering less than one week a month or for a specific event. Compared to regular volunteers who handle the day-to-day operations of a library, such as shelving and book circulation, one-off volunteers sign up to be part of a group or organization that does "not require a regular commitment for activities which are run at particular times during the year for a short period of time" (Volunteer Now, 2011, para. 2).

Check with the Administration, School District and Union

The school environment can complicate the use of volunteers. Schools need to insure student safety and your district may require background checks, project approval, or other oversight. Before deciding on a project or selecting volunteers, be sure to check with your district and county regulations and restrictions on using volunteers in the school building. Additionally, you'll want to clear any such project with your administration and/or union. Throughout the process, make sure your school administration knows what you're doing, when you're doing it, and who is going to be involved.

This essay focuses on identifying one-off volunteers and designing projects for them to complete in the school library. Your thinking should be on larger projects that you never have time for, but always want to do.

Five Steps to a Completed Volunteer Project

Now that you're finally ready to tackle that major project, you need to consider: What do you want to get done? What is a good project for volunteers? Is your project too ambitious? Will the volunteers feel they are participating in something helpful and worthwhile to your students? We start by defining the project. We then discuss finding your volunteers, scheduling your project, completing the overall project design, and creating the ideal volunteer experience. Following are five relatively simple steps to get that major task permanently off your to-do list.

Step 1: Define Your Project

As in any process, you should start by defining the volunteer project. It's important to have a clear idea of what you're doing when your volunteers arrive, otherwise they either do nothing, or even worse, whatever they want. You don't have to have each step of the project in place, but you must have a big idea. If you have one, we strongly recommend that you consult the students and staff on your library advisory board to help brainstorm ideas and prioritize projects.

Concrete Project Ideas

Moving shelves and furniture: The layout of your library is a mess. Students are constantly running into things, the shelves don't flow, and the tables and chairs are cramped. First determine the best layout for you and your school, make sure you stick to items that can be moved relatively easily, and determine how many volunteers you will need. Steer clear of uprooting built-in shelves and anything requiring more than four people to lift, as it could be too dangerous.

Shifting the collection: Shifting is a major undertaking and difficult to do on your own. With some instructions and each person assigned to a specific section, a squad of volunteers could knock out the task in an afternoon. Be sure to create a solid plan for where everything will go before getting started.

Basic book repair: You don't want to simply buy a new book when one is damaged, but you don't have time to make them "new" again. Give each volunteer a specific repair task and watch the assembly line work.

Redecorating: A little facelift goes a long way toward making the library space more appealing, and the students enjoy it, but it's always such a chore. Create a vision and a plan for the redecorating task. Gather the materials and request that volunteers bring supplies and tools. Then, let them loose to display their creativity.

Other projects for volunteers:

- Crafting templates and pieces for lessons
- Creating and updating websites (for the more tech-savvy volunteers)
- Designing advocacy templates (e.g., newsletters)
- Developing a volunteer manual (for the ambitious small group)

It's important to note some projects aren't appropriate. Don't ask them to do something that takes several days or can't be done without your expertise. They won't have your knowledge for something like cataloging and you certainly shouldn't expect them to create or design lessons.

Step 2: Finding Your Volunteers

Once you have the idea for your project, it's time to find volunteers. You may be thinking, "Shouldn't I finish designing the project first?" You could do that, yes. However, you want to tailor the project to the volunteers with whom you'll be working. Some volunteer groups have particular requirements and before you get down to the nitty-gritty of schedules, tasks, and instructions, it's best to know just who will be helping you with your project.

You don't have to recruit on your own. Many websites dedicated to volunteer work connect organizations with groups or individual volunteers in order to complete a specific project. You go to the website, create a profile and project, and let the recruitment begin. Here are some examples of organizations that will help connect you with volunteers:

- All for Good (allforgood.org)
- Get Involved (getinvolved.gov)
- Idealist (idealist.org)
- deed (indeed.com)
- Volunteer Match (volunteermatch.org)
- Volunteer.gov (volunteer.gov)

Each of these organizations has their own way for you to submit your project proposal to recruit volunteers. View their tutorials to understand exactly how you should design, recruit, and schedule your project for optimal turn-out and completion. We won't go into any further detail on that part of the process, as each website is a little particular and their instructions will provide better guidance. You might also look at the "Guide to Volunteer Opportunities Online" on About.com.

There also may be local organizations similar to these in your area. For instance, in our area of Maryland and Washington, D.C., we can look to Volunteer Maryland (volunteermaryland.org), Single Volunteers of DC (svdc.org), Hands On Greater DC Cares (greaterdccares.org), and Hands on DC (handsondc.org).

Step 3: Scheduling Your Project

Ideally, the entire project should be completed in one session. One-off volunteers are less likely to sign up for a project if they have to be present for more than one day. It might be possible to get different people to come on separate days, but this can be problematic. You will have to train more than one group of people and you increase your chances of no-shows. Whenever you can, stick with one group of people in one session on one day.

The best day of the week for volunteer projects will be on the weekend, with Saturday preferable to Sunday. If your school cannot be open to you on the weekends, consider after school projects on weeknights. Entice your volunteers with food if you're asking them to help after their workday. This is highly recommended and creates happy and agreeable volunteers. Holidays, such as Thanksgiving, Memorial Day, Veteran's Day, and Earth Day, are also ideal and people are often moved to volunteer on these days.

You must clear your scheduling plan with your administration. Your school may have unexpected activities in the evenings and on weekends (I was surprised to find out halfway through my first year that my school was used every Sunday for church!). Make sure the school building will be open and available, and ask if anyone in the administration would consider making an appearance. Volunteers love to work with the individuals running the school and it would be of great benefit to your project.

STEP 4: DESIGNING YOUR PROJECT

You've now nailed down your overall task, the volunteers to be recruited, and when your project will take place. With all these in mind, it's time to finish designing your project. To begin, break your project up into many steps. A few things to remember:

- Understand the limitations of your volunteers. It would be unwise to ask them to do anything too complicated (such as designing a web page) without first knowing their abilities.
- Do not ask of others what you would not do yourself. These volunteers are not your maintenance staff and therefore should not be expected to scrub all your windows (unless your project is a beautification of your library).
- Structure and time each step. Giving people a general task for the entire day may not end well. But if you tell volunteers, "I would like you to move all of these boxes to the marked location on the second floor within the hour, if possible," then that task is far more likely to get completed exactly as you prescribed.
- Don't micro-manage. Once you've given specific instructions to volunteers, let it go. Volunteers will do the best they can and while mistakes will be made, the goal is to get things done, not get things done perfectly. If volunteers need constant supervision, then they probably shouldn't be attempting the task in the first place.

If you create the project with some flexibility built in, it is a great opportunity to let your volunteers show their creativity. Some people will love the chance to show what they can accomplish and how they can help your students. However, don't let a volunteer derail your goals with outlandish changes. Make sure volunteers understand your parameters for the project and the best ways for them to assist you.

STEP 5: CREATING THE IDEAL VOLUNTEER EXPERIENCE

The success of your project is measured by the completion of the project and the volunteer experience. People want to feel as though they contributed to something worthwhile. Though this step takes a little extra effort, it is worth it.

When setting up the project, try to make sure no one has to work alone for too long. Volunteering is a social activity and builds ties within the local community. Some tasks are solo, but set up as much work as possible in pairs or groups. If someone does want to work alone, however, do your best to accommodate their wishes, such as a simple side project.

The most important part of creating the ideal experience for your volunteers is by saying thank you. Say "thank you" before the project begins, throughout the entire event, and in multiple ways after completion. Before the event, a simple e-mail or contact reminder will do. During the event, give your volunteers a verbal shower of compliments. Provide food or refreshments, and if you're working with a large group, you might consider giving away door prizes or gift certificates. It doesn't need to be fancy, just exciting.

After the event is over, the best way to say thank you is to stay in touch with visuals. Perhaps your project has some dramatic before and after photos. Use these to create a small newsletter, online video or slideshow to share with your volunteers. If students are involved, ask them to write a thank you note, expressing their gratitude for the change in the library. If you have another event scheduled, invite your volunteers so they can see their handiwork in action. Also visuals can be shared with administration and community stakeholders. Whatever you do, make sure your volunteers feel as helpful and appreciated as possible.

Conclusion

The big project is done, and you can check that major stressor off your list. But before you put your feet up, lay out a roadmap for future projects. Reflect on and evaluate what worked and did not work during the one-off event. Ask your volunteers what they would do again and what they would change. Based on the feedback you get and your most pressing needs, plan your next major project by simply repeating steps 1 through 5.

The goal of this essay was to position volunteering as a way to reduce stress. Take a deep breath and be proud that you have successfully used many hands to make light work. Your volunteers and you have released built-up anxiety by good old-fashioned manual labor and completing a finite list of tasks within a set amount of time. The school library is a place of change—a constantly evolving information space with new needs surfacing almost every day. Instead of fighting these changes, efficient librarians will address these challenges head on. By making the most of organized volunteer groups, you have created an invested community of stakeholders who understand the mission of the school library, and that may be the biggest accomplishment of all.

References

American Library Association (ALA)/American Association of School Librarians (AASL). *Empowering Learners: Guidelines for School Library Media Programs*. Illinois: ALA Publishing, 2009.

Association for Educational Communications and Technology (AECT), and American Library Association (ALA)/ American Association of School Librarians (AASL). *Information Power: Guidelines for School Library Media Programs*. Illinois: ALA Editions, 1998.

Barack, Lauren. "Are There Any Volunteers? A Pain-Free Approach to Getting the Very Best Out of Parents." *School Library Journal* 56, no. 12 (2010): 40–43.

Dickinson, Gail. "LMC 1-Question Survey: How Do You Use Volunteers in Your Library." *Library Media Connection* (May June 2011). Accessed July 30, 2012. http://www.librarymediaconnection.com/pdf/main/survey_results/1qs_May_June2011.pdf.

Farmer, Lesley. "Teen Library Volunteers." *Public Libraries* 42, no. 3 (2003): 141–142.

Fritz, Joanne. "Should Nonprofits Save Money by Replacing Staff with Volunteers? A Reasonable Recession Tactic or Not?" *About.com: Nonprofit Charitable Orgs Guide*. Last updated 2012. http://nonprofit.about.com/od/volunteers/a/replacestaffvol.htm.

Jacobson, Alan. "Those Who Can, Do. Those Who Can Do More, Volunteer." *American Libraries* 41, no. 5 (2010): 39–41.

McCauley, Elfrieda. "Volunteers? Yes!" *School Library Journal* 22, no. 9 (1976): 29–33.

McHenry, Cheryl A. "Library Volunteers: Recruiting, Motivating, Keeping Them." *School Library Journal* 34, no. 9 (1988): 44–47.

Nicol, Erica, and Corey M. Johnson. "Volunteers in Libraries: Program Structure, Evaluation, and Theoretical Analysis." *Reference & User Services Quarterly* 48, no. 2 (2008): 154–163.

Tikam, Madhuri. "Library Volunteerism Outcomes: What Student Volunteers Expect." *Library Management* 32, no. 8 (2011): 552–564.

Volunteer Now. 2011. Occasional Volunteering: Helping Out from Time to Time. http://www.volunteernow.co.uk/fs/doc/publications/occasional-volunteering-information-sheet-nl.pdf.

VII: Overcoming Challenges

Being an "Only One":
The Sole Minority on Staff

Charlcie K. Pettway Vann

This essay is intended to give suggestions on how any member of an "only one" under-represented group in an academic library can keep his or her "Righteous Mind." In this document, the "only one" under-represented group member is defined as any librarian of color (African American, Asian, Latin, Middle Eastern, Multiracial, Pacific Islander, etc.) in a predominately White academic library. However, a White librarian can be the "only one" employed at a Historically Black College or University (HBCU) or in a predominately Hispanic library or any library he or she is considered a minority and they are the only member of a particular nationality or race represented at their place of employment.

Age can also be added in the "only one" under-represented group. Many librarians who are members of the "Baby Boomers" generation may find their colleagues are younger and she or he may be the "only one" librarian old enough to have marched in the civil right movements of the 1960s and 70s or remember the Vietnam War or The Cold War in their youth. Moreover, being visibly different than your colleagues can be viewed as a badge of honor, a burden of responsibilities or a combination of both. Either viewpoint can generate stress. Stress does not discriminate. People of all ethnicity, nationality, age and gender can experience stress.

According to Webster's Dictionary, the definition of stress is: "physical, mental, or emotional strain or tension" (Webster's Unabridged Dictionary 2001). Experiencing anxiety or being overworked may cause stress. Along with diet, stress is a contributing factor in causing high blood pressure or depression (Encarta Dictionary 2011). Learning techniques to thrive in an environment where no one else looks like you, sounds like you, and/or possibly thinks like you may appear to be simple but when you are in that situation; it can be anything but simple. Those of us employed are thankful for our positions and are in no means complaining about working when so many of our fellow citizens are unemployed or under-employed. Obtaining good mental health will contribute to our physical health as well as healthy library careers.

Current literature concerning "only one" minorities in academic libraries in scholarly journals is extremely low in number. In the 2007 the American Library Association (ALA) compiled and revised information taken from the 2000 U.S. Census concerning the library profession. The ALA along with the Office for Research and Statistics and the Office for Diversity developed a report entitled Diversity Counts. The report includes the percentage of academic librarians by Race/Ethnicity as follows:

- 85 percent of academic librarians are White
- 6 percent of academic librarians are Asian Pacific-Islander
- 5 percent of academic librarians are African American
- 2 percent of academic librarians are Latino
- 1 percent of academic librarians are two or more races
- Academic librarians were slightly more ethnically diverse than their counterparts in public and school libraries, with a representation of 15 percent non-white.

Now we know the reason many of us find ourselves in "only one" situations is because there are not many of us (non-white races/ethnicities) employed in academia or in academic libraries. Job satisfaction and retention are factors which must be addressed to increase the recruitment of underrepresented academic librarians in predominately white colleges and universities (Curry 1994). If you do not feel safe, wanted, or accepted in an environment, you will probably not stay there. If you do stay, you will quickly leave when a better opportunity comes along.

It is questionable if most academe hiring procedures and professional development systems are inclusive to all races and ethnicities although most job announcements, web pages and brochures may state otherwise. The lack of diversity is evidence of that fact. Underrepresented librarians have been commenting and writing about this fact for nearly 40 years or more. Dr. E.J. Josey, a pioneer author of social consciousness of librarianship, academe, and civil rights was one of the first librarians to compile essays about American minorities in librarianship. Josey is the author of more than 400 articles in library, educational and history journals. He has written and edited 12 books in the field of librarianship, including *The Black Librarian in America* in 1972; *New Dimensions for Academic Library Service* in 1975; *Opportunities for Minorities in Librarianship* co-authored with Dr. Kenneth E. Peeples, Jr. in 1977, and *The Black Librarian In American Revisited* in 1994, just to name a few. The main themes in these publications were diversity is beneficial to the library profession, academic libraries, their institutions, and most of all, diversity benefits all librarians. Dr. Josey and his peers spoke about how the profession needs to improve recruitment and retention procedures and that celebrating differences of cultures, races and philosophies helps in the creation of paradigms shifts. In the meantime, "only one" librarians cannot afford to wait for their libraries to have their "ah ha" moments" to decrease or eliminate stress, we must find ways, like the generations before us, to thrive in academic librarianship in spite of the flawed system.

Tips for "Only One" Librarians to Decrease Stress

All librarians are responsible for their own good mental health. Our environment contributes to our mental state. Success can be achieved both because of and in spite of our environments. Although some environments may not be ideal, the atmosphere of self-assurance and peace can be achieved. During my quest to find inner peace as an "only one" African American academic librarian in a predominately white institution in Alabama, I have learned:

1. Be grateful. Give thanks to your supreme power for life. Realize there is a spirit higher than your own. All good things come from a supreme power; I am just a willing vessel.

2. Be honest. Realize that you are like your colleagues and in some ways and that you are different than your colleagues in other ways. Recognize the "Pink Elephant" in the room.

3. Be accepting. Admit your talents and focus on improving them. Accept the "Pink Elephant."

4. Be flexible. Be willing to adjust. Improve your attitude about yourself. Make the necessary changes to decrease negativity in your life. This is an on-going process.

5. Be humble. Recognize you are where you are because someone helped you get there. In return, help someone else achieve their goals.

You may be the "only one" member of an underrepresented group at your academic library but you are not the only one in the world. Join professional organizations and network with others. The famous author Zora Neale Hurston said, "Not all my skin folk is my kin folk." This means people of any race or culture can encourage, care and love you. Anyone who is a positive force should be welcomed to encourage you. Do not discriminate when it comes to supporters. Meaning, campus housekeepers as well as assistant deans can be a part of your supporters. Do not allow a person's economic status hinder you from the encouragement you will need.

An African proverb which states, "Each One Teach One" became prevalent in the United States during slavery, when Africans and African Americans were legally denied many basic rights, including the right to learn to read. Many slaves were kept in a state of ignorance about anything beyond their immediate circumstances. When a slave was fortunate enough to learn to read by a compassionate owner or another kind-hearted slave, it became his/her duty to teach someone else, personifying the phrase "Each one teach one." Passing on wisdom is customary in most cultures. The academic library culture is also a world where wisdom is needed and shared.

Here are a few physical stress relievers for librarians especially if you are the "only one" librarian in your library:

• Walking. Exercise improves your health both mentally and physically.

• Calling or visiting loved ones increases the lines of communication with others and can eliminate the feeling of isolation as an "only one" academic librarian.

• Listening to music. Melodies and tones have a way of mellowing any stressful situation.

- Watching comedy. Humor has saved my sanity and not taking "me" too seriously has been wonderful. Laughing at myself makes situations less harmful and more educational.
- Writing in a journal. If you are unable to find anyone to talk to journaling is a great way to communicate your thoughts.
- Take a long bath. Taking the time for a soothing bath is rare for most of us, yet it is great to help us to relax.
- Read encouraging magazines and books.

Reading or listening to motivational and inspirational books will psychologically prepare any "only one" academic librarian to triumph over challenges. Some inspirational books are the Holy Bible (any version that you find suitable and comprehensive), The Torah, The Qur'an, Talmud, and Tao-te-ching, just to name a few. Learning inspirational scriptures or quotations to recite and meditate on will allow its meaning to get into your mind and spirit. This will inspire your attitude and help develop purpose and clarity of life. Motivational books can also be entertaining and insightful. The best-seller, *In the Meantime,* by Iyanla Vanzant, has many thought provoking sayings which may prompt you to not only analyze your physical environment; but also helps you think about your contribution to your physical as well as mental well-being. Some of Vanzant's quotations from the Website Good Reads are:

> "...We cannot outperform our level of self-esteem. We cannot draw to ourselves more than we think we are worth."

> "Your willingness to look at your darkness is what empowers you to change."

> "One way to eliminate self-negating thoughts and behavior is by gaining more understanding through realizing that you cannot force others to see that what you feel is real."

Humor is also a great tool for relieving stress. None of us are perfect and even the best librarians make mistakes. Unshelved comic stripes by Gene Ambaum and Bill Barnes are witty comedic anecdotes about libraries, librarians and library users. Additionally, the International Federation of Library Associations and Institutions (IFLANET) webpage has a list of funny one-liner library jokes. Also watching comedy TV, internet shows or reading popular journals can be fun. I subscribe to my favorite magazine in print and online so I can always have access even when I am on the go. The magazine focuses on women of color and entertains me as well as informs me on the "news in the street" and cultural fashion.

Good Mental Health and Physical Well Being

Practicing good mental health is crucial to our mental and physical well-being.

Christian counselor, minister, public administrator, mentor, and mother, Patricia Pettway provides steps to practicing good mental health which are:

1. Enthusiastic acknowledgment of your supreme being.

2. Say aloud, "Good morning" and thank your supreme being for life. Where there is life there is hope.
3. Affirmation of self, say aloud, "Good morning, this is a new beginning. I'll be better, kinder, and more understanding to myself."
4. Embrace your support of family, friends, colleagues, spiritual leaders, or pets.

Many academic librarians have the responsibilities of being: a tenure track faculty member, an instruction librarian, an active church/community member, a daughter (a son), a sibling, an attentive spouse, an active and concerned parent. Successfully completing the fore-mentioned responsibilities while being the "only one" member of an under-represented group in your library can be a challenge. Completing professional duties and being a "team player," staying physically and mentally healthy while simultaneously honoring your ethnic and/or cultural identity can be an even bigger challenge.

More literature on under-represented teaching professors at predominantly white institutions has been published than those of academic librarians. In the 1980s and 1990s articles were published in scholarly journals concerning prejudice and discrimination of minority librarians particularly African American women librarians in academic libraries. However, recent research articles dealing with stress and minority librarians are difficult to find. Articles concerning diversity or lack of diversity in academic librarianship have been written, yet stress articles of under-represented academic librarians' articles are minuscule. Is the lack of "only one" academic librarian articles due to the fact that it is not relevant or is it because librarians are just too stressed to write about it? It may be accurate to conclude the latter as true.

In the article, "Your Worries Ain't Like Mine: African American Librarians and the Pervasiveness or Racism, Prejudice and Discrimination in Academe" written by Deborah A. Curry, a compelling description of the "new racism" is given. Curry credits Professors Anthony Platt and Robert Staples as saying racism is not in its old format with white sheets and cross burning, yet it may be stylish and "even sits at a computer" (Platt 1990, 34). Staples explains the new racism is a "pervasive denial of the existence of racism and the non-acceptance of responsibility for it..." (Staples 1984, 2). Curry states many well represented colleagues feel as if under-represented colleagues are "overly sensitive to acts or perceived prejudice and discrimination" (Curry 1994, 301). It is difficult to believe that all of the underrepresented teaching professors and academic librarians are too sensitive and have over analyzed the discriminative atmosphere of their institutions, especially when they are the "only-one" of their race there.

To learn if individuals who are the "only one" in their academic library have experienced stress and if they have, how they deal with stress, I e-mailed this question to the Black Caucus of the American Library Association (BCALA) listserve. Reading the responses from fellow librarians was therapeutic and learning that the subject is relevant was enlightening. In some cultures, discussing stress is often viewed as a sign of weakness. However, in this case, sharing experiences was helpful emotionally as well as professionally. Emotionally, the experiences shared were relatable and professional, providing coping mechanisms opened my mind to creative techniques which could be shared in other "only one" academic professions. The following are inspiring comments given by a the former BCALA president Dr. Sekou Molefi Baako. Dr. Baako is a fellow BCALA member and the Executive Director of Queens Library's Langston Hughes Community Library and Cultural Center in Corona, New York, he advises:

- Believe in yourself above all else.
- Get a mentor who you can bounce ideas and strategy with, who will help you deal with a hostile workplace or when you start to question your own professionalism.
- Never stop learning. Having the MLS or other pedigree does not mean you can't learn new skills and develop new knowledge to do your job better. Attend training sessions, conferences and webinars. Always be willing to grow.
- Don't try to prove how good you are. Let your work speak for itself.
- Join organizations which will give you a sense of family such as Black Caucus or church for a support system.

Robert McClain, educator and minister, once said, "Every member of the body is important. Your difference decides your importance." In turn, every member of a library is important and our differences decide our importance. McClain adds, "Commonalities make us comfortable yet difference create our reward." Recognize differences and do not minimize your difference and contributions. Differences do not make you less than or better than anyone else. Celebrate the differences in yourself and appreciate the differences in others! (McClain, Sunday morning message June 3, 2012.)

References

Acree, Eric Kofi, Sharon K. Epps, Yolanda Gilmore, and Charmaine Henriques. "Using Professional Development as a Retention Tool for Underrepresented Academic Librarians." *Journal of Library Administration*. (2001): 45–62.

Curry, D.A. "Your Worries Ain't Like Mine: African American Librarians and the Pervasiveness or Racism, Prejudice and Discrimination in Academe." *The Reference Librarian*. (1994): 299–311.

Each One Teach One. (2010, April 10). Retrieved February 10, 2012, from Wikipedia: http://en.wikipedia.org/wiki/Each_One_Teach_One.

Gray, Jody. "A Different Approach to Diversity Outreach." *College & Research Libraries News*. (2010): 76–79.

Josey, E.J., ed. *The Black Librarian in America*. Metchuen, NJ: Scarecrow Press, 1994.

Josey, E.J., and Kenneth E. Peeples, Jr. *Opportunities for Minorities*. Metchuen, NJ: Scarecrow Press, 1977.

Office for Research and Statistics Office for Diversity and Office for Diversity. *Diversity Counts*. Statisical Report, American Library Association, 2007.

The Trailing Spouse:
A Portable Career

KIMBERLY SWANSON

Moving is stressful. Moving for your spouse's job is even harder. About twenty years ago, after I moved for my husband's job for the first time, I ran across an article about "trailing spouses" and had a small epiphany. There was a term for my situation! Not only did the situation have a name, experts recognized it as a difficult one. I was not alone, and if you are a trailing spouse or are contemplating becoming one, neither are you.

Social scientists who study family mobility consistently use the word "stress" to describe the emotional impact of moving on a trailing spouse. None of the research on the topic fails to mention it. What can you expect if you trail your spouse? In a word, stress. Researchers note it is not unusual to experience anger, anxiety, resistance, resentment, loneliness, depression, addiction, shame, low self-esteem, loss of identity, and relationship difficulties. Male trailing spouses are especially prone to losing confidence because of the difficulty involved in defying social norms.

Here are the problems in a nutshell:

- You lose your support network of friends and/or family
- You lose your familiar home and community
- You lose your job
- You are at risk of losing your sense of self

We all make life choices that seem sensible, or possible, at a particular place and time. In 1994 I earned a Master's degree in library and information studies at the University of Wisconsin-Madison. Earlier I had earned a Master's degree in American history from the same institution and had worked at a university institute devoted to German-American studies. My aim in going back to school was to launch a career in academic librarianship. While in library school I was lucky enough to obtain a half-time position as assistant to the campus administrator responsible for collection development, a job that gave me terrific experience, an influential mentor, and money to pay my bills. In school I took interesting classes and attended cutting-edge workshops with titles such as, "The World Wide Web: Where Is It? What Is It?" These were the years before Google, before Explorer, before even Netscape. (The workshop was an introduction to Mosaic.) I was 27 years old. My future looked bright.

Then I got married.

I am not knocking marriage. I have been married to the same guy for eighteen years. But marriage involves compromise — as those of you who are married know perfectly well — and in our case I agreed to compromise my career. My husband finished his PhD in the same spring as I finished my library degree, and we immediately embarked upon an adventure that took us, in the course of time, to three new universities in three different states. In each move we prioritized my husband's soaring academic career. I was the trailing spouse. I was the trailing spouse three times.

Some people dislike the term "trailing spouse" and prefer "tied mover" or "relocated partner" or a similar title with greater dignity. I have no objection to the traditional term and will continue to use it. It describes how I felt: Second-class. I use the word spouse broadly and mean to include all committed partners, including gay and lesbian couples, but the research on family mobility does focus more narrowly on heterosexual married people.

Work, Family and Moving

Dual-career couples are a modern phenomenon. Although most people believe American women began working outside the home during the 1970s, women's labor force participation has actually been on the rise for more than a century. The postwar era saw a dip in female employment, but this was an anomaly, a brief reversal of an unstoppable trend. Something new did happen during the 1960s and 1970s, though, and it explains the sheer volume of women who took jobs for pay during those decades and beyond. For the first time in our country's history, large numbers of married women went to work. Even married women with children went to work, an unprecedented shift that changed — and complicated — work life and family life for almost all of us in one way or another (Moe and Shandy 2009).

During the decades in which married women began working, moving for a job also became commonplace. Today nearly one third of long-distance moves are for career advancement, and the people most likely to move are the well-educated and the well paid (Moen and Roehling 2005, 117). Career success depends on many factors, but it is abundantly clear that full-time work, uninterrupted work, and the ability to work long hours all contribute toward it. This helps explain why mothers who scale back their hours or leave the workforce entirely, whether briefly or for many years, are at a disadvantage and unlikely to rise in the professions or in the corporate world. Trailing spouses are at a similar disadvantage because their employment is often irregular and lacks focus (Hardill 2002, 8). Many of us, of course, face a double hurdle: Motherhood and trailing-spouse status.

Trailing spouses have been, and undoubtedly still are, overwhelmingly wives. Librarianship has always been a female-dominated profession except at the highest levels, and for this reason alone we are more likely to trail a spouse at some point in our lives than practitioners of many other fields. Husbands do follow their successful wives, of course, and one hopes this will become more common, but it has not been typical. Researchers who study the economic consequences of family relocation have found that women are less likely to receive offers to move in the first place and are hesitant about taking such offers if it means uprooting their families (Moen and Roehling 2005, 117–118). The research indicates that gender roles play a large part in moving decisions, larger even than financial motives. When a family moves, the husband's salary usually increases and the wife's decreases, the pattern holds true even when the wife has a high earning potential due to education or experience. Among the majority of moving families, the husband's career comes first (McKinnish 2008). In my case as in so many others, my husband's career demanded geographic mobility, especially in the early years, and we assumed each time we moved I would be able to find some kind of work in our new home.

Trailing spouses may very well have no job lined up upon arrival. Once settled, they often take jobs for which they are overqualified, accepting a lower salary or lower prestige or both. Some trailers choose to start on the lowest rung of their fields again. Others change careers or stop working altogether to raise children (Bayes 2010, 284). "I started at the top," explained Virginia Nordin, a Harvard Law graduate and trailing spouse who spoke to the Wall Street Journal (July 20, 1993), "and worked my way to the bottom." Men who follow their wives, on the other hand, are more likely to receive help and to find comparable work in their new homes. This may be because female breadwinners are more likely to resist moving unless the entire family benefits (Moen and Roehling 2005, 120). My own experience has not been unusual: All of my library jobs, seven in total, have been entry-level despite nearly twenty years as a working librarian. Most of my jobs were term appointments, and several were part-time.

It is normal, statistically speaking, for the wife to follow the husband. It is or will be normal for you, the trailer, to derail your career to some degree. It is also normal to feel resentful sooner or later. "What about me?" you might ask.

A fictional character in a short story by Jessica Francis Kane feels typically unmoored:

> In the mornings, watching Nick dress for work, she admired his energy, the verve of the primary spouse. The leading spouse? She had asked the professionals, but they said there was no term. While he left every day at eight o'clock, it was all Tessa could do to put on her hat. She had nowhere to go, no one knew where she was, no one anywhere in London was expecting her (140).

Here Is My Advice in Five Points

1. Think It Through Before You Move

You do not have to go. More specifically, divorce is not the only alternative. If you simply cannot stomach the proposed move, consider asking your spouse to decline the job offer.

Would you be willing to live apart temporarily, permanently, or part-time? A commuter relationship may not be ideal, but plenty of couples have made this choice, even families with children.

Would telecommuting work in your situation? After our third move I did part-time consulting work for JSTOR, the scholarly digital archive and my former full-time employer, from a home office for a year. JSTOR sent me boxes of journals to evaluate via Federal Express, and I mailed them back. I submitted my work and conducted all correspondence via e-mail. A great deal of library work cannot be done from a distance, of course, but perhaps you do the kind of work that can.

If you decide to go, be honest with yourself and your spouse about how you feel during and after the move. Some trailers want to meet family and social expectations— or their own expectations— and feel surprised, or even ashamed, when the transition is not easy. Trailers may hesitate to complain to their spouses after moving for fear of alienating the only person they have left. At the same time, it is very important to acknowledge and accept that you made the decision to move. Your spouse cannot and did not, force you to go.

It might be helpful to make a deal with your spouse that the next move will benefit you, if not your career, then in another way you find meaningful.

2. Ask Your Spouse's Hiring Institution or Company for Help

Many organizations have policies related to dual-career couples. If you are not married, ask whether unmarried domestic partners, including same-sex couples, are included in these policies. Even if no formal policy exists, the organization may be willing to help.

Corporations offering to relocate employees on a regular basis are the most proactive in helping dual-career couples to manage. They do this because employees in these relationships frequently resist assignment to a new geographical location. Don't expect the company to offer a second job outright. Opportunities to apply for in-house positions may be available, but companies often help by offering leads and arranging contacts.

Colleges and universities recognize that helping dual-career couples is important to recruitment and retention. Even in the absence of a formal policy, more than a quarter of academic institutions without policies say they will help if asked. The institution will be more inclined to help if your spouse is a faculty member, especially a faculty member who is a person of color, a full professor, or a woman. From the institutional perspective, these recruits are worth extra effort. The institution will be more inclined to help at the initial hire, so ask your spouse to negotiate on your behalf immediately after he or she receives an offer. Colleges and universities usually provide help in the form of contacts within the institution or outside it. If you are very lucky, they may offer a non-tenure-track job such as an adjunct or administrative position (Wolf-Wendel, Twombly and Rice 2004, 16–46).

3. Use Your Research Skills to Find Work and Make a Life for Yourself

As a librarian, you have an advantage over other trailing spouses: You know how to find information. Put your skills to work for yourself! Investigate employment opportunities. Find groups of people who share your hobbies and interests.

After our first move I sat down with the American Library Directory and systematically called every local library to inquire about job opportunities. In this way I learned about a part-time cataloging position that had not been advertised. I was the single interviewee, received an offer quickly, and soon began work in my first professional-level position. I was friendly in the interview and had relevant qualifications, but most significantly I was in the right place at the right time.

You can use your skills in a similar way to settle yourself into the new community whether you seek a new babysitter, a good restaurant, or a few book-club buddies. Look online, read the newspapers, and ask the people you encounter for advice, including the local librarians. Use your creative thinking — the kind of thinking you use to solve puzzles and problems at the reference desk — to make yourself at home.

4. Be Flexible If You Want to Continue Working as a Librarian

It is very difficult, if not impossible, to maintain a consistent and upward career arc if you move frequently. Your experience may prove to be different, but I have found it helpful to be open to any and all kinds of library work in pursuit of employment. I have worked as a cataloger at a private graduate school; in public services for an undergraduate library at a major research university; and in production for a nonprofit digital archive. Most recently, I was the interim (adjunct) liaison to six social science departments at a medium-sized university library.

You may feel medical librarianship is your calling — or perhaps it is music cataloging or children's literature or digital preservation. If you stay in one place long enough you may be able to work yourself into a position that really suits you, but I would caution against choosiness when you first arrive in town. Take the work that is available, make contacts, get references, and enjoy the opportunity to stretch yourself and learn something new. An eclectic career may appear less successful from the outside than a meteoric rise to the director's office — you will earn less money and enjoy less prestige for certain — but a career that zigzags offers real, though less obvious, rewards. The trail you forge will be interesting and will not grow dull. Working in different jobs and types of institutions will help you develop diverse, marketable skills. In addition, your broad experience will give you an understanding of libraries and librarianship that is a form of wisdom in its own right.

5. Be Hopeful and Curious

I know very well this advice is easy to dispense and at times difficult to follow. However, a positive attitude really can go a long way toward helping you to adjust and to adapt. If you have made the decision to follow your spouse, try to view the move as an adventure. How can you get something out of it that you want? How can you make it a fun experience, or at a minimum not a miserable one? I have lived in four college towns during the course of my marriage and library career. Although you might consider this experience to be somewhat lacking in diversity, each place has been truly unique and delightful in its own way. Political activism! Fantastic weather! Rich culture! Stunning mountains! Many people love their hometowns and would never move, but I have found living in a variety of places to be both enjoyable and eye-opening.

One mobility researcher I read cited his father's nugget of wisdom: "You should not confuse your career with your life," (Harvey, Novicevic and Breland 2009). Personally, I find this sentiment irritating. Doesn't it seem self-serving coming from a male author when women have made most of the sacrifices in family relocations? On the other hand, it is hard to deny its inherent truth.

Summary of Suggestions for Trailing Spouses

- Explore your options before becoming a trailer
- Get assistance in job hunting and relocating from your spouse's employer
- Do what you do best, seek information. Investigate jobs, hobbies, and activities to build a new life for yourself
- Be flexible and respectful and make professional contacts to find work
- Find a way to make the move feel like an adventure

I admit readily I have not had the career I intended when I completed my own library degree, and I still experience the occasional twinge of regret. Nonetheless, my disappointment is balanced by the fact that I have met many wonderful people, worked for some very creative organizations, and gained countless skills through the course of a disjointed career. Who knows what the future will bring? Maybe I will try something entirely new. My advice boils down to this: Enjoy the journey. It may sound trite, but work and personal life can't be controlled fully. Make peace with your decisions, do your best, and be kind to all people.

References

Hardill, Irene. Gender, Migration and the Dual Career Household. London: Routledge, 2002.
Harvey, Michael, Milorad Novicevic, and Jacob W. Breland. "Global Dual-Career Exploration and the Role of Hope and Curiosity During the Process." Journal of Managerial Psychology 24 (2009): 178–197. http://dx.doi.org/10.1108/02683940910928874.
Kane, Jessica Francis. Bending Heaven: Stories. Washington, DC: Counterpoint, 2002.
McKinnish, Terra. "Spousal Mobility and Earnings." Demography 45 (2008): 829–849. http://www.jstor.org/stable/25651478.
Moe, Karine, and Dianna Shandy. Glass Ceilings and 100-Hour Couples: What the Opt-Out Phenomenon Can Teach Us About Work and Family. Georgia: University of Georgia Press, 2009.
Moen, Phyllis, and Patricia Roehling. The Career Mystique: Cracks in the American Dream. Maryland: Rowman & Littlefield, 2005.
Wolf-Wendel, Lisa, Susan B. Twombly, and Suzanne Rice. Two-Body Problem: Dual-Career-Couple Hiring Practices in Higher Education. Maryland: Johns Hopkins University Press, 2004.

So You've Been Laid Off, Now What?

Lara Frater

Imagine you are hard at work when the library director walks by the reference desk and tells you to meet her in her office immediately. You wonder what is going on. You tell her you would have to leave the reference desk, but it doesn't faze her. However it is your boss, so you go.

When you arrive, you are disturbed to find that Mr. Deals of Human Resources is also there. You know Mr. Deals, because every time he visits the library you lose another staff member. Mr. Deals isn't a librarian. He knows nothing about library science and thinks Google offers everything for free. Mr. Deals doesn't say anything and your boss tells you to sit. You do, but your heart is pounding. You know exactly why Mr. Deals is here, but you can't admit it until one of them actually says something.

"I'm very sorry," your boss says as your heart sinks in your chest. "It has not been a good year financially. I'm afraid we have to let you go. We are very sorry. You do a very good job but…"

You aren't hearing what she is saying. A million thoughts are now going through your head. Your thoughts can be anything: "How could they lay me off?" "I've worked really hard," "Why can't they lay off someone else?" "How can I get another job?" "How will I pay my rent?" You can become angry, sad, numb or confused. These are all normal emotions to feel when you've been let go.

They ask if you have any questions, you may have some or not. Or, perhaps the only questions you can think of are R rated. You may want to leave without a word and go home. You may want to scream and yell they are making a big mistake and that your boss is terrible and Mr. Deals is Satan.

I have gone through two layoffs in my 16 year library career. Neither layoff had to do with job performance since I have a collection of performance evaluations calling me outstanding. Both times the reasons they claimed were financial.

So what do you do now? The job market is so bad even burger flippers have trouble finding work. You think of horror stories of other librarian friends. The ones who have been laid off for a year or those right out of library school who have been searching for a librarian position or anything only to come up empty. Congratulations you are now one of them. As I am writing this, I am also one of you.

The Grieving

Losing a job is almost as stressful as death and you can go through a grieving process, especially if it is a job you loved. Chances are you have gone through one or all of these stages. It's natural and normal. Following are the stages and emotions you might go through:

- Denial — You are told you are laid off but know the library will fall apart without you. You think this is a scare tactic to get some administrator to cough up more money and soon you will happily have your job back.
- Anger — What the hell do they think they are doing getting rid of me? The library will collapse without me! They really think Google can do everything?
- Bargaining — Maybe if they get rid of this person, I can keep my job. Maybe they can find money. Maybe they can keep me on a little bit longer so I have more time to find another job.
- Depression — Why do they hate me? Did I do something wrong? I'm the one who lost this job. I should have worked harder.
- Acceptance — My job is over, but my career isn't. I have to move on and find a new position.

Can you save your job?

I don't want to tell you not to fight. You should, as hard and heavy as you can. Don't go down without a fight. There is nothing wrong about telling your employees in a non-hostile manner how foolish this decision is, nor is there anything wrong with talking to HR, labor relations, your union if you have one, or a lawyer. However, I can tell you by experience saving your job is highly unlikely. I had a job with union representation, researchers who sent letters to the administrators to reinstate me, and even one letter from a politician, but my employer refused to budge.

However, successful campaigns have been waged not only to save libraries but librarians. For example in 2007, the Environmental Protection Agency (EPA) began closing some regional libraries and planned to close more. This plan included laying off librarians and support staff (unfortunately librarians at EPA libraries are contracted out so they have no federal protection against layoffs). When the Government Accountability Office heard about this, they investigated and found significant problems with the closings. Fortunately, most of the libraries remained open and librarians kept their positions (Keiser 2008). The Barr library in Minnesota that was supposed to close in October 2010 is still open (Anonymous 2010). However these are rare occurrences. You can try talking to other staff members or other librarians to see if something can be done. Let your patrons know what happened.

Should You Contact a Lawyer?

Especially if you think you have been discriminated against and if you're willing to shell out $200 or more for a consultation with a labor lawyer, it can't hurt to see if you have any legal options. However even if the lawyer thinks you have a case, it may be years before it's settled and may cost more than it's worth. You might not get your job back and at best you might get back salary. Remember this, if you do manage to win your job back, how much longer would you be willing to stay?

Breathing Room and Resisting the Urge to Sabotage

If your employer has given you advanced notice, you have some breathing room to look for another job. Employers don't expect laid off employees to work at peak efficiency. Use this extra time to search for jobs and work on your resume. I don't suggest submitting applications at work and make everything discreet. And remember to breathe. Take a deep breath and hold it for seven seconds, then release.

Professional or not, getting laid off may result in the desire to sabotage the job. Change passwords, delete important documents, steal the pencil sharpener, and write inappropriate messages on the bathroom wall are a few ways to get even. This sabotage might make you feel better briefly, but not in the long run. It won't help you let go of your anger. Also, you don't want to alienate your library co-workers or director. Believe it or not, you leaving makes them feel guilty not only for still having their job but your absence will increase their workload. You don't want to burn bridges. You'll never know when you'll need them in the future.

This Isn't Your Fault

When some people are laid off they can react outwards, inwards or both. Some people blame the higher ups, while others blame themselves or go back and forth between the two. It's normal to have these feelings and to blame yourself. Librarians get it the worst because we are an undervalued and overworked field. Also, it is a field for introverts. I once read a post in a library forum where a person (an actual librarian) accused librarians for their own job losses for not speaking up. He was wrong. This isn't your fault. According to *Reader's Digest*, a 2010 poll found that 39 percent of mayors wanted to reduce or close libraries to save money (Kavner 2010). One of the places where I worked, the people in charge of funds had no clue how the library worked and didn't care to know. Any public service positions such as schools, libraries, parks, firefighters or police are usually the main target when times are bad. Simply put, it is because we are a public service rather than a money maker so when revenues are not coming in, then we get the cuts. Maureen Sullivan, president-elect of the American Library Association (ALA) said: "People don't realize how essential their local public library is until it's too late. When it comes to making budget decisions—'Should we cut funds from the police department or the library?'— local lawmakers are putting the library at the bottom of the totem pole, and state governments are not stepping in to save them." (Kavner 2011)

Many of those who decide layoffs may not have any idea how much a librarian does and think it's an easy cut. A Pew Center Trust study discovered library usage is up, but so are library layoffs. For example in Phoenix, despite a 2 percent increase in visits and a 13 percent increase in circulation, hours were cut by 37 percent and full time staff was cut by 25 percent. (PEW 2012). Cuts like this are across the board in cities such as Charlotte, Los Angeles, Chicago, and New York. NEVER blame yourself in a layoff. Both my layoffs occurred in recessions. Don't worry about the people who made the decision, they look at dollar signs not service. Remember the people you have helped over the years for they are the ones who will feel your absence.

Therapy as a Resource

For weeks after I lost one job that I felt highly invested in, I felt depressed, angry, numb, and humiliated. Not only was I out of a job, but I was taken away from a collection I helped build. Feeling numb is normal as well; your mind is calming itself. I found some days, life was tolerable, other days I felt like everything was out of control. If you find yourself not improving, please talk to a therapist. I did and she helped me through my layoff. As I write this, I am now 10 weeks out of a job that I had for 7 years. I still have bouts of anger, depression, and numbness. It does get better and I feel I can soon let go and move on.

Okay, Now How Do I Get Another Job?

You may find that being stressed over feelings from losing your job may even effect your motivation for finding a new one. Here are some tips and suggestions to *motivate* yourself:

1. Start your job search immediately. Don't wait or decide to take time off. The job market is bad and you may discover it is months before you find something. That's a lot of time to be off.
2. Apply for unemployment as soon as you can.
3. Prepare for the interview even if you don't have one. Get a haircut, get a manicure, and buy new interview clothes. Ask your friends for tips to look your best. Think about what questions you want to ask at an interview and how to best represent your skills.
4. Pretty up the resume. Ask other librarian friends to look it over and give you some tips.
5. Stick to a daily routine. Most jobs are 9–5; try to stick to something like that. It's easy to fall into staying up late, but keeping a schedule will keep up the routine of job searching in the morning. You want those resumes out ASAP. When you get a job, it will be easier to transition into it.
6. Check job listings every morning. Some places you can find job listings are with library associations such as the American Library Association, Special Library Asso-

ciation, Medical Library Association and Association of College and Research Libraries (ACRL). The online resource, I Need a Library Job (INALJ), is available as a newsletter and via LinkedIn group. Search online for library headhunters. If you see something you like, immediately prepare your cover letter and resume and send it. Don't procrastinate. Even if you aren't sure the job will fit, worry about that later. If it doesn't work out, at least you'll have some interview practice. Sometimes you might interview for a job and not get it, but you might get a call back for a different position.

7. Enjoy your time off. Once you get a job you won't have as much free time, so use it wisely. Do activities such as joining a gym, work on projects you put off, organize the house, go to the park, spend time with the kids, friends and relatives, or see a movie.

8. Network, network, network. Even if no one if offering jobs, make sure they remember your name and that you're looking for work. There are plenty of articles out there to help you learn networking even it if it isn't your thing. (Check out I need a Library Job (INALJ) for several good articles on networking).

9. Be willing to relocate. If you can relocate, look into it. There might be a fabulous job for you in another state.

What Happens When the Job Market Is Bad?

I'm not going to sugar coat this. The job market is horrendous right now. The first time I dealt with a layoff, I had 6 weeks' notice and had a new job lined up before the six weeks were up. The second time around I got four weeks' notice and by the time the four weeks were up, I only applied to one job (To be honest I was more choosy than the last time but I am seeing less jobs posted.)

Don't get discouraged when no one calls back right away. Late call backs are common. Many libraries are being inundated with resumes; they have to sort through resumes to find ones suited for the position. If you know someone at the library be sure to let them know you applied. It might not get you the job but it might get your resume out of the sorting pile. Don't wait on a job, even if it's your dream one, continue to apply.

So let's say you've been looking for a new job and have gone on a few interviews. Even though you are good, do all the right things (ask questions, thank everyone, write thank you notes).With so many applicants, there is always someone better or who meshes better with the staff. If you have gone on interviews, you know which ones you have done well on. When I was first looking for a job out of library school, I went on an interview where after 20 minutes I realized I was way over my head. However for all you are doing you have not yet gotten a job. Here are some tips to keep up your resume, help network and help find work until you finally land a position.

- Volunteer at a library. This will help fill gaps in your resume. For example I knew someone looking for a job who volunteered to work on his church's archives and newsletter, allowing him to put it on his resume. Volunteering gets your name out there and that you are looking for work. If a job happens to open up where you are volunteering, then you'll have a much better shot at it. Most libraries love to have volunteers.

- Volunteer for library organizations. Look up local chapters of organizations that represent library work you are interested in. It is another experience you can put on a resume to make it look more fabulous. Plus you get to network with librarians in your area and you might hear about job openings.
- Stay friendly with former colleagues at previous jobs. You never know when a job may open up or they have a friend who knows a friend, who knows about a job. Even if it only gets your resume to the top of the pile.
- Be willing to do temp or work at a non-librarian job. For instance, take a civil service test in another field. I had a civil service position and when I was laid off at one job, I got another job in the same system with the same benefits—just not a library job. While I took a pay cut, at least I had something.
- Be willing to take a job different from librarianship but something you are qualified to do. For example: researcher, organizer, fundraiser, grant writer, website designer, or customer service. If you have done any of these during your career, you can transfer your skills to another position.
- Keep up with library and technology trends for the field you are interested in, even do side projects on the web. Submit to library journals. Again this helps to fill the gaps in your resume and spruces it up.
- Social network: join library related groups on Facebook and LinkedIn. Some terrific ones are libraries need librarians (a good place to get support after your layoff) and I Need a Library Job (INALJ).
- Go back to school. If you are a seasoned librarian, it might be a good idea to go back to school to enhance and catch up on current library skills (Many library schools offer advanced certificates). More librarian jobs require web based skills. Learn XML, PHP, CSS, Access, SQL and how to use social networks. Libraries are moving to virtual reference and social networking and want librarians to know the technology for upkeep. Much as we grumble about eBooks and online journals, they are the wave of the future and librarians will be the ones to make them easy to navigate.

Whatever happens, try not to be discouraged. I know the market is bad now but something will come along. It might take some time but it will happen. Keep a routine and updated resume at the ready. Use your skills which come naturally to a librarian when networking, online searching, and job hunting. Recessions eventually end and jobs come back.

References

Anonymous. "MAPE News for September, 2010: Barr Library: budget ax closes this important Resource." *MAPE News* 1, no. 9 (2010). Accessed July 27, 2012. http://www.mape.org/news/mape-news-sept-2010-barr-library-budget-ax-closes-important-resource.

Ellen Keiley. "How to Network Well: It's Not All About You." Boston.com. (January 23, 2012). Accessed May 25, 2012. http://www.boston.com/business/blogs/global-business-hub/2012/01/how_to_network.html.

Ellen Mehling. "Networking Tips for the Reluctant Networker." INALJ (May 10, 2012). Accessed July 27, 2012. http://inalj.com/?p=2864

Kavner, Lucus. "Library Budget Cuts Threaten Community Services Across Country." *Huffington Post.* (November 16, 2011). Accessed July 27, 2012. http://www.huffingtonpost.com/2011/11/16/can-the-american-library-_n_1096484.html.

Keiser. Barbie E. "EPA Library Closures: Management Incompetence or Something More Sinister?" Information Today INC., NewsBreaks. (March 17, 2008). Accessed July 27, 2012. http://newsbreaks.infotoday.com/NewsBreaks/EPA-Library-Closures-Management-Incompetence-or-Something-More-Sinister-41260.asp.

Pew Charitable Trust. "The Library in the City: Changing Demands and a Challenging Future." (March 7, 2012). Accessed July 27, 2012. http://www.pewtrusts.org/our_work_report_detail.aspx?id=85899373217.

The Over-Underemployed Librarian: The Full-Time Stress of Multiple Part-Time Jobs

Zara T. Wilkinson

In the current economic climate of slashed budgets and dwindling resources, more and more recent LIS grads are unable to find full-time jobs and are having to settle for one or more part-time positions. According to *Library Journal*'s 2011 Placements & Salaries Survey, 25 percent of all jobs reported by 2010 library school graduates were part-time positions. In 2007, only 16.3 percent of graduates reported taking part-time positions. That number rose to 22.8 percent in 2009, revealing a sharp, steady increase (Maata 2011). When applying for very few entry-level positions, newly-minted librarians have to compete with more experienced librarians who are out of work. As a result, they may have to resort to working part-time in order to keep themselves afloat in a difficult job market, as well as to build a resume impressive enough to land that much-desired, first full-time librarian position.

Part-time employment does offer some benefits to librarians, especially new librarians. Working part-time may provide a librarian with the chance to get very specialized experience. In many cases, a part-time reference librarian spends far more hours each week on the reference desk than would a full-time reference librarian, whose workload may include instruction, collection development, programming, liaison duties, and research in addition to any variety of other duties. Therefore, while part-time librarians are often not able to develop as many different competencies as their full-time counterparts, they can acquire experience and invest a lot of time into one specific area. In this respect, part-time work can be useful for developing new skills or for exploring new areas of librarianship and may be a good option for a new librarian who had no or little library experience before attending graduate school. Exposure to multiple libraries and management styles, along with the opportunity to meet and work with many different professionals in the field, can be very beneficial to a librarian who is in the job market and looking to improve his or her professional network. In addition, part-time employment offers a librarian a great deal of flexibility and makes it possible to schedule working hours around other commitments, such as family care or non-library employment.

Despite the potential benefits, working part-time positions for extended periods of time can be immensely stressful — especially if you have more than one. Certainly some librarians are happy with a part-time job that represents a fairly small time commitment from week to week, while some librarians may be taking on a part-time position in addition to full-time work. However, numerous librarians are getting by with *only* part-time work, cobbling together multiple jobs into a pale approximation of a full-time position. Of the new librarians who told *Library Journal* they were working part-time library jobs, 32.9 percent had more than one part-time position (Maata 2011). These part-time librarians juggle two, three, or four positions at different libraries or wear multiple hats at the same library. They commute long distances and work long hours including evenings, late nights, weekends, and holidays. They work on their own, sometimes with a great deal of responsibility, and may be left in charge of whole departments or libraries when full-time staff has gone home. They settle for lower salaries than their full-time counterparts and receive few or no benefits — no sick days, vacation days, or health insurance.

For those librarians who find themselves with multiple jobs for the short or long-term, and for those who see the possibility looming in the future, this essay represents practical advice from someone who has been in the same situation.

The Schedule, or "I'll Have to Pencil You In"

I'd like to start with scheduling, which can seem basic but in fact represents the hardest part of juggling multiple part-time jobs. Part-time positions tend to require hours that full-time 9–5 staff do not or cannot work — those hours are evenings and weekends. A person with multiple employers may find each employer wants them to work the same basic schedule. Most people are not fortunate enough to have one daytime, evening, and weekend job — all clearly delineated and pre-determined. As a result, scheduling is often a non-stop game of keeping track of when and where you are supposed to work *now*, but also figuring out when and where you can work at a given point in the future.

Knowing where you need to be and when you need to be there is by far the most pressing concern when you work at multiple libraries. It can be the most difficult to keep track of, especially if your schedule changes from day to day and week to week. Anyone working multiple part-time positions needs to determine very early on what kind of scheduling system will be the most helpful for them. Some people might prefer a paper calendar or a day planner, something solid they can carry in a bag or hung on a wall. Others might prefer the calendar function on an iPod or Smartphone, secure in the knowledge they are able to carry their schedule with them at all times. Any of these could work well. Personally, I have come to rely on my Google calendar which I can access from any Internet-connected device. My calendar is incremented by hour and color-coded by workplace: dark blue, light blue, and purple for each of my three workplaces and green for the rare times when I can manage a personal appointment or non-work social event. The goal is to have an up-to-date copy of your work schedule available at any moment. Immediate access proves absolutely invaluable when agreeing to work extra hours, planning a get-together with friends and family, or simply remembering where to be and when to arrive.

A part-time librarian must be able and willing to share her schedule with each of her supervisors. Recently an acquaintance expressed surprise that I had three separate employers. He then commented my employment situation was "like dating three people" and asked if they each knew about the others. They do, of course, and I could not imagine trying to schedule my hours while keeping the reason for my limited availability a secret. People who have full-time jobs may be hesitant to reveal to their employers they are looking for work to supplement or replace their current job. For those struggling to balance multiple positions such transparency is not only recommended but, in my opinion, downright necessary.

Part-time librarians need to be able to communicate their schedules with all of their employers and should take extra care to keep everyone updated regarding availability and schedule changes. Keeping track of multiple part-time positions is hard enough for the person working them. Supervisors cannot and should not be expected to remember an employee's schedule at another library. Communication and transparency is vital. You still won't be able to say yes to everyone, and you still won't have the ability to be two places at once, but an informed supervisor will be better able to work with you to find a schedule suitable to everyone. You can accomplish two goals with clear statements such as "I can't work at X time because I am already committed elsewhere, but I can start at Y time." Most importantly, you will be able to schedule shifts that do not conflict with other jobs. At the same time, you will demonstrate to your supervisor that you are a dutiful employee who would give the same respect to *their* scheduling needs if the positions were reversed.

Survival 101: "Can I Have That to Go?"

Even a librarian with impeccable organization and time management skills would find the busy, on-the-go lifestyle of the over-underemployed challenging. When working an unusual and variable schedule, sometimes it's hardest to keep track of the basics. For example, part-time librarians often do not have scheduled meal breaks. If a librarian is combining short shifts at multiple libraries, she may find she is not eligible for paid or unpaid breaks at any of them. I was in such a situation for several months, and I learned to restructure my meals to accommodate my schedule (since I didn't have the option of restructuring my schedule to accommodate mealtimes). A combination of at-home breakfasts and packed lunches and snacks was the answer for me, even if I had to eat my packed meals on the subway or in my office in the few minutes before my shift started. A good rule of thumb is to always carry food, even if you have other plans for lunch that day. The unpredictable nature of part-time schedules means you might be asked to stay late at one job or come in early at another. Ideally, every part-time employee should carry such basic items as non-perishable food, water, an umbrella, a sweater, and extra cash. Circumstances aren't always ideal, of course, but if you can manage to have even a few of those items on hand, do.

On any given day, a part-timer's schedule can include seemingly unending stretches on the reference desk, large gaps between shifts at different libraries, not large *enough* gaps between shifts at different libraries, and long commutes to, from, and between jobs. Part-time librarians, like adjunct professors, often piece together an income from as many different sources as possible, and these different workplaces are not typically very close to one another. Working a forty or forty-plus hour week sounds fairly usual, and so does a daily commute, but adding a commute between jobs can result in transit representing a significant percentage of a part-time employee's time. For example, you may have a half an hour commute to one library, a forty-five minute commute from that library to the other where you also work, and then a forty-five minute commute home. Depending on how many days a week you work, you would be spending between ten and fourteen hours a week in the car or on public transportation. For some people, two hours a day is a rather conservative estimate. On an average day, I travel an hour to get to my first job and work three hours at the reference desk. I then take public transportation to a second library. That trip, including time spent waiting for the subway, takes approximately an hour. I have one free hour before I am scheduled to work, then spend another four hours at the reference desk. When I'm finished, I travel an hour home. As a result, my transit time (plus unscheduled time) is sometimes equal to or more than half of the time I spend on the clock on a given day.

Such a commute can be expensive and exhausting. However, a smart commuter can learn to use her transit time wisely. Time spent driving or taking public transportation can be an oasis in an otherwise busy day, rather than yet another source of stress. The commute becomes a time to breathe, be out of the public eye, relax and recharge. Those who drive can listen to a favorite radio station, create playlists of energetic music, or "read" an audiobook — perhaps even one checked out from the library. Those who take public transportation have a little more freedom; music and audiobooks are still an option, but so are paperbacks, phone calls, power naps (sometimes inevitable, but not recommended), snacks, and staring out of the window and watching the trees go by. Some part-time librarians will find their schedules don't align perfectly and will, as a result, have time "left over" after their commutes. Time between jobs doesn't have to be time wasted and can instead be thought of as a scheduled mid-day break. For example, taking a walk in nice weather or finding somewhere to sit and eat a packed lunch can be a welcome change in one's daily routine.

Saying No: "I Wish I Could, But..."

Part-time librarians, particularly those who are over-scheduled, also need to be careful not to take on too many hours or responsibilities. The kind of experience sought by hiring managers is not always readily obtainable for part-time employees, specifically those who work during off-hours. Therefore, any additional tasks, projects, or hours can represent a chance for part-time librarians to develop or learn new skills. More work may require more hours, which in turn guarantees a bigger paycheck.

Librarians are helpful people, and part-time librarians are even more so, particularly when every "yes" adds a much-needed and appreciated line to a resume or a few dollars to a pay stub. Despite the appeal of professional development and the allure of being the employee giving 110 percent, an already overworked or over-scheduled librarian may be better off declining a new project or additional hours. Sometimes it makes more sense for a full-time librarian, someone who is already at the library, to teach a class or take an extra hour on the desk, rather than having a part-time librarian come in early or on a day when they were not otherwise scheduled. As with any scheduling concerns, such decisions should be made with complete transparency and as a consensus between the part-time librarian and the supervisor.

A manager or supervisor may not consider that part-time employees may have only a few hours a week at one institution, but have more hours or taxing responsibilities at another workplace. The employee is therefore responsible for making clear what "extras" a supervisor can and cannot expect. This does not mean an employee should always expect to dictate his/her schedule, or that the librarian should not make an effort to accommodate extra requests. A part-time librarian should always work their regularly scheduled hours and complete regular duties to the best of his/her ability. However, you should also take care when agreeing to any additional work. You do not want to jeopardize your physical or mental health or your ability to complete your regular duties at another workplace. Working multiple jobs at multiple workplaces already makes a part-time librarian more likely than full-time counterparts to experience burnout. Taking on extra duties or working more than a normal full-time workweek on a regular basis increases the chances of becoming overwhelmed. A part-time librarian, whose position may provide no insurance for medical or psychiatric services as well as no time off, must take extra care not to add to the strain already being placed upon them.

Juggling Acts: "I Have the Name of This Library Written on My Hand."

Having multiple jobs can leave you feeling like you are being pulled in many directions at once. A lot of the stress of over-employment is due to the time commitment involved, but switching between workplaces with different duties and cultures is also mentally and emotionally taxing. Workplace responsibilities and stresses can bleed into other, unrelated jobs, especially if one position is more difficult than another or you are already feeling tired or stressed.

Some part-time librarians may benefit from compartmentalizing, or keeping their workplace identities as separate as possible. We live in an electronic world, which is always on and connected, but being "plugged in" can be detrimental to people who are trying to juggle multiple jobs. A librarian should be 100 percent mentally present at the library where she is physically present. That may require not checking e-mail for another job while at work and not logging into staff wikis or calendars from another workplace. Not doing other kinds of library work can also help keep you from getting distracted or from having to quickly switch gears. For example, a librarian who is cataloging at the reference desk or answering e-mail reference questions at the circulation desk may find it startling when a patron asks a question or wants to check out a book. Some part-time librarians work multiple part-time positions at the same library, which can make compartmentalizing very challenging. Sometimes duties will overlap, and sometimes part-time employees are expected to wear all of their hats simultaneously. In these instances, part-time librarians may still find it helpful to impose their own restrictions and to attempt to do certain types of work only in certain contexts.

Communication: "How Am I Doing?"

Working multiple part-time jobs, while stressful, can be a great opportunity, particularly for a newly minted librarian. As previously mentioned, part-time employment is a way to get experience, network, and find mentors. However, these benefits are not always readily apparent, and they certainly do not always come easily. Part-time librarians do not always have access to a workplace support system or to professional development opportunities. They have to work harder to get the same experiences and opportunities afforded to full-time staff, and they have to work harder to stay in touch with colleagues and supervisors they may see rarely or not at all.

Librarians working the traditional evening and weekend part-time schedule may feel (or are) left out of the day-to-day operations of the library. Because part-time employees work off-hours or have unpredictable schedules, they often do not have the opportunity to participate in staff and departmental activities or meetings. They may feel their concerns are not being heard or their input is not needed or appreciated. Ideally a part-time librarian should interact regularly with full-time library staff, whether in person or via e-mail, with the goal of remaining in touch with the rest of the department, keeping up with ongoing issues, and staying informed about impending policy changes. In person is best, but electronic communication is a wonderful tool for the modern day off-hours employee. If a department relies heavily on e-mail or a listserv, you should request to be added ASAP. If they don't, consider asking your supervisor and/or your colleagues how they would prefer you communicate with them.

Part-time librarians should embrace e-mail as a way to communicate needs to their employers, ask questions, keep track of schedule changes, and document difficult patrons or reference questions. The asynchronous property of e-mail makes it an excellent way for part-time employees who work evenings and weekends to stay in touch with and learn from their weekday colleagues; they can carry on work-related conversations and get valuable feedback without being physically present. One of the ways I built up my confidence as an off-hours employee was to directly ask the others in my department for input. After every weekend decision I was unsure of, I would send an e-mail that said, roughly, "This is what happened, this is what I did, and this is why I did it. How should I handle this next time?" On Monday morning, I would have a response. Whether it was positive or negative, I felt as if I was benefiting from the guidance and support of unseen, but more experienced colleagues.

Communicating electronically is only one way to participate within a department. I make a special effort to check my work e-mail addresses at least once a day and to reply to messages from co-workers and patrons, even if I have to do so from home. I don't want to be left out, so I do my best to communicate that I am an engaged and interested colleague. To feel or be more involved in a department, a part-time librarian may also, depending on her schedule, arrange to work during normal daytime hours one day a week or one day a month or to attend meetings or special events for staff. She may also wish to periodically check in with a supervisor or mentor regarding her quality of work and progress on the job. Additionally, requesting to have annual or semiannual evaluations similar to those performed for full-time employees can be a more formal way for a part-time librarian to get feedback, as well as a chance to discuss opportunities for advancement, additional training, or professional development.

References

Maata, Stephanie. "The Long Wait | LJ's Placements & Salaries Survey 2011." *Library Journal*, October 14, 2011.

Stuck in Security: The Mid-Career Frustrations of the Tenured Academic Librarian

Beth Evans

According to a 2006 survey, librarians in tenure-bearing jobs make up one third of the librarians who work in academic libraries (Bolger and Smith 2006). The path towards tenure is known to be grueling, and it is natural to expect the pace to change once you reach the goal. In reality, finishing a tenure track will feel more like coming off of a treadmill after a very long work-out. You step off but feel like your legs need to keep going. You know you are no longer on the treadmill, the timer has stopped, and you have achieved the miles run/calories burned goal you aimed for when you came to the gym. Nonetheless, finding out how to walk now that you are off the treadmill is an unexpected challenge, especially after a long period of vigorous walking.

As a post-tenure library faculty you will face new stresses and challenges as you adjust to a work life much different from the one you were recently living. Achieving tenure seems by its nature to be defined as satisfaction. It was a difficult goal to reach and it brings with it many benefits. But as with achieving any goal, savoring the sweet moment is brief and life demands the winner move on. Having reached your post-tenure life, you are now on a path that is less clearly defined than the path most recently traveled. The stresses on the post-tenure path may be less obvious than the stresses you faced daily during the years leading to this point. Consequently, because what may cause stress is now less clear, figuring out how to overcome these obstacles and find new sources of satisfaction can be a difficult challenge.

The landscape of the post-tenured job includes elements marking the pre-tenured world as well as some elements that are new. Moreover, some of what has always been a part of the job changes in its nature once you have achieved tenure. The post-tenure work-life is likely to include:

- Colleagues
- Opportunities for engagement within the library
- Opportunities for engagement on campus and beyond
- A professional world outside of the job

- Scholarly and other writing opportunities
- An evolving personal life
- Time after work

Examining each of these elements closely will shed light on how each may be a stress factor, but will provide approaches and suggested attitudes that will enable you as an academic librarian at the post-tenure point in your career to move forward more happily in the job and beyond.

Colleagues

An academic librarian is usually working with colleagues while on the path towards tenure, but the relationship with your colleagues is likely to change once tenure is achieved. Before tenure you may have seen senior faculty standing on the sidelines watching as you scrambled for deadlines in order to prove yourself willing and capable. Those who already had tenure might have been good sounding boards to help when you were still a junior faculty member and needed to understand the politics of the organization. Senior colleagues may also have been there to offer expert advice on how to master something unfamiliar. In the best of times, the senior faculty were encouraging. In the worst of times, they may have seemed aloof and unsympathetic. You may have imagined they were thinking that they had their turn struggling as a newcomer, and now it was your turn to struggle.

Being new on the job for so long, no one is more surprised than you to turn around one day and notice that one, two, or more librarians have since been hired after you. These newer colleagues, who may just be starting on the tenure path where you had struggled for so long, will be favored candidates for taking on new responsibilities. Library directors are interested to see what these newer hires can do, and the new librarians are equally eager to prove themselves. You yourself lived in this role for a number of years. Consequently, you may see not being called upon to take on a new task as rejection and a cause for some envy. You spent years on a daily basis showing your enthusiasm for new opportunities. Being passed over now for a junior colleague is not an occasion you are practiced in welcoming.

One solution for the feelings of rejection you as a recently-tenured faculty member may have to accept is the new role as a senior faculty member and offer yourself to junior colleagues as a mentor. Making the switch from being the advice-seeker to the advisor could require the same sort of adjustment that a child makes whose birth order shifts from being the youngest to becoming an older sister or brother. Just as children who are repositioned when a new sibling enters the family may take time to appreciate their new place, finding comfort in a new work position can take some time. Getting over what you have given up, namely the special attention of being the last in, will be replaced with the positive feelings of maturity when those less experienced will turn to you for help and advice.

An additional problem that may surface in the relationship you have with colleagues after achieving tenure is the result of the dual hierarchy in place in an academic library. College librarians work within an academic hierarchy and an organizational hierarchy. Tenure and promotion, part of the academic hierarchy, come as a result of teaching, service and scholarship. Achieving tenure is the first hurdle in the academic hierarchy. Promotions to any level above assistant professor, usually after achieving tenure, are great goals to achieve, but keeping your job does not usually depend on these promotions as achieving tenure does. Hence, achieving tenure brings a certain level of job security and is a decided accomplishment.

Most academic libraries get the work done that needs to be done by having in place an organizational hierarchy functioning concurrently with the academic hierarchy of the professorate. Academic libraries are typically divided into various work units and each unit is managed by a head. Whereas achieving tenure or even a promotion to associate professor is an elevation in your academic career, it is not a promotion in the traditional sense to a job with more responsibilities. In fact, it may not feel like a promotion at all. Depending on the hierarchy in place, there may be few jobs in the library that are considered senior, and there are not enough of these jobs for all who get tenure.

A weak economy discourages many, including librarians from retiring. With senior library faculty staying in their jobs longer, there are fewer opportunities for you to advance to more challenging work in the same library where you have gotten tenure. When colleagues in management positions do retire, their jobs will open and, typically, a librarian who has already gotten tenure will take on this position in an acting role. Your stress will increase if there is significant competition for the temporary position. Moreover, if you are fortunate and offered the job, you are likely to be required to apply for the job when it is posted even after having served in the acting position. Whether you are offered a more responsible, temporary or permanent job at your current institution, you may be reluctant to leave your job and go through the tenure process again in order to take a more responsible position in another institution.

Opportunities for Engagement within the Library

Despite feeling tied to a workplace where challenging new responsibilities are given first to those hired after you, and there are limited opportunities to move into more demanding, responsible positions within your institution, as a creatively thinking librarian you can enrich your job experience in many ways. By finding your own new projects, you will look forward every day to going to work and making a meaningful contribution.

As a fully engaged, academic librarian, you have never failed to stay in touch with new ideas and trends happening within the profession and more broadly throughout higher education. Moreover, your daily experience of being a working librarian has served as a constant reminder of the needs of those you serve. You have always been a librarian who takes the time to consider what is going on in the field and in academe as you experience it daily. You have stayed in touch with how others report anecdotally on their experiences and your reading has continued to inform you of the scholarly analysis of what is happening in the field. Your open ears and open mind will give you ideas of how to do things differently or innovatively in your own workplace. As a post-tenure librarian, less often tasked directly by your boss, you now may have more leisure and a degree of confidence to suggest changing an approach to a long-established service. You are now in a good position to pilot an emerging new idea, not yet well-tested or widely practiced, but one that may hold great possibilities for your particular institution.

A library in a college or university where librarians earn tenure is seen as a department in the larger institution rather than as an administrative office. As a department, the library is likely to have in place a committee structure existing concurrently with the administrative hierarchy. As a tenured librarian looking for a vehicle to allow you to air a new idea, you may use the library committee structure as a way to find an appropriate sounding board and a vehicle for action. Your ideas pertaining directly to the library may take off in a library committee.

Mechanisms for bringing about change that will benefit library services exist outside the library as well. Having had many years of experience in your library and at your college by the time you achieve tenure, you will know quite a bit of the institutional history, have participated in college-wide committees and know a good many of the players both inside and outside of the library. You stand in an excellent position to recognize who in the library and who on campus are the best to approach for organizing around a new idea and getting it off the ground. You will find great satisfaction with the ease with which you can bring together from a number of places on campus those best suited for trying a new project where the library will play a significant role. The years you spent earning tenure will have been a time during which you have earned the trust and respect of others on campus. Their faith in your ability to carry through on a challenge will give them the comfort to join you in making a project successful.

Moving forward to try out something new may not come as a responsibility directly from the director of the library. Nonetheless, the feelings you may now have since getting tenure of being outcast and less favored for the new jobs in the library will change with the opportunity to exercise an increased degree of independence. Instead of feeling the pressure of needing to follow through on projects assigned by your boss, or frustrated you have not been given a compelling new project, you may now feel exhilarated with your own decision to initiate and take on the full responsibility for the success of something that goes beyond the standard program in place for the library or the college.

Academic library directors have the opportunity for providing newly tenured library faculty with opportunities to take on higher levels of responsibility. New requirements may call for the need to establish ad hoc committees or task forces. Tenured, experienced faculty may be ideal as chairs of such committees. A library director may even consider rotating leadership positions in the functional work units of the library. This will alleviate the possibility of senior members of the staff becoming entrenched in how they approach their jobs. Also, it will give those who more recently got tenure an opportunity to work at something new and approach the job from a fresh perspective.

Opportunities for Engagement on Campus and Beyond

Often as a tenured librarian you may look outside of the library to find ways to contribute to the work of the college you serve. Committee service in areas not directly related to the work of the library can offer insight into the operation of the college that may broaden your view and give you a better understanding of the jobs of non-librarian faculty and the lives of the students whom you serve. Librarians typically have brief encounters with students and faculty either at the reference desk, in a one session class, or through a few e-mail exchanges, chat sessions or phone calls. Serving on college-wide committees gives library faculty a chance to examine close at hand admissions and graduation requirements, changes needed in the curriculum, issues of academic integrity and academic freedom, facility and technology infrastructure planning, grade disputes, disciplinary matters and the other business constituting the work of the college. Learning how the different pieces fit together to make things work can be engaging. Providing input towards the running of the broader institution, furthermore, can be refreshing after a period of time focused on concerns specific to the library.

Often a college may be part of a larger university system or have established alliances with other similar or complementary institutions. Established committees and newly-formed working groups will require cooperation across campuses or institutions. As a tenured librarian you will be an invaluable participant in any of these groups, whether the work involves multiple libraries or a variety of campus departments and offices. As with other opportunities found outside of your own library, the chance to work with colleagues from other institutions puts your professional life into a larger perspective.

A Professional World Outside of the Job

Another option available to any professional seeking enriching, relevant and rewarding work beyond your daily responsibilities is to get involved in a professional association. Hundreds of library and related associations provide prospects in getting involved with local, regional, state-wide, national and international opportunities to connect with similarly focused individuals. Committees, roundtables and other divisions within each organization do outreach, provide support, develop programming, and allow for networking. With your time now freed from the focus of proving yourself on the job and meeting the requirements of publication, you can build a career through association that parallels your everyday work.

Association work is typically voluntary, and identifying talented and committed volunteers can be a challenge for any group. Those who serve are likely to find the work gratifying and very likely to be rewarded for their time with leadership positions. In addition to gaining additional respect from and finding pleasure in working for an association, as a tenured librarian with a number of years of work behind you, you may find yourself more economically comfortable and better positioned to support professional organization conference attendance than an untenured librarian might be.

Scholarly and Other Writing Opportunities

In your time spent working towards tenure, you were well aware of the stringencies of the publishing requirement. Not only is research and writing required, but whatever you write must pass through peer-review before it is published. Following completion of the tenure process, a larger publishing universe opens up for you. You may continue to write to meet the rigors of peer review, or you may now gear your writing for a venue with a more relaxed editorial policy. You may choose to start a blog or find opportunities to write as a guest blogger or a guest columnist in a trade-oriented publication. The expository writing will be less stressful than writing for peer-review and the "do or die" requirement once pressuring you to get published will now be absent.

An Evolving Personal Life

During the time you have spent getting tenure, your life moved ahead in a number of other ways. You may have delayed some activities to accommodate the time demands of the tenure process, or you may have pursued other personally demanding life commitments simultaneously.

Regardless, the end of the pressure and stress of getting tenure will bring with it the new stress of finding yourself at a decision-making point in life. Moving ahead with a new, major life decision such as changing jobs, committing to a partner, beginning or adding to a family, relocating, buying a home, embarking on another degree, or any other of life's big decisions will surface at this time.

For those whose lives became even more filled with commitments during the time working towards tenure, many things may now tie you more strongly to a place and your job than you ever felt tied before the years of working through the tenure clock. Any discouragement felt by real or imagined marginalization as a tenured person on the job must be measured against the strength of the ties that make leaving the job feel like a difficult if not impossible choice.

A job chosen because your parents are nearby may seem even more important to keep than ever as your parents age and begin to require care. Children who entered the family before or during the tenure process may be at an age where they resist moving and leaving a settled life, school and friends. In addition, because going through the tenure process itself was so draining, if you are discouraged with your job at this point, you will have to decide which choice will be the least stressful. Should you stay in a job that has begun to feel stale or change jobs and go through the tenure process once again? Staying in your job but focusing your energies on building other commitments will fill out your life and keep the job in perspective, but is also likely to add its own stress and demands. Maintaining a realistic perspective on what ties must be maintained, what ties can be severed and what new ties you are ready to build will help you as a tenured librarian under stress make the most rational and healthy decisions.

Time After Work

Faculty working towards tenure rank high among individuals claiming to have very little free time. With your pre-tenure evenings and weekends consumed with research and writing, you turned down invitations to take up Salsa, learn a new language, join a book group or help with the PTA. Now that you have been liberated from such tight time constraints, you may find yourself at a loss as to how to fill your free time. You are not used to the luxury of being able to choose something solely for the pleasure it will give you and may feel guilty about finding time on your hands. The greatest gift you can give yourself regardless of the commitments and responsibilities placing demands on your time is the gift of some free time to pursue something for the pleasure it gives and for no other reason.

If you continued to pursue a hobby or passion developed before the tenure process, or dropped it and returned to it after getting tenure, or if you have taken up something new after reaching the tenure goal, time spent in such a way is well-deserved and soothing for the soul. Doing something just for fun may be the biggest reward of having come through one of the most stressful processes. Knitting, biking, singing karaoke or whatever it is you choose to do will ameliorate the discovery that you have made it to the point where you thought the stress would end, but, in fact, new stresses have appeared. Believing you now have the time, where you did not believe you had it before, to incorporate pleasure into your life, is a fortunate reality of the post-tenure life. Acknowledging this found time will do much to cut down on your stress.

As Philipsen, Bostic, and Mason suggest in *Helping Faculty Find Work-Life Balance: The Path Toward Family-Friendly Institutions*, it is ultimately the ingenuity of faculty that will help them survive whatever stressors they find in academia (2006). By being creative in looking for stimulating opportunities in familiar and unfamiliar places after you achieve tenure, you will continue to be challenged by the work you do, valued in your institution, and enriched as an individual who has come to a new plateau in your life.

References

Bolger, Dorita F., and Erin T. Smith. "Faculty Status and Rank at Liberal Arts Colleges: An Investigation into the Correlation Among Faculty Status, Professional Rights and Responsibilities, and Overall Institutional Quality." *College & Research Libraries* 67, no. 3 (2006): 217–29.

Philipsen, Maike Ingrid, Timothy B. Bostic, and Mary Ann Mason. *Helping Faculty Find Work-life Balance: The Path Toward Family-friendly Institutions*. New Jersey: Josey-Bass, 2010.

No Time Like the Present: Proactive Retirement Planning

Aline D. Wilson

Last year I retired from my position as Reference department supervisor in a public library after working there for 12 years. I had not planned to retire for another 2–3 years, but changing circumstances led me to re-evaluate my priorities. Due to budget cuts and reductions in our workforce, I was doing more — and definitely enjoying it less. For the sake of my health and well-being, I decided to retire. While I had done some planning for retirement, my plan was by no means complete. My experience and the last-minute decisions I was forced to make taught me much about the importance of advance planning.

Most people think of retirement as one of the happiest events in a person's life. No more alarm clocks, deadlines, reports or meetings, and no more worrying about meeting someone else's expectations. In retirement we are finally free to pursue our dreams and spend time on activities we never had time for while working.

While the above is true, it is equally true that retirement and planning for it can be very stressful. In fact, on the Holmes and Rahe social readjustment scale, retirement ranks number 10 of 43 (Gross 2001, 18). Surprised? Think about it: retirement is a major lifestyle change, as is marriage, divorce, and starting a family. The good news is taking certain steps now — whether you are 25 or 55 — will ease your planning and eventual transition into retirement. In this essay you will learn several steps you can start taking now to make your retirement planning focused and stress-free. By identifying your retirement goals in advance, you will be closer to making this phase of your life as enriching as you hope it will be.

Step 1: Do Your Homework

The best way to start planning your retirement is to do what you, as a librarian, do best: research. You need to first educate yourself on all of its facets. Begin by making yourself a binder or file folder dedicated to your retirement. Start gathering articles about retiring from popular magazines, newspapers, trade and scholarly journals, and even neighborhood newsletters. Find books in your library; take notes to keep in your file, and consider purchasing books you think you will refer to often. Search the Internet and periodical databases. You'll find there is no shortage of information out there, especially now that baby boomers are starting to retire.

Much of what you will find focuses on finances and how to fund your retirement by saving and investing. Of course, this is an important part of planning for retirement, but it is only one part. You should also look for information on retirement lifestyles, downsizing, and interviews with or articles by current retirees. Reading about retirees' lifestyles and retirement planning strategies is instructive and often entertaining. If you know any retirees, talk to them about their experiences and any advice they might share about what to expect and mistakes they made you can avoid.

As part of this first step, you need to familiarize yourself with the resources available to you from Social Security and your pension plan. As of May 1, 2012, the Social Security web site included information on planning for retirement, a retirement estimator and calculator, forms, a FAQ page, contact information, and more. Bookmark this page on your computer, because you will refer to it often in the months (or years) ahead. Of course, you should do the same for your pension plan. If you cannot find their web page, check with your employer to get the web address and telephone number. While reviewing their site, be sure to look for information on any upcoming pre-retirement workshops. These can be very helpful and will facilitate your planning by addressing issues you may not have considered.

Here I mention a note of caution about Social Security and pensions. In the current economic climate, laws and regulations governing Social Security and pension plans are under scrutiny. In its 2011 session, the Florida legislature passed a law requiring employees hired before July 1, 2011, to contribute 3 percent to their retirement; previously, employees were not required to make any contribution. At this writing, a lawsuit has been filed. On its web site, viewed May 21, 2012, it states that the law has been struck down in Florida Circuit Court. For the present, then, the law has been stayed until it is reviewed at the appellate court level (www.myfrs.com). In your planning, then, you will need to be vigilant and keep abreast of any changes that will affect your social security and pension.

It's a good idea to meet with someone in both your pension and social security offices to review rules, regulations, and deadlines. I met with a representative from Social Security a few months before retiring, and I learned something I had overlooked in my research. I was told if I worked after retiring, my benefits might be reduced! If you plan on working after you retire, you may have $1.00 deducted from your social security for every $2.00 you earn over the annual limit. As of May 11, 2012, the Social Security web site listed the limit as $ 14,160.

Step 2: Dare to Dream

Now is your chance to think about what you would like to do with all of the free time you'll have in retirement — because if you have no plans, you're probably going to be bored. The first days and weeks of retirement are definitely exhilarating. However, the novelty does wear off. Because I took retirement earlier than expected, I had made only a few plans for how I would spend my time. Now, having done some research, I understand the structure, sense of purpose and community that working provides leave a vacuum and need to be replaced by meaningful activities. In fact, researchers' report 1 in 5 people find the transition from working to retirement so difficult they become depressed (Zelinski 2011, 103).

Is there something you've always dreamed of doing — when you had the time? Have you always wanted to travel, learn another language, return to college, or learn to quilt? Or would you like to give back to the community by becoming a volunteer? Consider part-time work as a way to increase your retirement income and keep you busy. If you are ready to leave your full-time job, but want to keep active in the library profession, you might think about joining the American Library Association's Retired Members Round Table. As a member of the round table, you'll have a chance to network with colleagues and collaborate in developing programs and training for retirees from all types of libraries (American Library Association 2012).

If you have trouble coming up with ideas, there are ways to tickle your imagination. Remember the binder or file you started in the first step? Go through it, pick out articles or pictures representing possible activities for you to do in retirement, expand on them, and group them all in their own folder or section of the binder. No matter how wild, silly or expensive something appears to be — include it. No one ever said dreams have to be sensible!

Another, more creative approach to identifying potential retirement activities is to draw a Get-a-Life Tree (Zelinski 2011, 80–81). By drawing a diagram with your goal in the center and principal and secondary lines (branches) coming from it, you generate a list of ideas. For example, you might put book group in the social category, along with sailing club, shopping with friends, or joining a political active retiree group. Under the spiritual category (spiritual as used here means whatever nurtures your spirit) you might write, attend church services, learn yoga, meditate, or watch the birds. Remember: this is your life and your list, so there is no need to worry about doing it right.

If you are more of a traditional list-maker, you can simply keep a written list. Keep a small pad with you so you can jot down ideas when and wherever they occur to you. If you find you need some inspiration, Zelinski has created a list of some 300 suggested activities for retirement (Zelinski 2011, 85–91). You'll find many of his suggestions are not unusual, like gardening or learning a foreign language. Others are, well, rather silly, like learning to walk backwards!

The Internet is a great resource for suggested activities for retirees. Type retirement activities in the search box; your search will yield thousands of hits. Do the same with search terms like: retirement and work, retirement and volunteering, retirement and travel; your results will number in the hundreds, if not thousands. Be sure to look at the AARP's web site (www.aarp.org). Because it is a national organization for anyone over 50, its web site includes news, information and links to all topics of interest to retirees. The Work and Retirement section offers tips on finding a job or changing careers, and a list of the best employers for workers over 50; also it provides links to several discussion groups for job-seekers. From the home page there is a volunteer link you can follow to find articles and blogs about volunteering. Enter your zip code in the search box on this page to find volunteer opportunities in your area.

Step 3: Do the Math

Once you have a pretty good idea of what you want to do when you retire, you need to set financial goals now to be able to afford it. Does this sound daunting? Don't worry; there are tools available making this process painless. To complete this step you will be:

- Estimating expenses
- Estimating income
- Making a financial plan

Estimating Expenses and Income

Start by writing down your projected expenses in retirement. Separate these into: nondiscretionary and discretionary expenditures. The former are pretty well fixed, as: mortgage or rent, groceries, transportation, health care, taxes, insurance premiums, and utilities. Retirement planning experts recommend that you have a 3–6 month emergency fund, to cover unexpected expenses. Your nondiscretionary expenses are variable; you have the option of cutting back on these, or stopping them completely (Bruno 2012, 44).

After you've calculated your retirement expenses, you'll need to estimate your income. Social Security has an estimator on its web site allowing you to see what your benefits will be at different ages (www.ssa.gov/estimator). Check your pension plan's Web site to find a tool to estimate your pension income. Or contact them and request they send you an estimate.

When calculating income, include all income sources you will have when you retire, among these: savings accounts, deferred compensation or 401k funds, other investments, inheritances, and salary if you plan to work after retiring. Financial planners recommend that your income in retirement be approximately 70–80 percent of pre-retirement income. The percentage you choose will depend on your own personal plan. Now deduct your expenses from your income. If you're one of the lucky ones, you may have a surplus. But, if you are like me and probably most librarians, your results will show a shortage of funds.

It's a good idea to complete one or more online calculators, in addition to the calculations you've completed manually. Why? You can compare your results with theirs and get a clearer picture of how you can pay for the retirement you want.

While there are many calculators on the Internet (search for retirement calculator), I mention three here which are easy to use.

- The Employee Benefit Research Institute's Ballpark Estimate is a 2-page worksheet that can be completed online or printed out (*www.choosetosave.org/ballpark*)
- The AARP's calculator (www.aarp.org/work/retirement-planning/retirement_calcu lator/ asks you a series of questions and then produces a graph depicting how long your income will last in retirement.
- CNN Money has several calculators on its web site (search cnn money)

MAKING A FINANCIAL PLAN

Once you know how much you'll need in retirement, you need to make a plan. You can save more, downsize, or do a combination of both. If you currently have a lot of debt, especially credit card debt, your first priority must be to pay it off before saving. It doesn't make sense to be paying 15–25 percent interest on credit cards while you try to save. First, put everything you can each month on paying the cards until that debt is cleared.

If your employer offers a defined contribution plan, such as a 401k or a 457 deferred compensation plan, you can sign up and have money automatically taken out of each paycheck and deposited into the account. You do not pay taxes on this money until you start using it.

There are other available options. You might decide to open an IRA, or start investing. Take advantage of your library's resources and read everything you can about investing, stocks, mutual funds, or bonds enabling you to make an informed decision. The Internet has a lot of information on investing basics; here are some sites you'll want to review:

- www.bankrate.com Financial information site with new investing section
- www.money.cnn.com Money magazine online
- www.investopedia.com Online investing encyclopedia
- www.investor.gov U.S. Securities & Exchange Commission
- www.finance.yahoo.com Yahoo Finance's Education page

DOWNSIZE

If you think you may want to live frugally in retirement, below are some tips to get you started. Remember, too, you can start living frugally now and carry the habit over into your retired life. While I am retired, my husband is still working, but we've starting looking at how we can downsize. After my husband retires, we hope to sell our home and move into a smaller one. The following are ways we have downsized our everyday expenditure:

- Pay off credit cards
- Dine out less
- Use coupons
- Sell your home and buy/rent a smaller one

- Move to a cheaper town/state/country
- Trade in car for a cheaper one with better gas mileage
- Cancel cable
- Cancel Internet and use library computers
- Shop for lower cost car and/or homeowner's insurance
- You may have your own ideas you can add to the list. Or you can search the Internet with keywords frugal retirement or retirement downsizing.

Step 4: Construct a Timeline

As librarians, you are undoubtedly familiar with historical timelines. For our purposes, your timeline is a document that tells you what you need to be doing and when, in order to keep on track with your retirement goals.

Although your retirement may be twenty or thirty years away, you can start a timeline now. The Minnesota Department of Human Services, in partnership with the Minnesota Board on Aging, has made a very helpful Timeline to Retirement available on its web site. To access it, type Project 2030 into the search engine, and you'll see a link to this PDF document on their homepage. Their timeline outlines actions you need to take now, every year, every five years, 10–15 years and 1–5 years before you plan to retire, and in your last year preceding retirement. If your employer sponsors a retirement plan, you can see if that web site has a timeline.

Here are some examples of what you should put on your timeline. It's not complete; you can add items which apply to your situation when you learn about them.

What you can start doing now:

- Pay off debt
- Start saving now; set financial goals
- Enroll in or increase your contribution to a 401k or 457 deferred compensation account
- Read about your pension plan and options you might have to select
- Read about social security, forms, deadlines, etc.
- Start learning about investing

Every five years:

- Review your annual Social Security statement; notify them if there are discrepancies
- Request an estimate from your pension plan; review it
- Review your financial goals; determine if you need help from a financial planner

10–15 years before retiring:

- Think about what you will do for health insurance when you retire
- Look into long-term care insurance

- Attend pre-retirement seminars or workshops
- Review your savings and investments; increase contributions

   1–5 years before retiring:

- Review your personal and financial retirement plan; adjust as needed
- Review your expenses
- Decide where you want to live when you retire; discuss with spouse

   The year you plan to retire:

- Notify supervisor about plans to retire
- Talk with Social Security, your pension plan, and your Human Resources office to decide the best time to retire
- Prepare a post-retirement budget
- Check social security and pension estimates for accuracy
- Schedule annual health exam and any needed tests
- Schedule dental and vision checkups

   4–6 months before retiring

- Apply for social security benefits
- Notify pension of last day before retiring
- Start cleaning your work paper and computer files
- Prepare a list or manual for your successor at work — with deadlines
- Apply for health, dental and possibly vision insurance

   1 month before

- Turn in resignation letter
- Notify staff (if you supervise) of your retiring
- Take personal items from office
- Make sure Social Security and pension forms are completed
- Prepare for exit interview

Step 5: Make a Checklist

I mentioned earlier my retirement was rather sudden. I had just 5 weeks to wrap things up at work and at home. While I was excited about retiring, I was also terrified. My greatest fear was I would forget some crucial deadline or fail to complete all the required forms. What saved me and dissipated my anxiety was making a checklist. Using the list as my guide, I was able to get everything done — with no mistakes or delays.

Although you may not know now what your retirement day or year will be, you can start your checklist now. Look at your timeline and copy items, with deadline dates, to your checklist. It is useful to leave space between entries, so you can mark items completed with dates.

Step 6: Plan for the Unexpected

You may be thinking this last step sounds like an oxymoron. After all, how can you plan for something, if you don't know what's going to happen? What I mean here is that you need to be flexible and adapt your plans if necessary. Some things cannot be predicted, such as the death of a partner or family member, illness, or a downturn in the stock market. You just don't know what might happen that would require you to work longer, or to take retirement earlier than planned. If you tell yourself now you will be able to deal with whatever happens, then you will be prepared for the unexpected.

The six steps described here are designed to make your retirement planning virtually stress-free. Knowing in advance what you want to do, how you will pay for it, and when everything needs to be completed will give you a sense of confidence. When you wake up the first day of your retirement, you will be able to declare I'm going to do whatever I want today! As a retiree, I can tell you it is a wonderful feeling. So—what are you waiting for? There's no time like the present to start planning your ideal retirement.

References

AARP. "AARP Retirement Calculator." Accessed May 16, 2012. http://www.aarp.org/work/retirement-planning/retirement_calculator/.

American Library Association. 2012. "Retired Members Round Table (RMRT)." Accessed May 11. http://www.ala.org/rmrt/.

Bruno, Maria A., CFP. "Your Income in Retirement: Steps to a Solid Spending Plan." In *Pre- & Post-Retirement Tips for Librarians*, edited by Carol Smallwood, 41–51. Chicago: American Library Association, 2012.

Gross, Richard. "Holmes and Rahe (1967) the social readjustment rating scale." *Psychology Review* 8, no. 2 (2001): 18.

Social Security. "The Official Website of the U.S. Social Security Administration." Accessed May 1, 2012. http://www.ssa.gov/.

Social Security Online. "Retirement Planner." Accessed May 11. 2012. http://www.socialsecurity.gov/retire2/whileworking.htm/pubs/whileworking3.htm.

Zelinski, Ernie J. *How to Retire Happy, Wild, and Free.* Edmonton: Visions International Publishing, 2011.

About the Contributors

Amy **Bodine** received an MLS degree in 2008 from the University of Maryland College Park. Since 2009, she has worked for the Office of Minority Health Resource Center (OMHRC) in Rockville, Maryland, as the technical services librarian. Before coming to OMHRC, she worked for Smithgroup, an architecture and interior design firm, and the Everglades National Park.

John **Boyd**, associate professor and information literacy librarian at Appalachian State University, Boone, North Carolina, since 1995, obtained an MLS from Kent State University, and an EdS in adult education from Appalachian State. He is a member of the American Library Association and has written for six encyclopedias published by Salem Press including *Great Events from History: Gay, Lesbian, Bisexual, Transgender Events, the Encyclopedia of American Immigration* and recently in *International Leads* about his visit to Appalachian's sister library in Cochabamba, Bolivia.

Sharon M. **Britton**, library director at Bowling Green State University Firelands, in Huron, Ohio, since 2007, earned an MLS from the University of Rhode Island. She is a member of the American Library Association, Association of College and Research Libraries, and the Academic Library Association of Ohio. She has been featured in *American Libraries* and *AURCO Journal,* and has contributed book reviews for *Library Journal.*

James B. **Casey** has been director of Oak Lawn Public Library in southwest suburban Chicago since 1992. He holds a PhD in librarianship from Case Western Reserve University (1985), an MLS from SUNY Genesee (1973), and an MA in history from Cleveland State University (1979). He has worked in public libraries since 1973. He has served four terms on ALA Council and received the Librarian of the Year award from Illinois Library Association in 2005.

Kathleen **Clauson** is the unit coordinator, at the Physical Sciences Library at Western Illinois University, of the highly successful Forensic Series and Mock Crime Scenes. She has a BA in German and a MA in economics. She spent many years as an editor, feature writer and book review columnist, and has published numerous short stories and a novella. She is working on future forensic and astronomy programs and outreach.

Elizabeth **Cramer** is lead catalog librarian and collections librarian for foreign languages and literatures at Appalachian State University in Boone, North Carolina. She has an MLS from Kent State University, an MA in French and a doctorate in educational leadership from Appalachian State. She is active with the ALA International Relations Round Table. She and John Boyd have a blog, Librarians on Bikes: librariansonbikes.blogspot.com/

Jeffrey **DiScala** is a PhD candidate in the College of Information Studies at the University of Maryland. With an MLS from that university he became a middle school librarian in Prince

George's County, Maryland. He is co-principal investigator on the Lilead Project, a national study of school library district supervisors. His research interests include the evolving role of the school librarian and school library programs; information, technology, and education policy and standards; evidence-based teaching practices; and social media in education.

Su **Epstein** has an MA degree in humanities from Wesleyan University and holds a doctorate in sociology from the University of Connecticut. She began her career teaching criminology. She earned an MLS from Simmons College and worked in a variety of libraries as well as the newspaper *Springfield Union News*, and at Greens Farms Academy. She has also worked at the West Haven Connecticut Public Library and is the director at the Saxton B. Little Free Library in rural Columbia, Connecticut.

Beth **Evans** is an associate professor in the library of Brooklyn College of the City University of New York (CUNY). She holds an MLS from Queens College, CUNY, a degree in English literature from Brown University and a BA from Brooklyn College. Her job includes implementing and promoting electronic resources and services, overseeing virtual reference services and coordinating the library internship program. In 2007 she was named a *Library Journal* Mover and Shaker for her work with social networking.

Stacey R. **Ewing** is an assistant university librarian in Library West, the humanities and social sciences branch of the University of Florida libraries. She coordinates the Information Commons and specializes in outreach, instruction, social media and emerging technologies. She received an MLIS from the University of North Texas where she was an Institute of Museum and Library Services fellow in the digital image management program. Her "Building a Participatory Culture: Collaborating with Student Organizations for 21st Century Library Instruction" appears in *Collaborative Librarianship*.

Barbara **Fiehn** is an assistant professor in library media education of Western Kentucky University and has an MS and EdD. Following years as a school librarian and media services coordinator, she taught in library media education at Minnesota State University at Mankato and Northern Illinois University and has published articles in *Multimedia and Internet@ schools*, *2Tech Trends*, and *Dragon Lode* and essays in *Educational Media and Technology Yearbook*, *Library Management Tips That Work*, and *How to Thrive as a Solo Librarian*. A member of ALA, she has served on its Intellectual Freedom committee.

Lisa A. **Forrest** is an associate librarian for SUNY College at Buffalo and the founding member of the school's Rooftop Poetry Club. She is the recipient of the 2008 Excellence in Library Service Award from the Western New York Library Resources Council. Her scholarly writing has appeared in a variety of journal and book publications.

Jonathan **Frater** received an MLS from Queens College in 2005 and has worked in electronic resources and as a systems librarian. His essay appeared in *How to Thrive as a Solo Librarian* in 2011. He has been the technical services librarian for Metropolitan College of New York since 2007 and lives in Rego Park, New York.

Lara **Frater** received an MLS from Queens College (in 2000) and has worked in libraries for a number of years including at the New York Academy of Medicine, the Environmental Protection Agency and the New York City Department of Health and Mental Hygiene. Her essay "The Lonely Librarian: A Guide to Solo Weeding" appeared in *How to Thrive as a Solo Librarian*.

Kymberly Anne **Goodson** earned an MLIS in 1998. With a background in user services at the University of California San Diego library and elsewhere, she served since 2007 as the UCSD library's decision support analyst. In 2012 she assumed the role of program director for the library's new Learning Spaces Program. She has published articles in library science and political science journals.

Shirley A. **Higgins** is the assistant head of the Metadata Services Department of the University of California San Diego libraries. She has worked in cataloging and metadata services for many years, starting as a student employee and working her way up through the library assistant ranks. She joined ALA in 1992 and is the founder of StressBusters, now two decades old.

Samantha Schmehl **Hines** received an MS in library and information science from the University of Illinois Urbana-Champaign in 2003. In 2004 she became the social science librarian at the University of Montana Missoula library and is the distance education coordinator and head librarian for the College of Technology on that campus. She is the author of *Productivity for Librarians* (2010) and has written and presented widely on the topics of productivity and time management.

Kim Rush **Lynch** is a certified nutritional consultant and health coach and the founder of Cultivating Health, which provides coaching, education and support for individuals and organizations learning about healthy eating. She also served as the Director of the Washington Youth Garden at the U.S. National Arboretum. She is the co-founder of the Greenbelt Farmers Market and chairs the Herb Study for the Herb Society of America's Potomac Unit.

Sheri Anita **Massey** is the assistant MLS program director for the school library specialization at the University of Maryland College of Information Studies. She received an MLS and a PhD from Maryland's iSchool with a focus in school library media programs. A former D.C. public schools teacher and Montgomery County public schools librarian, her research explores the history and development of urban school library media programs.

Maryann **Mori** has presented on a variety of topics at several national library conferences, including ALA and PLA. She has been published in various library journals, ALA books, *Social Networking Communities and E-Dating Services* (2008), and most recently in *Serving Teen Parents: From Literacy to Life Skills* (2011). She is a district library consultant for Iowa Library Services, and holds an MSLIS from the University of Illinois.

Beth **Nieman** has a decade of public library work experience and is youth services librarian at Carlsbad (New Mexico) Public Library. She has written a popular weekly book column for her local newspaper since 2008 and collaborated with others on two books including *Writing and Publishing: The Librarian's Handbook* (2010). She also serves on the nominations committee for the Land of Enchantment book award on behalf of the New Mexico Library Association.

Pamela **O'Sullivan** obtained an MLS from SUNY Buffalo and is head of integrated public services at Drake Memorial Library, the College at Brockport (New York) since April 2008, after two decades in public librarianship. A member of the SUNY Librarians Association and the Jane Austen Society of North America, she is a regular reviewer for *Library Journal*. Before joining the staff at Drake Library, she was a public librarian for over two decades. She is also a professional storyteller.

Marcia E. **Rapchak**, a librarian at Duquesne University, teaches a course on information literacy and coordinates instruction efforts. She has presented at LOEX and published in *Library Trends*. Previously, she taught classes on communication, composition and information literacy in the Department of Communication at the University of Kentucky. She completed an MA in English at Ohio State University and received an MSLS in library science at the University of Kentucky.

Carol **Smallwood** received an MLS from Western Michigan University, and an MA in history from Eastern Michigan. *Librarians as Community Partners: An Outreach Handbook* and *Bringing the Arts into the Library* are two of her anthologies. Other publications are *Women on Poetry: Writing, Revising, Publishing and Teaching*; *Marketing Your Library*; and *Library Services for Multicultural Patrons*. She has worked in school, public and academic libraries and in administration and as a consultant, and is a poetry Pushcart nominee.

Aislinn Catherine **Sotelo** (with an MLS from UCLA) is the coordinator of technical services for the Mandeville Special Collections Library at the University of California San Diego. She is the author of the "StressBusters Recipe of the Month" column in the libraries' staff newsletter, and has participated in numerous StressBuster activities. She is an active member of the Rare Books and Manuscripts Section of the Association of College and Research Libraries Bibliographic Standards and Seminars Committees.

Kimberly **Swanson** has worked in a wide range of public and technical services positions since earning an MLS from the University of Wisconsin Madison in 1994. Her employers have included the Institute of Transpersonal Psychology in Palo Alto, California; the University of Michigan in Ann Arbor; and the University of Montana in Missoula. She is a member of the American Library Association and the Montana Library Association. She holds an MA in American history from the University of Wisconsin Madison and has published in this field.

Cristina Hernandez **Trotter** is head of the reference department and the Heritage Center at the Laurens County Library in Dublin, Georgia. An ALA Spectrum Scholar, she earned an MLIS from Louisiana State University in 2005. She started her library career as a student worker at Tulane University, where she received a BA in Spanish. While managing the library at the Newcomb College Center for Research on Women, she learned how to cope with work-related stress firsthand during Hurricane Katrina. Her writing has appeared in *Library Worklife* and *Versed*.

Charlcie K. Pettway **Vann** has filled a number of positions, including assistant professor and reference and general instructional librarian at Jacksonville State University. She obtained an MLS from North Carolina Central University in 1996. She is a member of the Black Caucus of American Library Association, and former president of the Alabama Chapter of the Association of College & Research Libraries. She helped initiate the Multicultural Information Roundtable Committee of the Alabama Library Association and her work has been published in *Reference Services Review, Reference Librarian, Alabama Librarian,* and BCALA Newsletter.

Linda Burkey **Wade** obtained an MLIS from Dominican University and an MS in instructional design from Western Illinois University. Her writing has appeared in the *Journal of Interlibrary Loan, Document Delivery, & Electronic Reserve; Pre- and Post-Retirement Tips for Librarians* (2012) and *Jump-Start Your Career as a Digital Librarian: LITAGuide*. She is the unit coordinator of digitization at the Western Illinois libraries and was elected to the Brown County

Library Board. She received the 2010 Distinguished Service Award for innovation and dedication to service and the 2012 Community Service Award.

Janelle **West** is a music catalog librarian at the University of North Texas. In addition to the cataloging of music books, scores, and sound recordings in various formats, she coordinates materials for the College of Music. She received an MLS and a master of music degree from the University of North Texas and has been an active performer of early music for more than fifteen years.

Zara T. **Wilkinson** is a reference librarian at the Camden campus of Rutgers University. She also has an MA in English literature from West Chester University. She obtained an MLIS from the University of Pittsburgh in 2010. The inspiration for her essay was a period in which she had three library jobs: part-time reference librarian at Rutgers-Camden, part-time reference librarian at Temple University, and weekend access and lending services supervisor at Swarthmore College.

Aline D. **Wilson** earned an MLS from the University of South Florida and an MA in French from Southern Illinois University. She became a librarian late in her career, with the assistance of several University of South Florida staff scholarships and a grant award. She retired from her position as reference department manager and library management team member at the Hernando County Public Library in 2011.

Leigh A. **Woznick**, a media specialist at Bridgewater-Raritan (New Jersey) Middle School, received an MLIS from Rutgers and is a member of ALA, YALSA, New Jersey Association of School Librarians, Mystery Writers of America, and the New England Historic and Genealogical Society. Her publications include: *Living with Childhood Cancer: A Practical Guide to Help Families Cope* (2002), and a *Libraries and Culture* cover story. She received the 2012 Distinguished Service Award from her school district.

Index